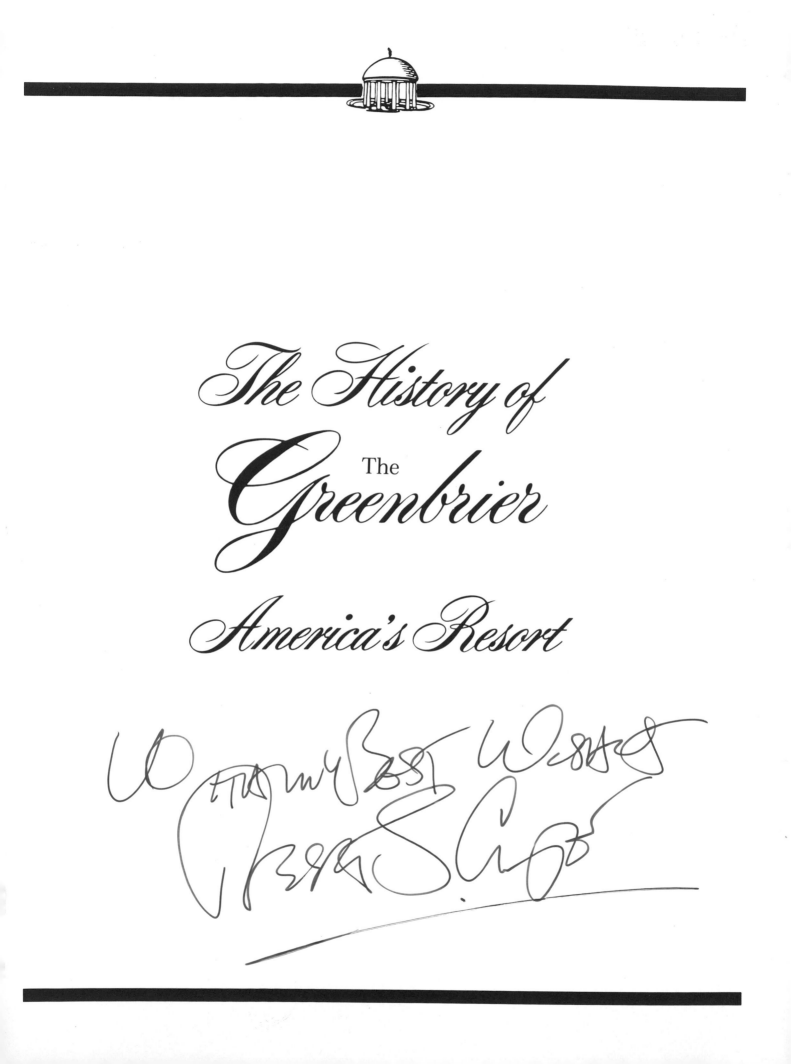

The History of
The
Greenbrier

America's Resort

With my best wishes

The History of
The
Greenbrier

America's Resort

by

Robert S. Conte

LIBRARY OF CONGRESS CATALOG CARD NUMBER 98-67086

ISBN 0-929521-14-5

ALL OF THE PHOTOGRAPHS AND ARTWORK IN THIS BOOK, EXCEPT WHERE NOTED IN
CAPTIONS, ARE FROM THE GREENBRIER'S ARCHIVES OR PUBLIC RELATIONS DEPARTMENT.

PUBLISHED FOR THE GREENBRIER BY PICTORIAL HISTORIES PUBLISHING COMPANY, INC.,
1416 QUARRIER STREET, CHARLESTON, WEST VIRGINIA 25301

PRINTED IN CANADA

Introduction

Entering the grounds of The Greenbrier, you sense immediately a place rooted in a time well before our own. The stately white hotel, the neat rows of cottages, the spacious lawns shaded by ancient oaks, all bespeak a romantic past that continues to float elusively in the collective memory of America. In fact, the history of The Greenbrier colors the recollections of not one, but numerous generations as it weaves its way through the many eras of the country's past. The purpose of this book is to tell the stories that have always surrounded the place, to follow the people who created the resort and those who sustained it, as well as the many legendary characters who frequented it over the years.

Because it is history, what follows is about change over time. We are separated by many years from the early homesteaders who first used the mineral water, from the ante-bellum Southern society that assembled here each summer, from the world of travel by train for two weeks of golf each spring and autumn. But much has not changed—including the simple fact that for over two hundred continuous years there has been a resort at White Sulphur Springs. Since 1778 the spring of mineral water in the middle of the grounds has been the center of resort life, even though the rituals and routines of this life have varied considerably in those centuries. Only two times in The Greenbrier's long history was it closed to the public: for a short time during the Civil War and then again during World War II. Other than that, the business at White Sulphur Springs has always remained the same—that of being a resort of unusual beauty and old world grace.

The word "resort" literally means a place to which people go for rest and relaxation, a pleasant escape from the demands of daily cares. It also connotes community, a gathering spot in a unique location. The mountains surrounding The Greenbrier and the soothing waters of the mineral spring have been constant features of the resort's setting, the context where the whirl of social life has evolved within the fluctuating whims, fashions and habits of American society. It is this ongoing interplay between what has changed at The Greenbrier and what has remained that is the subject of the pages ahead. The long and glamorous history of this venerable resort is, in short, living testament to William Faulkner's famous words, "The past is never dead, it's not even past."

The Indian Legend of White Sulphur Springs

An ancient Indian legend explains the origin of the White Sulphur Spring by a tragic tale of two young lovers who came often to this valley to escape the notice of their elders. One day they met in the forest, unaware that an enraged chieftain was secretly watching them from a nearby hilltop. The stern chieftain was so filled with wrath at the couple's idleness that he shot two deadly arrows down upon them. The first arrow hit its mark, piercing the heart of the young boy. The second narrowly missed the young girl and sank into the earth. When the distraught young girl pulled the errant arrow from the ground, the sulphur spring burst forth. It is the poignant yearning of this lonely maiden that draws us back year after year, the legend concludes, because her lover will be restored only when we have drunk the last drop of water from the spring.

THE SPRING.

Contents

The Lure of a Wilderness Spring

The Greenbrier stands in what was once a vast virgin forest, in a small valley tucked away amidst the subtle yet awesome contours of the mighty Appalachian Mountains. For generations visitors have traveled to this valley on horseback, by stagecoach and railroad, in automobiles and airplanes, but to the English colonials who settled tidewater Virginia in the seventeenth century, this land was far beyond the frontier of civilization. Because these seemingly limitless mountain ranges appeared to stretch westward farther than their imaginations, the earliest cartographers labeled this region on their maps "The Endless Mountains."

By the middle of the eighteenth century, explorers began to penetrate the river valleys and gaps and to tentatively make their way through the maze of creeks, foothills, passes, towering peaks and fearsome rhododendron thickets. The forests were patrolled, however, by Shawnee Indians in search of game. For hundreds of years various Indian tribes had moved through the mountainous terrain from river settlements to hunting grounds and back again. Near the center of the valley now occupied by The Greenbrier, the Shawnee found an ideal hunting spot—a small marsh that migrating deer, elk and buffalo used as a "lick." Upon closer inspection they determined that the source of this marsh was a spring of strong-smelling mineral water. Stories passed down from the earliest European settlers indicate that the Indians valued the curative powers of the water, but precisely how they used the spring for medicinal pur-

poses was never recorded. Most likely it was the Shawnee, then, who taught Mrs. Anderson, one of the first homesteaders in the area, about the wondrous mineral water. She put it to the test on her chronic rheumatism.

In 1778 Mrs. Anderson was carried fifteen miles on a litter from her home to the wilderness spring. A tent was set up for her comfort and, following Indian custom, a bathing tub fashioned by felling a nearby tree and hollowing out the log. The improvised tub was filled with spring water, which was heated with hot stones. Mrs. Anderson bathed in the water; she also drank directly from the spring, and in a few short weeks the pain of her rheumatism receded dramatically. In fact her recovery was so complete that word of the potent sulphur water spread rapidly to other settlers in the region, and since rheumatism was a common frontier complaint many followed her lead. In the next few years numerous log cabins were built in the vicinity of the spring. Within a decade, each year a small but enthusiastic crowd could be found—at least during the warm months—gathered to take Mrs. Anderson's "cure."

But this peaceful discovery of health-restoring waters was an unusual event in western Virginia at a time when a bloody struggle was underway between encroaching colonial settlers and Shawnee Indians. From the 1740s

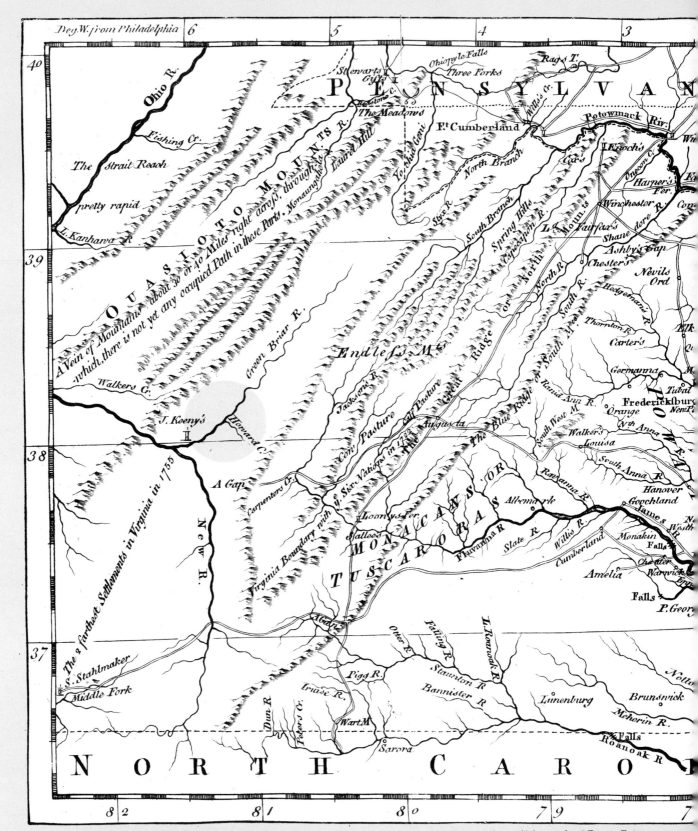

On this 1761 map of Virginia the site of The Greenbrier is where Howard's Creek branches off from the "Green Briar River" west of the Endless Mountains.

through the 1770s, the history of the area was one of explorers—guided mostly by river beds and animal paths—probing the endless mountains, with backwoods settlers following in their wake. These pioneers carved out simple homesites, which were then periodically abandoned in the face of terrifying Indian attacks. The fact was that good land was growing scarce in eastern Virginia after a century of colonization. Population pressures were driving migrants—mostly German and Scotch-Irish—beyond the Shenandoah Valley and up into the Alleghenies where affordable land could still be found, though the price was high in terms of hardship and danger. Settlement was further complicated by the French and Indian War (1756-1763), which closed off the country west of the Alleghenies to English settlement for the next decade. It wasn't until October of 1774, when General Andrew Lewis defeated the majestic Shawnee Chief Cornstalk at Point Pleasant on the Ohio River, that homesteaders began to feel secure.

Twenty-four years earlier, Andrew Lewis had been the surveyor for the Greenbrier Land Company, a consortium of speculators who organized the first explorations of the Greenbrier region, having been granted 100,000 acres on the condition that they survey and eventually settle the land. It was Lewis, some say, who named the major river "Greenbrier" after the profusion of tangled and clinging vines that surely impeded his way. Others claim that the name was given originally by earlier French explorers, who called it "Ronceverte," which was later anglicized to "Greenbrier." At any rate, the river was known as the Greenbrier (variously spelled on the early maps "Green Brier," "Green Bryar," and "Green Briar") by the time the earliest settlers arrived.

The first settler on the land that included the spring of sulphur water was not connected to the Greenbrier Land Company. Rather, Nicholas Carpenter parted company with relatives who established a fort on the Jackson River where Covington, Virginia, now stands, moved westward into this valley and took possession of the land by means of what was then called "Corn Rights"—that is, he who plants the first corn owns the land. Carpenter claimed his parcel of land on a tributary of the Greenbrier River, Howard's Creek, about 1750. The story becomes a bit confused at this point, tending to blur between fact and folktale, but apparently Carpenter returned to the Jackson's River fort a few years after his move, and was killed there in an Indian attack. His wife Kate and their infant daughter Frances remained behind at the homesite on Howard's Creek until they too were attacked, whereupon Kate escaped with the baby in her arms to the top of a mountain overlooking the creek. According to legend, the mother and child hid in a hollowed-out log while marauding Indians searched all around them.

This statue of Andrew Lewis, an early explorer of the Greenbrier region of western Virginia, stands on the grounds of Capitol Square in Richmond, Virginia. (Courtesy Virginia State Library)

Somehow Kate was able to keep the baby silent, sparing them from capture or death. To commemorate this woman's courage, the mountain standing across from The Greenbrier's main entrance still bears her name, Kate's Mountain.

However sketchy this account of Kate Carpenter and her daughter Frances may be, it is clear that afterwards they moved to Staunton, where little Frances grew up and in 1766 married Michael Bowyer. Captain Michael Bowyer, Jr. was a member of large and influential Virginia family. Even in the late eighteenth century the Bowyer family could proudly trace its roots back to one Edmund Bowyer who came to Jamestown with the first English settlement in 1607. Michael Bowyer, born in 1730, was a man of varied occupations. He was a lawyer, a church vestryman, the owner of a general store in Fincastle, Virginia, an officer during the Indian Wars, a farmer, and a captain in the Revolutionary War.

But Bowyer showed no interest in his wife's family land until after the end of the Revolution, when in May of 1783 he obtained the first legal deed to the land. Given the vague history of the property, however, it is no surprise that his claim was disputed, presumably by assignees of the Greenbrier Land Company. The Virginia Court of Appeals in Richmond ruled in his favor on February 21, 1784 and Michael Bowyer received a clear title to 950 acres along Howard's Creek, which passes through today's golf courses. There is no way to know if Bowyer was aware of Mrs. Anderson's experience with the sulphur water, but surely he had heard stories of people visiting his land, and that probably prompted him to seek legal ownership.

Thomas Jefferson, though he never visited, also had heard about the spring. He wrote the first published mention of the mineral waters in his *Notes on the State of Virginia* (1784): "We are told of a sulphur spring on Howard's Creek of Greenbriar." Jefferson, incidentally, took a characteristically skeptical view of the virtues of the mineral water on Bowyer's property, as well as those of the nearby Warm Springs, Hot Springs and Sweet Springs. "None of them," he wrote, "having undergone a chemical analysis in skillful hands, nor been so far the subject of observations as to have produced a reduction into classes of the disorders which they relieve, it is in my power to give little more than a enumeration of them."

The "Since 1778" slogan has been used in Greenbrier promotional material for many years. This design is from the 1930s.

This view of Kate's Mountain from Howard's Creek appeared in an 1878 issue of Harper's Weekly.

Frances Carpenter Bowyer died in either 1784 or 1785, and that left Michael Bowyer in Staunton with the couple's seven children; so in 1787 he hired a Mr. and Mrs. Leven Gibson to manage his fledgling health resort. Many years later, the Gibson's son told the story: "Mr. Bowyer, being anxious that the property should be occupied, employed my father to take control of the Springs property and to make such arrangements as best he could for the persons who resorted there for the benefit of their health." Gibson wrote what seems to be the earliest description of conditions and life at White Sulphur Springs: "The Spring, then in its natural state, emptied its water from between two flag rocks about twenty inches wide and about four inches apart, falling into a pool about three feet deep. I never saw the spring muddy—the changes of the weather had no effect in increasing or diminishing the quantity of the water. At the time my father moved to the White the only improvements on the property were a few small log cabins—the principal one of which was to be occupied by the family. Most of those who came to the Springs brought tents, provisions and cooking utensils on pack horses—no arrangements being yet made to board visitors. From twenty to thirty persons came during the warm season. My parents remained there three years. . . . After my father's departure, Mr. Bowyer moved his family and occupied the Springs property."

Michael Bowyer was sixty years old when he moved up to the springs property with his four sons and three daughters. Along with his children he brought two friends, a Mr. and Mrs. Wiley, and each family lived in a log cabin. Although the danger of Indian attacks had subsided, life on the frontier was still wild and rough. Indeed, wolves and panthers were seen prowling about the cabins in broad daylight. The spring itself was still bubbling forth from the middle of marsh and on one occasion Mr. Wiley's horse sank deep into the mud until only its head and ears were visible above the swamp. One particularly nasty feature of the backwoods was noted by visitors during this period—the size and number of rattlesnakes.

Despite these drawbacks, the reputation of the water drew more and more health-seekers. Wiley, it seems, was the first to grasp the money-making possibilities of catering to travelers and invalids; soon after his arrival, he moved his family into the stables and rented out his own cabin. Still more visitors arrived and pleaded through the cracks in the stable's walls for Wiley's permission to sleep in the hay. The budding commercial venture, however, was dependent on transportation improvements and it is significant that Bowyer paid little attention to the springs until the first road was hacked through the wilderness. Roads in this region, as elsewhere, developed from Indian trails, which in turn had followed routes created by migrating animals, particularly buffalo. To have called the oversized trail wending through Greenbrier county in 1782 a road would be overstating the matter. Massive boulders and huge trees remained intimidating obstacles. In 1790 the Commonwealth of Virginia, concerned that western goods could not reach their markets in the east, constructed what came to be known as the Old State Road. For the first time, wagons—in good weather at least—might roll from the Kanawha River valley to the piedmont and tidewater sections.

Although this road remained primitive for over thirty years, it was more than a mere obscure mountain route, for it represented part of a grand vision of the nation's future. As early as 1784, George Washington brought the Virginia legislature's attention to the great prospects for commerce via this road. The broader scheme behind the building of the Old State Road was to connect the James River basin, which ran through the center of Virginia, to the Kanawha and Ohio River Valleys, thereby creating a trade corridor extending from the Atlantic coast to the Mississippi River. In Washington's words, "But smooth the road and make easy the way for Western settlers and see how amply we shall be compensated for any trouble and expense we may encounter to effect it." In fact, a great deal of trouble and expense was encountered surveying practical routes, building portions of the combination canal and turnpike, and most of all, finding the means to finance the project. On August 21, 1785, the James River Company was organized, George Washington was elected the first president of the company, and for almost a century thereafter, various schemes, proposals, and plans were submitted and attempted to create the great connection between east and west. An all-water route, mixing navigable rivers, canals, locks and dams, was never achieved, but a decent turnpike did reach Greenbrier County by the 1820s.

Unfortunately, these improvements in transportation came too late to help Michael Bowyer's business. He died in 1808 at the ripe old age of seventy-eight leaving precious little information about the living conditions and social life at the sulphur spring during the eighteen years he had lived there. The primeval resort was known to travelers at the time as "Bowyer's Sulphur Spring," although many referred to it simply as "Sulphur Spring." Years later, an elderly gentleman recalled his 1790 journey from Alexandria and described the visitors as "horsemen who carried their entire spring wardrobes in saddlebags, with a bottle or so of prime French brandy, a pack of cards, and a convenient pistol and rifle for venison." Obviously, travelers so equipped were not suffering ter-

This Buffalo Trail monument stands alongside the roadway from the hotel to the golf clubhouse. The inscription reads: "The Great Buffalo Trail between the Atlantic coast, the valley of Virginia and the Ohio valley, here crossed the Allegheny Mountains. And over the pass was the war trail of nations, one of the chief warrior trails of the American Indians, which was last used by the Indians of the Ohio valley when attacking the settlements of Virginia. Through it was constructed the James River and Kanawha Turnpike, the great thoroughfare connecting the James River and the west over which flowed from the south and east an important portion of the settlers who founded and developed the states of West Virginia, Kentucky, Ohio, Indiana, Illinois and Missouri, and who were potential factors in the life of other states of the Republic west of the Ohio River. This road for a century has been the scene of many of the most important events in the history of our country. This monument was erected February 1st, 1916 by William A. MacCorkle, former governor of West Virginia, George W. Stevens and Decatur Axtell of Virginia, Joseph E. Chilton of West Virginia and General Edward P. Meany of Kentucky."

ribly from rheumatism, so it seems that even before the beginning of the nineteenth century, visitors were coming to socialize—note the brandy and playing cards—and not solely to cure their ills.

Perhaps the best evidence of Michael Bowyer's scope of operations while proprietor of the springs is the appraisal of his estate made a month after his death. This document lists all his possessions including nine slaves—four adults and five children—seven head of cattle, eleven sheep, and nine hogs. In addition, the following items indicate that he was providing meals and lodgings on a fairly large scale: fifty-two blankets, twenty-three mattresses, thirty-eight cots, eleven wash bowls, 125 plates of various kinds— including twenty-one soup plates, twenty-seven dinner plates and seventeen breakfast plates—twenty-three stem glasses, forty-three candlesticks, four dozen knives and forks, twenty-five small tables, seven large tables, twenty-two tablecloths, thirty-five pairs of sheets and eight chamberpots. All of this, and much more, was appraised at $3,709.59. Bowyer's other activities on his property are documented in a separate deed noting "all the houses, barn, and stables adjacent together with the grist mill and saw mill." That he was definitely working the land as well as entertaining visitors is shown on the deed by the nine horses, two wagons, one oxen yoke, gardening equipment, axes, saws, augers and hammers.

It is difficult to imagine what might have become of Bowyer's sulphur spring property had not three young Baltimore merchants wandered into the area in 1795. James Calwell and his partner, William Bedford, arrived at the springs with their clerk, John Copeland, while taking a break from their shipping business. They found Michael Bowyer's resort and hospitality, but more important, they discovered that Bowyer had three daughters. As one Greenbrier County historian phrased it years hence, "How little did Mr. Bowyer realize of the bright future in store for his three rosey-cheeked, barefooted daughters that huddled behind the door when these shipping merchants were taking their first meal in his cabin." In other words, the three Baltimore shippers each successfully wooed one of the daughters. Frances Bowyer became Mrs. William Bedford; Elizabeth Bowyer Mrs. John Copeland; and Mary Bowyer— usually called Polly—Mrs. James Calwell. Of these matches, the most significant was that between Polly Bowyer and James Calwell, for Calwell was to reign as the sole proprietor of the resort for most of the first half of the nineteenth century, and their children were to be associated with it for fifteen years after the Civil War. Although Michael Bowyer deserves credit for hacking out the site of a potential spa, it was James Calwell, in fact, who oversaw its transformation from a clearing in

the wilderness, to the South's grandest resort.

James Calwell swept Polly Bowyer off to Baltimore, where they were married on December 12, 1797, and over the next twenty-three years had nine sons and three daughters. For the two decades following his marriage, the ambitious Calwell energetically pursued his burgeoning shipping interests, which involved shipping grain to Europe and then filling the returning ships with fine French garments for the home market. From surviving letters it is clear that at times he or Polly made trips back to the mountains to visit Michael Bowyer, while the other spouse remained at their Eutaw Street home in Baltimore.

The year he died, Bowyer foresaw the need for a larger and more permanent building to improve the collection of log cabins, so he commenced construction of a tavern, with a dining room and a few guest rooms, on a hill just above the spring. This structure, completed in 1808, served for many years as a dining room and later the reception room, and it, plus the miscellaneous cabins, barn, stable, and mills, constituted the improvements on the 950-acre plot of land that was deeded to eldest son, James Bowyer, in 1809. The acres were then divided

In the mid-1780s, the "resort" was in fact a collection of log cabins and tents surrounding the sulphur water spring. This painting by William Grauer is one of the Virginia Room murals.

Portraits of James and Polly Calwell, probably painted in the 1820s. (Courtesy of Mrs. Clarence Colton Milton, a direct descendant of James Calwell.)

equally among the seven children, with a small portion held in common. That son-in-law James Calwell had his eye on eventually running the springs business was clear because he systematically purchased most of the items listed in the appraisal of Michael Bowyer's estate, especially all the furnishings and equipment necessary to operate a resort.

For ten years after Bowyer's death, James Calwell consolidated his holding in the mountains. The transition from Bowyer to Calwell was a slow process because the Baltimore merchant was shuttling back and forth between his established business and his potential business. As early as 1810, he hired a Mr. Herndon to oversee the operation at the sulphur spring. One condition of the lease was that Herndon build ten hewn-log buildings eighteen by twenty feet, finished with shingle roofs and brick chimneys. These cabins stood close to the spring near Bowyer's tavern, and they were the first of a style that would come to dominate the grounds, that is, individual cottages strung together in a row, each row with its own name. Business must have been brisk because Herndon hired his nephew James Frazer as superintendent, and Frazer began the policy of housing overflow guests in nearby farmhouses.

James Calwell's Baltimore shipping business was dealt a disastrous blow during the War of 1812. First commerce was interrupted by the fighting, and then all his ships were either lost or captured. Calwell joined the ranks of Americans defending the homeland against the invading British, and was wounded in the arm during the battle for Fort McHenry in Baltimore harbor. It was during this battle that Francis Scott Key, imprisoned on a ship in the harbor watching the bombardment, was inspired to write *The Star Spangled Banner*. Later, Key was a guest at Calwell's resort and wrote a poem about its charms.

Stung by his reversals during the war, Calwell turned a more serious eye to his prospects as a resort proprietor. Between 1816 and 1819, he purchased the land of the six other Bowyer heirs, except about one hundred acres kept by his sister-in-law Elizabeth Copeland. In 1817, he persuaded eight Baltimore friends to sign notes for a $20,000 loan, about the amount needed to pay for his land acquisitions. Calwell realized that the central attraction offered by his new resort endeavor was the sulphur spring, and he was an astute enough businessman to recognize that symbolism conveyed a comforting message to those taking the water. Therefore, sometime after 1815, he built the first springhouse—a symbolic altar of health—enclosing the source of the water. This first springhouse was a frame structure with wooden columns and a square roof. On top of the roof stood the neatly carved image of an Indian queen in costume, a bundle of arrows in her extended right hand, a large bowl in her left. About this time the resort took the name it would be called for more than a century, White Sulphur Springs, a name derived from the white deposit left by the sulphur water on the surrounding rocks.

Not until 1818 did James Calwell, now forty-five years old, move his family to a permanent home at White Sulphur Springs. A few remaining letters from the years immediately before this move illustrate his concerns. In August 1815, he wrote to his wife Polly that he hoped prices would go down with the end of the War of 1812 and increase the number of visitors. He noted that one night "100 sat down to supper" and that there was a ball every other night. Later in the month he told Polly that "there still continues a large company here and would be many more if there was room." A letter written the next August shows that Calwell had his eye on the competition—Sweet Springs, Warm Springs, and Hot Springs— which was developing in the area: "We found a tolerable good company here which continues, and am in hopes will have a good season taking the lead of all the springs, say double the number of any other." A few weeks later he proudly stated, "We have been much crowded with company ever since and the neighborhood now all full waiting their turn to get in. A very flattering prospect of a good season." In the same letter Calwell mentioned the visit of a distinguished guest, one of hundreds who eventually frequented his resort, the celebrated naval hero of the Barbary Wars: "Commodore [Stephen] Decatur and his lady is here, they intend giving him a ball."

The oldest document in The Greenbrier's archives is an account book for the seasons 1816 and 1817, and it is a most interesting source of information about the details of travel in those early years. For instance, the majority of accounts are for single men traveling alone on horseback, since the road permitted only a few carriages. A typical entry reads: "Doctor George French, servant and two horses arrived to dinner, 5th August." In a smaller number of cases the presence of a woman is indicated: "Edward C. Goodwin, Lady, two servants and three horses arrived to dinner 30 August."

The going rate during those two seasons was about $1.15 per day, or $8.00 per week, although a few were charged $1.50 per day, perhaps for better accommodations or because of their shorter stay. Servants, horses and children (and the last were not common) were all charged the same rate—half price. Most of the gentlemen arrived with one servant and two horses, so the average bill amounted to $20.00 per week, or less than three dollars per day. It was, as might be imagined, liquor that drove an account upwards. The most extravagant spender in this book was a Thomas Watson, who managed to pile up a bill totaling $336.55 for an extended stay of four weeks and five days. The bill for himself, his servants, and two horses was $94.50 and the remaining $242.05 was primarily for juleps, wines, drams and grogs plus a few "segars."

Although a small number of those arriving at White Sulphur Springs were on their way farther west and stayed only two or three days, the majority clearly had the springs as their destination, since they stayed from one to three weeks. Because the account book does not cover the entire seasons of either 1816 or 1817, no accurate count of the total number of visitors is possible, but for July and August of 1816, certainly the most popular months, there are accounts for 374 guests accompanied by 167 servants. The accounts for 1817 begin on June 10, and for the next ninety-seven years, that is until 1914, White Sulphur Springs opened more or less in mid-June and closed at the end of September or in early October. James Calwell, then, needed to pack his business into the prime eight-to-ten week period from mid-July through mid-September.

This account book also contains the list of charges for two of the most prominent men of the day, Stephen Decatur and Henry Clay. Commodore Decatur was a national hero in 1816, following his military rebuke of the Barbary pirates in 1804 and again in 1815. Calwell not only noted his presence in a letter to his wife, but filled in the account book for a sixteen-day stay, from August 20th to September 4th, for a total cost of $87.45. Decatur's bill included an item overlooked today: extra grain for the horses upon departure. He purchased twenty gallons of grain for $3.32. The account for Henry Clay, at that time the Speaker of the House of Representatives, is recorded for a three-day visit in July of 1817. Clay's group consisted of himself, a servant and three horses. A look at his bill shows the pleasures a guest paid for: room and board at $1.50 per day (total $4.50), lodging for his servant ($2.25), stabling his horses ($6.75), two gallons of grain ($ .33), nine more for the trip home ($1.50), a dozen cigars ($ .25), clothes washed ($ .68½), three drinks for his servant ($ .25), all for a grand total of $16.51½. The surprising part of Clay's account is the lack of any charges for his own use of liquor. The only explanation for this absence is that Clay was a favored guest of Calwell. Indeed for the next thirty years, Henry Clay and James Calwell greeted each other almost every summer at White Sulphur Springs.

THE WHITE OR BOWYERS SULPHUR SPRINGS,

Greenbrier county, Virginia.

THESE highly and justly celebrated waters, together with the buildings and a part of the landed estate appertaining thereto, have been leased by the subscribers; who mean to exert their utmost power to prepare for the reception and comfortable accommodation of as many as a want of health, or a wish to preserve it, may induce to visit these well known Fountains of Health, the s lutary effects of which they hope and believe will be much increased by the additional comforts in the accommodation which the subscribers mean to afford   The season will commence on the *First day of July*, 1810; but a good Tavern will at all times be kept open for the reception and accommodation of Travellers and others, under the care of *Mr. James Frazer*, a most respectable man, for whose good conduct the subcribers pledge themselves.

WILLIAM HERNDON & Co.

June 15—4w.

The earliest known advertisement for the resort appeared in the July 4, 1810 issue of the Washington, D.C. National Intelligencer. (Courtesy of Mr. Carl Wolfe)

Henry Clay of Kentucky,
the unofficial host at
White Sulphur Springs for
over three decades before
the Civil War.

Michael Bowyer's original tavern, which stood on the site of today's croquet court.

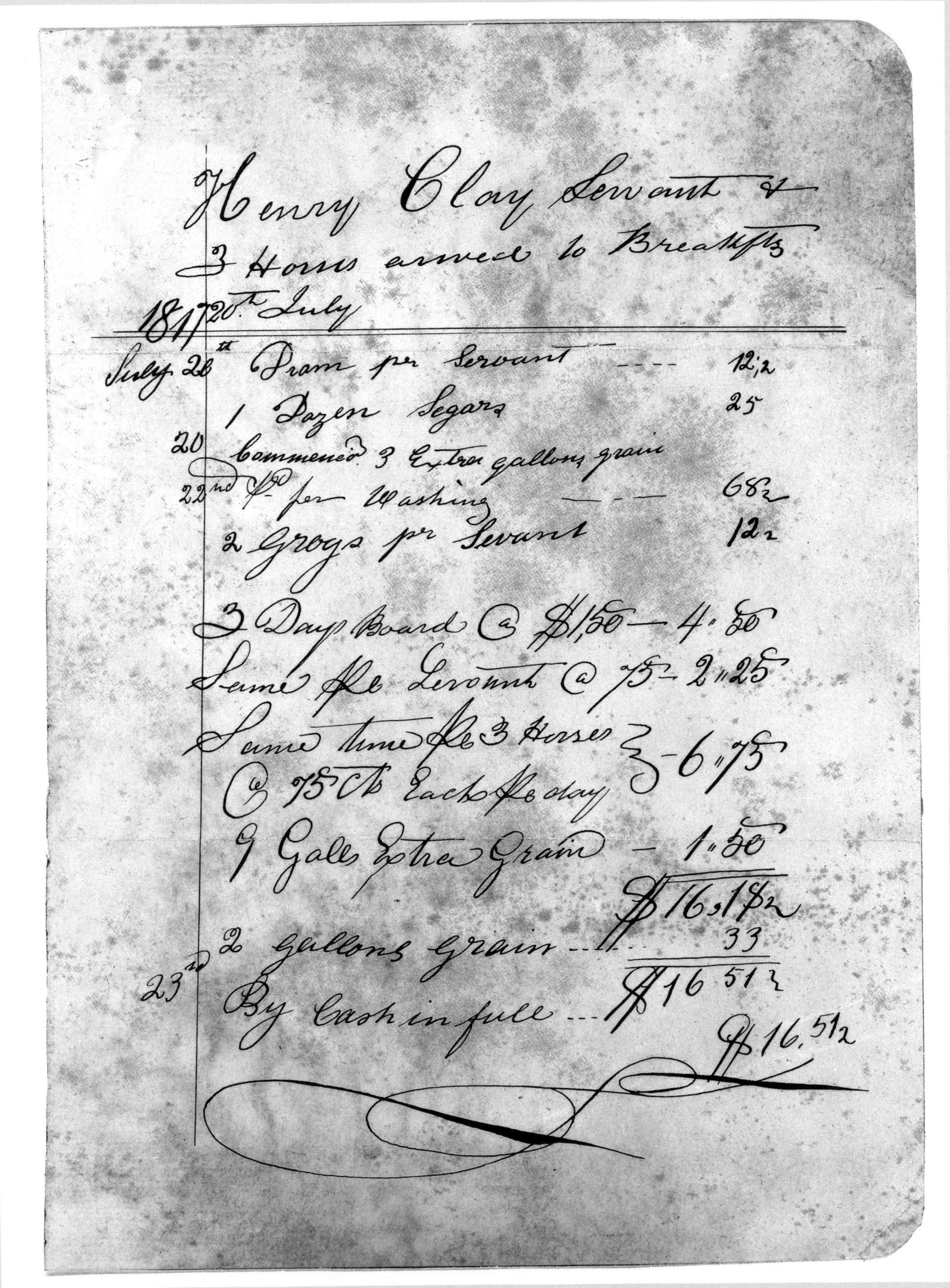

Henry Clay Servant &
3 Horses arrived to Breakfst
1817 20th July

July 20th   6 Dram per Servant   ---   12½
          1 Dozen Segars   25
    20   Commenced 3 Extra gallons grain
    22nd do per Washing   ---   68½
          2 Grogs per Servant   12½

          3 Days Board @ $1,50 — 4. 50
          Same for Servant @ 75 — 2"25
          Same time for 3 Horses
          @ 75 Cts Each per day   } — 6"75
          9 Galls Extra Grain   — 1"50
                                        $16,17½
    23d   2 gallons grain ...   33
                                        $16 51½
          By Cash in full ... $16 51½

                                        $16.51½

Henry Clay's account for his stay of July 20-23, 1817.

Those who knew James Calwell described him as small in stature, with a ruddy complexion and well-liked for his pleasant disposition. The Resident Physician at the springs wrote that Calwell was "one of the finest and best men I have ever known and the very finest sample I have ever seen in manners, dress and general character of the polished gentlemen of the old school." Another local citizen said that he was "honest, kind, generous and benevolent, universally loved by all classes." James Calwell seemed perfectly suited for his role as genial host to prominent gentlemen, generals, politicians, lawyers, writers and social leaders, all of whom accepted him as a gentleman among gentlemen. To resort guests who sometimes complained about the rates, lodging, or food, he had a ready answer which always ran something like this, "You are paying me eight dollars a week for the use of the waters; I am giving you your food and lodging free."

After the middle of the 1820s, James Calwell left the day-to-day management of the resort to his son William, who was then in his early twenties. In later years William B. Calwell was referred to as "the best-known private citizen in America" because of his association with White Sulphur Springs, which lasted until his death in 1880. While William operated the resort, "the elder Calwell," in the words of a Richmond writer, "presided with grace over the economy of the grand watering place, and was the general object of the respect and friendship of his generous guests." James Calwell built a home on the hill above Michael Bowyer's tavern and there attended to long-range planning and to entertaining his special guests.

One of the 300-year-old white oak trees that has graced the lawns of The Greenbrier throughout its history.

Two of those special guests began their visits to White Sulphur Springs about the time James Calwell moved his family there, and these two men—Colonel Richard Singleton of South Carolina and the Honorable Henry Clay of Kentucky—set much of the style and tone of social life at the resort for years to come. Richard Singleton first came to the springs in 1818, and by his death in 1852, he had become the outstanding resort figure of his time. Historian Perceval Reniers, in *The Springs of Virginia*, described Singleton as "the paradigm, the bright and shining example of what a spring-going gentleman should be and do. For thirty years he was the outstanding social figure at the White Sulphur, the Spring of springs, an eminence which he achieved by his unshaken loyalty to the waters, by a gracious and unobtrusive personality, and by his amiable willingness to lend money."

Colonel Singleton represented just the kind of customer Calwell required if he was to develop a fashionable resort. Not only was Singleton the owner of a huge cotton plantation and a respected horse breeder (a passion that Calwell shared), but he was enormously wealthy and quite influential in South Carolina social circles. Beyond that, he was a steady source of loans for Calwell. For example, in the early 1820s the Baltimore creditors who had signed Calwell's $20,000 note back in 1817 were calling for their money, and Singleton was persuaded to pick up that debt. In 1817 Calwell wrote to Singleton that he feared he might fall nearly $3,000 short of his commitments. James sent his son William to nearby Sweet Springs to inform Singleton that in fact the $3,000 was not enough and that perhaps an additional $4,000 would turn the tide. Singleton gladly agreed to both requests since he saw dramatic improvements at White Sulphur Springs and prospects for even more growth.

In 1825 Singleton built the first of two cottages he owned at White Sulphur Springs. This first cottage no longer stands, but it was located directly in the center of the present grounds, forming a right angle to Paradise

Row. The construction of Singleton's cottage began a custom followed by many prominent Southerners who visited the resort annually, that of owning a private cottage on the property. As White Sulphur Springs became ever more popular, getting accommodations was a major feat. At best, the alternative was staying in a boardinghouse nearby, or taking a room in a local farmhouse. To insure good lodging in a favored location then, it was wise to own a cottage. The owner paid the construction costs, and the cottage was built by Calwell, who thereby controlled the continuity of architecture by forming neat rows of similarly designed units. An owner paid the same weekly rate as any other guest, but he or she was assured of lodging upon arrival. However, if a private cottage was not in use Calwell would rent it out to other guests. No record remains of Singleton's purchase, but in 1832 his brother-in-law, Tucker Coles, built one next to him for $200.00. The same year a Mr. George Harrison bought a cottage in Paradise Row for $150.00.

The other special trend-setting guest of James Calwell was Henry Clay who, during his long political career, served as Speaker of the House, Senator from Kentucky, leader of the Whig party, as well as being a perennial presidential candidate. Clay often stopped at White Sulphur Springs on his way back and forth from Washington, D.C., to his home in Kentucky. It was during these visits Calwell and Clay became fast friends, exchanging numerous letters throughout the year concerning politics, family matters and mutual friends. In his letters to Calwell, Clay confided intimate details about his wife's health, his political hopes and disappointments; and sent eminent guests to the Springs, including Lord Morpeth from Britain, Charles Gayarre, the prominent New Orleans judge and Louisiana historian, and Abbott Lawrence, the founder of the industrial town of Lawrence, Massachusetts.

Henry Clay's presence galvanized the social life at the Springs. As one historian wrote about Clay: "He had the gift of winning friends and influencing people especially by his wonderful oratorical voice. His warm and genial nature attracted friends to him, and his love of pleasure was another bond of union with the mass of men. He was fond of drinking Kentucky whiskey, playing cards, dancing and being the lion at White Sulphur Springs." While Clay was at the resort, he was always the center of attention and was widely recognized as a kind of unofficial host. Yet even Henry Clay knew the difficulties of obtaining a good cottage on the grounds. He wrote from Staunton in 1832 that he was on his way and wished to stop. "The rumor is that you are overflowing and can take in no more. On the other hand, our friend Judge Brook told me that you were reserving a cabin for me. I hope this information was correct." Ever considerate, Clay added a postscript: "Supposing you would like to know who I have with me, I transmit this inventory: Mrs. Clay, a little grandson and myself compose the members of our party. Then we have four servants, two carriages, six horses, a jackass, and a shepherd dog—strange medley, is it not?" Demonstrating his warm feelings for James Calwell, Clay sent him a gift of prized Durham cattle raised on his plantation from imported stock and a portrait by the noted Kentucky artist, Matthew Jouett.

Rheumatism.

THE employment of the White Sulphur water in the treatment of rheumatism first drew attention to its great value as a remedial agent, and the reputation thus early acquired has been established and confirmed by its successful use in this disease.

The relation of the water to the treatment of the disease is so evident that nature could hardly explain more clearly than she has done, by laying open to us this great means of cure, in what manner we shall act as her ministers in driving out the foe that has settled in the organism.

Who is not acquainted with some member of that great army of diseases gathered together under the standard of "Rheumatism"—Rheumatism of the Joints, Rheumatism of the Muscles, Rheumatic Neuralgia, Rheumatic Bronchitis, Rheumatic Colic, Rheumatic Anæsthesia, Rheumatic Gout, Rheumatic Lassitude, Rheumatic Spasms, Rheumatic Ischiatica—all of which disappear by the use of these waters.

34

An 1882 brochure extolled the virtues of the sulphur water as a treatment for rheumatism.

This rather fanciful view of colonial visitors gathered around the springhouse is from the murals in the Virginia Room.

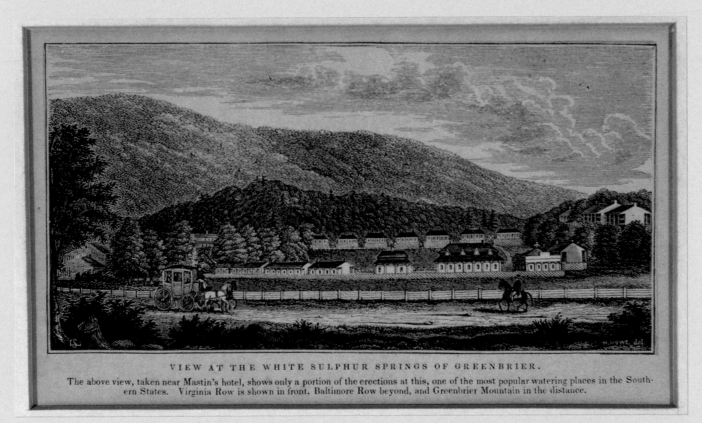

VIEW AT THE WHITE SULPHUR SPRINGS OF GREENBRIER.

The above view, taken near Mastin's hotel, shows only a portion of the erections at this, one of the most popular watering places in the Southern States. Virginia Row is shown in front, Baltimore Row beyond, and Greenbrier Mountain in the distance.

This print appeared in Henry Howe's Virginia, Its History and Antiquities, *published in 1845.*

Agreeable Society in a Mountain Garden

"There is an indefinable something at the White Sulphur Springs," wrote one doctor, "that swallows up the principal patronage of the great fashionable public far and near." By the late 1820s, just fifty years after Mrs. Anderson had been carried by litter to the wondrous spring of mineral water, word of that "indefinable something" had spread across the young nation, especially through the southern states. The evolution of White Sulphur Springs from an obscure mountain outpost into the most fashionable social resort in the South was on the verge of realization.

There were, in fact, a number of tangible factors that combined to make the resort something special. The natural beauty of the location was incomparable. Since most visitors were accustomed to expanses of flat countryside in the lowlands, the small valley sheltered by ranges of mountains and the "neat little village" of white cottages set into the hillsides were remarkable sights. And of course to visitors escaping the hot and muggy southern summers or the choking dust of the cities, the cool mountain air was exhilarating. More than a few writers of the day referred to the springs as a "Garden of Eden."

However attractive the setting, though, it took the right people frequenting the place to give it that "indefinable something." Above all, it was the society that congregated at White Sulphur Springs every July, August and September that fueled its reputation. Across the gravel paths under the oaks and maples strolled presidents, diplomats, foreign travelers, congressmen, military officers, lawyers, editors, ministers, writers, merchants and poets. White Sulphur Springs "is distinguished by the excellence and polish of its company," noted a Philadelphia physician in 1833. "Whatever Virginia has of wealth, talent, personal elegance or professional eminence finds itself represented, and by a proper combination forms a gay and highly finished aggregate." Even Ann Royal, known as the first woman journalist in America (and for her caustic comments on society) was prompted to comment that the visitors to the springs "are people of the first rank in the United States, they are people of fashion and taste, as well as great wealth."

In particular, it was the owners of immense Southern plantations who set the tone of social intercourse at White Sulphur Springs. While the number of slaveholding, large landholders in the ante-bellum South was actually quite small, their style of living was the ideal for the rest of the Southern population. Subsequent notions of life on an Old South plantation have become encrusted with romantic images over the years, but one fundamental reality of plantation life was that the manor homes were quite far from one another. Southern civilization was essentially rural and agricultural. Neither large nor small farmers lived near cities, so a common meeting place was a necessity. The summer season at White Sulphur Springs fitted that need perfectly. From tobacco plantations in Virginia, rice and cotton plantations in the Carolinas and Georgia, and sugar plantations in Louisiana, the Southern gentleman and his family migrated to the springs to pass their summers together. And later, as King Cotton moved west, they arrived from more distant plantations in Texas, Missouri and Mississippi.

At White Sulphur Springs the various elements of society mixed together in an atmosphere that lacked pretension and fostered free and easy sociability. The well-known Virginia writer, John Esten Cooke, once remarked that "the visitors were a single family, everybody knowing everybody else . . . there was no stiffness or ceremony whatever. The weeks passed in a round of enjoyment, and so strong a hold did this annual visit to the White Sulphur take on the old planter class, that to have been compelled to forego it for a single season would have been regarded by them as a real misfortune." Echoing that sentiment in more personal terms was the definitive statement of Richmond judge James Lyons: "If I can't go to The White as I am accustomed to do, well then, by George, I'll just stay home and die."

There is one other important factor explaining why White Sulphur Springs seemed to burst into national prominence so suddenly in the 1830s, and that was the economic boom that swept the country in that decade. The industrial revolution was still in its infancy, but the growing demand by Northern and British textile factories for more and more raw cotton spurred a tremendous expansion of production on the Southern plantations. The export value of the cotton crop stood at $25 million in 1831, $64 million in 1835, and $71 million in 1836. Tobacco, sugar and rice planters saw a comparable steep rise in the value of their products. These, indeed, were the "Flush Thirties." Not only did money expand, the American population almost doubled between 1820 and 1840, and that population poured from the towns, cities, and farms along the eastern seaboard to the Allegheny Mountains and beyond. The young nation was restless, and the transportation revolution in the second quarter of the nineteenth century channeled that energy into motion, building new turnpikes, canals, and eventually railroads. Virginia had its plans to partake in the frenzy of transportation improvements, and building the James River and Kanawha Turnpike was one part of that scheme.

For James Calwell's venture in the wilderness, the completion of this turnpike was the catalyst that brought together all the other elements critical to his success. A combination of the right water, the right climate, the right scenery may have been a powerful magnet, but un-

til the right people could reach his resort in relative ease, he was left out of the general prosperity. In 1821 Calwell permitted, quite gladly one must assume, the James River Company to build through his property. The road was generally twenty-two feet wide, with a raised center and sloped ditches for good drainage, and although not open year round, it was more than adequate in the summer months. The turnpike was open from the east to White Sulphur Springs by 1824, and by 1827 the first stage-coaches began rolling westward towards the Ohio River Valley.

By the late 1820s and early 1830s the James River and Kanawha Turnpike had become a very busy route. Salt in great quantities moved eastward on the road from the mines in the Kanawha Valley, and some of the 26,000 hogs driven to markets in the east in 1826 provided ham and bacon at the resort. For the wave of settlers heading westward to establish homesteads in Indiana, Ohio, Kentucky and Illinois, the turnpike was one of very few roads that ran in an east-west direction, that is, up and over the Appalachian Mountains. The James River and Kanawha Turnpike was, to say the least, a colorful road, as described by historian Lyle Bryce: "Twenty-four hours a day, seven days a week, landgrabbers, speculators, prospectors, trappers, traders, gamblers, fancy women, corn doctors, jugglers, magicians, small circuses, museums, and army officers headed west, and great fleets of covered wagon schooners hauling goods used this road." This "carnival," as Bryce aptly called it, rolled merrily along the turnpike carrying American dreams in the face of highwaymen, debilitating rains, fallen trees, strenuous inclines and treacherous declines.

A perhaps somewhat exaggerated depiction of stagecoach travel through the mountains to White Sulphur Springs from Edward King's 1875 book The Great South.

The Humpback Bridge, which still stands today near Covington, Virginia, spanned Dunlap's Creek as part of the James River and Kanawha Turnpike.

With the opening of the turnpike, entrepreneurs quickly connected all towns and villages of any size by stagecoach lines, and travelers from all directions bound for the springs poured over the mountains and through the passes. The journey by stagecoach was a major part of the White Sulphur Springs experience, and travel journals of the day devoted many pages to the routes taken, the tavern stops along the way, and the picturesque scenery. Travelers departing Baltimore or Washington rode most of the distance in a stagecoach, although in the 1830s Washington and Fredericksburg, Virginia, were connected by steamboats on the Potomac River. The trip from Washington by stage and steamboat lasted about four days, depending mostly on luck and the weather, with four or five transfer points along the way. They made a last stop at Callaghan's tavern, about fifteen miles east of White Sulphur Springs, to rest for the night and sample the famous fried chicken. Visitors from the west and southwest needed to get to the Mississippi River first, and from there they traveled upriver by steamboat without much trouble—except for a possible boiler explosion—into the Ohio River, where they disembarked at Guyandotte (present day Huntington, West Virginia). Families then boarded stagecoaches for a grueling three-day ride over the mountains to White Sulphur Springs. Many wealthy planters traveling overland from the Carolinas and Georgia organized elaborate caravans, for

it was the event of the year to travel up to the springs. The usual retinue, stretched out along the road for half a mile or so, included a fine private carriage for the ladies and small children, a baggage wagon containing the belongings of the family, and various vehicles bearing the older children, the ladies' wardrobes, and numerous servants. The planter and his sons rode alongside on their thoroughbreds, with a few select horses in tow for pleasure riding at the springs. A comment in *Harper's Weekly* explained the spirit behind this mode of travel: "In those days people did not come away from home so much as bring their homes, or as much as possible of their homes, with them."

Although travel by private carriage was not at all uncommon, as stagecoach lines improved, most visitors rode in individual commercial coaches and the travel journals of the day are filled with stories about the interesting, odd, and sometimes impressive characters met inside the coach. Edward Hill, a farmer from northern Virginia, kept a journal of his 1836 visit, which reveals some of the troublesome details of this means of transportation. Leaving his home near Fredericksburg, he endured riding backwards for nine hours and then a "miserably mean dinner" at a tavern in Gordonsville. The next morning he encountered the surprising custom of rising at three o'clock for the day's journey and found, moreover, that the coach traveled for three hours before stopping for breakfast. On his third day out, fifteen hours of dusty riding carried him only seventy miles—slower than usual, but then the average speed of a stagecoach was only six miles per hour. After getting up at three in the morning, he got to bed after ten at night and was up again the next morning at three. Edward Hill's stroke of bad luck came while descending a particularly steep and rocky hill where the coach broke down and everybody got out while the male passengers repaired the damage with a fence rail found nearby. Travelers of the day, presumably referring to suspension systems and road conditions, commonly called these stagecoaches "shakeguts."

Despite all these trials, the approach to White Sulphur Springs through the last few miles of rolling hills and wide meadows caused a rising pitch of excitement in all weary travelers. John H.B. Latrobe, a young Baltimore lawyer, described this final stretch in an 1832 letter: "As we descended the mountain there were various indications of our approach to the center of attraction in this part of the Union. A gay barouche drawn by prancing, foaming horses filled with ladies and followed by gentlemen on horses dashed by us, and inquisitive glances were exchanged with the stage passengers with parties looking for known faces. Then came a single cavalier with the servant in livery, then a carriage and four with curtains drawn and a laughing party within. Then three or four sulkies and buggies, then the more staid, sober hacks with people inside looking like invalids . . ." Finally, Latrobe could pick out signs of civilization as he crested the last hill and exclaimed excitedly, "There was *the spot*! Cottages hidden in the dark green foliage, long rows of white homes of all descriptions scattered here and there, and as we came into the precincts there on the right was the ascending lawn of the freshest verdure surrounded with its picturesque cabins with carriages of all fashions under its trees and gay groups laughing and running and walking across it."

Given the months of anticipation and preparation preceding the trip, and the many miles of rough road covered en route, the arrival at White Sulphur Springs was a magical moment. "There is something in the first view of the White Sulphur very prepossessing and almost enchanting," wrote a correspondent for the *Southern Literary Messenger* in 1835. "After rolling along among the mountains and dense forests, the wild and uncultivated scenery is at once exchanged for the neatness and elegance of refined society, and the bustle and parade of the fashionable world." Another writer, after days of riding from Washington, arrived to the sound of a band playing on the porch of the dining room as guests were streaming to dinner. "The whole face of things had the look of enchantment," she wrote. "It seemed to us

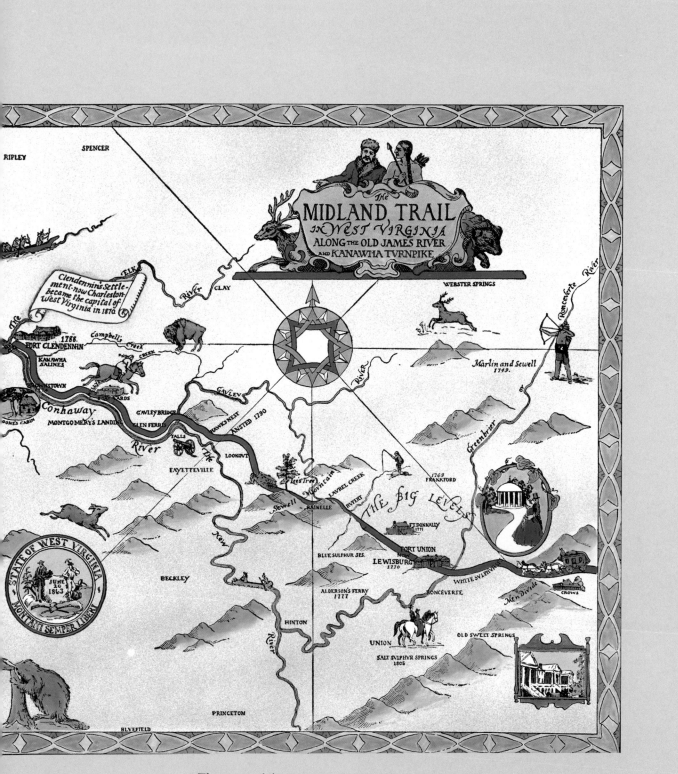

The route of the James River and Kanawha Turnpike
through West Virginia. In the 1920s it was renamed
the Midland Trail, or U.S. Route 60.

travelers, arriving at such a time, as if the inhabitants of some fairy isle were turning out to welcome the coming of expected strangers."

And what did the property look like to a visitor in the 1830s? That depended upon which year they arrived, because James and William Calwell were busily—indeed almost frantically—building new structures each year. The resort was more than three times as large in 1840 as it was in 1830; guest capacity grew from about two hundred to over seven hundred. White Sulphur Springs was a cottage resort, that is, each family or group occupied a single cabin within a row, giving the place the appearance of a well laid-out little town. A visitor in the mid-1830s saw a range of accommodations stretching through the valley that included old whitewashed log cabins (even then considered ancient relics of pioneer days), modest ivy-covered white houses with their indispensable front porches, and magnificent private residences perched on prominent hills.

A tour of the grounds began in front of Michael Bowyer's tavern, where visitors registered and some were assigned rooms upstairs. The tavern also functioned as the dining room in the early part of the decade, until a new one was built in front of it, in the middle of

the grounds. This was necessary because none of the cottages had kitchens, and all meals were taken in common in the dining rooms. Also in the center of the property stood the ballroom, where festive dances were staged nightly. Where the walkway now passes above the Springhouse to the Golf Clubhouse was the string of cottages James Calwell had ordered built in 1810. Next came a few older buildings called "Young Bucks' Row," which, no doubt, were the bachelors' rooms. Following the bend of the hill, where Valley View Estate House is located today, was Wolf Row. One writer warned visitors to avoid Wolf Row "unless you be young and foolish, fond of noise and nonsense, frolic and fun, wine and wassail, sleepless nights and days of headache." Large hunting parties assembled at Wolf Row each morning. In the evening, deer shot that day would be served in a room decorated with stags' antlers, bearskins, firearms and bugles. At night, Wolf Row was transformed into the gambling establishment. Gamblers—or "blacklegs" as they were called—laid their money down all night long at gaming tables, cards or billiards. "Those remarkably well-dressed, genteel men lounging about the cabin door," remarked John H.B. Latrobe, "are priests of the Temple of Fortune . . . you will find many whom you would not suspect among the votaries."

Below the springhouse, where the Indoor Tennis Building now stands, was the site of the original bathhouse. Sulphur water ran down a trough from the spring

Long after the days of stagecoaches, the old vehicles were used as reminders of years gone by. This 1920s photograph shows a coach that was used to bring guests from the train station to the entrance of The Greenbrier.

feeding the bathing pools inside. The White Sulphur Spring water issues at a fairly constant temperature—about sixty degrees—and thus it has always had to be heated for comfortable bathing. Guests clad in long robes frequented the bathhouse throughout the morning. However, to preserve decorum, separate bathing hours were maintained for men and women. Not far from the bathhouse were two large frame horse stables with eighty stalls in each. Some of the oldest buildings standing in the early 1830s were next to the stables. For that reason, they were known as "Flea Row" because those varmints were reportedly found there. About 1835 "Flea Row" was removed and replaced with Alabama Row and, where the present-day Golf Clubhouse is, new stables housing four hundred horses were built.

On line with Alabama Row was Paradise Row, the earliest of the cottages that still stand. The Row was built in small sections throughout the 1820s until they—like Alabama Row—evolved into attached units with a common porch. Originally Paradise Row was called Brick Row (these were the first cottages constructed of brick) and how the name eventually changed to "Paradise" is not clear. According to one writer, the cottages were up a considerable hill and like the heavenly paradise they were difficult to attain. Another theory is that these cottages had the best mirrors, along with other advantages, and were therefore the most coveted at the resort. John H.B. Latrobe called them "the most aristocratic" accommodations. Others have presumed that because these cottages were often occupied by honeymooning couples, it is that use that explains the name. In 1832 Samuel Hoffman of Baltimore and his father were assigned a two-room apartment in Paradise Row, due, Hoffman thought, to his father's long friendship with James Calwell. Quite pleased, he wrote to his wife, "In front is a beautiful view of the valley and the mountains, and all that is going on, on the lawn. A prettier spot I scarcely know—better sleeping accommodations I have rarely met with in this country." Of course, the name Paradise Row led to some wry comments over the years. In 1836 one visitor wrote home, "Mrs. Harrison, whom we visited this morning, lives in Paradise Row, I thought we never should find her house, so it seems paradise is not so easily found or entered, as some imagine." Years later a young man noted, "The Rector is here and was put in 'Paradise Row,' probably they thought he might as well be in that abode of bliss here anyhow!"

In 1835, Stephen Henderson, a Louisiana sugar planter, built the most imposing cottage on the property, choosing the high ground between Paradise and Alabama Rows. Henderson was relatively unknown to most of the visitors to the springs, and even today little is known about him except that he arrived from Scotland a

Baltimore Row in the 1830s, from a painting by John H.B. Latrobe.

Stephen Henderson's private house, the summer home of five presidents before the Civil War. Today, this is the President's Cottage Museum.

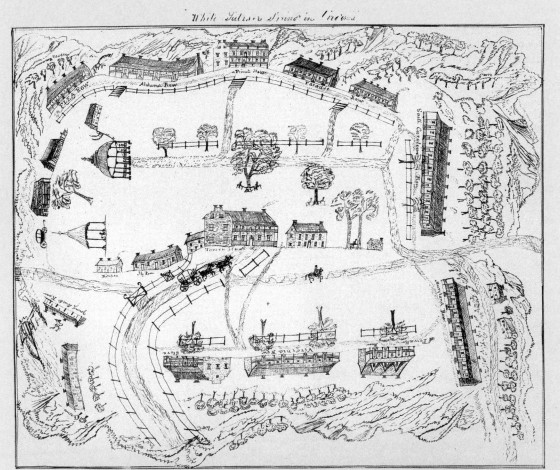

This unusual map is the oldest of White Sulphur Springs, probably drawn about 1835. Michael Bowyer's tavern is in the center. Directly above—labeled "a Private House"—is the President's Cottage Museum. Alabama and Paradise rows remain today. Note accommodations called "Flea Row," "Fly Row," and (upside down) "Young Bucks Row."

penniless youth, built a vast fortune as a merchant, and left a baffling will that was tied up in the courts for years after his death. In 1816 he married Elenore Zelia Destrehan, and later in the 1820s they inherited her family's one-thousand acre plantation on the Mississippi River. Henderson's two-story cottage (now the Presidents' Cottage Museum) offered a commanding view of the entire resort property. It was his proud statement that Louisiana sugar money had arrived and was the equal of cotton and tobacco wealth from Virginia and the Carolinas. As one historian has written, "Mr. Henderson's house was the first of the private cottages on the grand scale, the first to throw out its chest and raise its head and crow loudly of great riches." Unfortunately, Stephen Henderson did not live long enough to enjoy his summer retreat for more than a few seasons. Upon his death in 1838, James Calwell took over the cottage, reserving it for his most important guests, because it was the finest single cottage available. Among those guests, before the Civil War, were Presidents Martin Van Buren, John Tyler, Millard Fillmore, Franklin Pierce, and James Buchanan. Though the cottages was offered to the Presidents as a mark of respect, it was never officially designated the Presidents' Cottage at the time; rather, it was simply called the Henderson House.

All together the cottages shaded by noble oaks formed a large, hollow square facing inwards towards the lawn. Alabama Row, the Henderson House, and Paradise Row formed one side, the dining room and Virginia Row were on the other. Virginia Row was expanded throughout the 1830s. During part of the decade it was called "Compulsion Row," because guests were compelled to stay there even though the cottages were not entirely completed. Connecting the end of Paradise Row to Virginia Row were the handsome cottages of Carolina Row, including Richard Singleton's, and these formed the eastern side of the square.

By the mid-1830s, with the building of Baltimore Row, the collection of cottages was beginning to expand beyond this configuration. Some of the most aesthetically pleasing cottages to ever grace the grounds, Baltimore Row was started around 1834 when John H.B. Latrobe, the son of the famous architect Benjamin Latrobe, designed a cottage for himself and his new bride from Natchez, Mississippi. Building in the popular Greek Revival style, Latrobe's cottage set the architectural pattern for all the cottages that followed. Obviously James Calwell had kept up his Baltimore contacts because the seven cottages were soon purchased by residents of that city. One of the cottages was owned by Jerome Napoleon Bonaparte, who was the son of Betsy Patterson of Baltimore and Jerome Bonaparte, the brother of the French Emperor. Their marriage was short-lived because Emperor

Napoleon arranged an annulment so that his brother might make a more politically beneficial match, and eventually Betsy returned to Baltimore. She and her son and grandson became annual visitors at White Sulphur Springs, lending their glamorous name to the summertime society.

But the most ambitious cottage construction began in 1838, the project of two South Carolina cotton planters. One was the ever-present Colonel Richard Singleton, who wanted a new cottage to replace his original home. The other was Colonel Wade Hampton II, regarded at the time as the wealthiest man in the South. When these two gentlemen saw Stephen Henderson's house rise above the others, they recognized the challenge; both proceeded to flaunt their Carolina cotton money, building three stately cottages in a row, high on the hill above Baltimore Row. The Singleton family occupied one cottage, the Hampton family another, and the third (the one still standing) they shared to accommodate friends. Each structure boasted a double portico supported by six large, white columns, and all together they were called the Colonnades. "The effect was imposing," wrote one

A view of the Colonnades in the 1870s.

historian, "eighteen pillars in one long file, capturing some of the grandeur that was Greece, some of the splendor that was Rome." In the summer of 1838, Richard Singleton's youngest daughter, Angelica, was courted by President Martin Van Buren's eldest son, Abraham, in the shadow of the Colonnades. The couple was married on Singleton's twelve-thousand-acre plantation that November and, a few years later, he transferred the deed to his Colonnade cottage to his new son-in-law, Abraham Van Buren.

All of these cottages—from rustic log cabins to the miniature mansions of Henderson, Hampton and Singleton—stood in homage to the major attraction of the center of the grounds, the new Springhouse James Calwell had built in the early 1830s. Because the spring of sulphur water accounted for the resort's existence, the Springhouse was the physical and symbolic center of this summertime universe. And since the use of mineral water for health goes back to ancient Greek civilizations, Calwell chose a classical structure to mark the gift of nature that drew so many visitors to his property. The statue atop the Springhouse today is the second one to stand in that spot (the first was destroyed during the Civil War), but the original was the gift of Stephen Henderson. It was the Hygeia, the Goddess of Health. The donor wanted to ensure that everyone knew the source of his gift, so he had the following words engraved in gold around its base: "Hygeia, Presented by S. Henderson, Esq. of New Orleans." The best available description of this Hygeia on the Springhouse was written by a Philadelphian in 1836: "The statue is a buxom, hearty, handsome lass, with her bones of pine well covered with wooden flesh and drapery, and pigment of snowy white. Her left arm is folded in the coils of a serpent, which it is probable she has just poisoned with a draught of sulphur water out of a bowl which is in her right hand."

The earliest known photograph of the Springhouse, taken in the 1850s, showing the original statue atop the dome. (Courtesy of Mr. James S. Patton)

Certainly President Martin Van Buren's month-long visit in 1838 marked that season as one of the most brilliant in a decade of fabled seasons. However, the daily routine of life at White Sulphur Springs that year was, in truth, much the same as any other. Part of the charm, of course, was that life at the springs was quite simple; in fact, it was downright plain. With the exception of Henderson's house and the Colonnades, the cottages were not extravagant.

The highest compliment visitors might pay was that their accommodations were "particularly comfortable." The Virginia writer John Esten Cooke noted the incongruity between the social status of the gathered company and the simplicity of the cottages: "These men and women, accustomed to every comfort, were quite content with the split-bottomed chairs, the plain beds, the pine tables, and the rustic routine of the spot. It offered them—indeed much more than their fine homes could supply—health, high spirits, and an atmosphere so delightfully cool and bracing even in the 'dog days' that it made life a luxury."

Excitement at White Sulphur Springs was produced by the opportunity to meet a wide variety of people, especially as the resort's fame spread through the country. A Philadelphia bookseller, writing under the memorable pen name "Peregrine Prolix," was unmatched in his ability to compress into one sentence the social mix he saw during his 1834 visit: "From the East you have consolidationists, tariffites, and philanthropists; from the middle, professors, chemical analysts, and letter writers; from the West, gentlemen who can squat lower, jump higher, dive deeper, and come out drier than all creation besides; and from the South, nullifiers, union men, political economists, and statesmen; and from all quarters, functionaries of all ranks, ex-candidates for all functions, and the gay, young, agreeable and handsome of both sexes, who come to the White Sulphur to see and to be seen, to chat, to laugh and dance, and each to throw his pebble on the great heap of the general enjoyment."

How did the visitors pass their time to create this heap of enjoyment? A typical day at the springs began quite early with a visit to the Springhouse, where a gregarious crowd gathered under the dome to dip sulphur water from the spring into individual cups. The accepted routine was to drink three glasses of the water before each meal—although many insisted that if three glasses were good, then five, seven, or more were even better. A British guest commented that during this ritual, "One of

the greatest amusements was to listen to the variety of theories afloat about the properties and modes of application of the waters." Everyone then walked the short distance to the dining room for breakfast, which started promptly at eight. To take advantage of the coolest part of the day, visitors dispersed from the dining room to their varied activities.

Many chose to go for walks or carriage rides through the countryside because of the fine mountain views and grand expanses of natural scenery. Watching one riding party mount their horses, an 1835 visitor noted, "There are a great many beautiful rides and walks near here; the ladies ride a great deal on horseback, and several frights occurred, but no serious accidents: they only gave the gentlemen an opportunity of displaying their gallantry, and the ladies their bravery, or timidity, whichever they deemed most becoming." Also popular were excursions to nearby Lewisburg, where visitors could hear famous lawyers argue their cases before the annual sessions of the Virginia District Court. Others rode out along Howard's Creek, or further to the Greenbrier River, seeking a secluded fishing spot. Elaborate hunting parties, launched from Wolf Row and accompanied by hounds from the kennel of James Calwell's son, sped up, over, and around Kate's and Greenbrier Mountains, tracking the abundant game. For the gentlemen, James Calwell sponsored a horse market out in the meadows of bluegrass, where many a Greenbrier County steed—including Calwell's—was sold or traded.

But the great expanse of lawn surrounded by cottages was the social center during the daylight hours. Each morning Peregrine Prolix found it "humming like a beehive." Benches scattered about the lawn under full-leafed trees were filled with small groups engaged in conversation. Here youngsters heard heroic tales of the American Revolution; politicians and planters smoked cigars as they discussed elections and prices; many women played flutes and guitars to entertain friends; and children shrieked with delight as they played quoit. All anticipated the punctual visits of the cake-man, who brought trays of sweets, and the unnamed little boy in the straw hat, who carried buckets of maple sugar in from the mountains, not to mention the arrival of the daily stage, which always provoked a flurry of intense curiosity because it bore new guests to complement the company plus long-awaited letters from home. In this relaxed atmosphere, guests might mingle with well-known figures such as Dolly Madison, Daniel Webster, Davy Crockett, Francis Scott Key, John C. Calhoun, and, of course, Henry Clay.

Most visitors returned to the Springhouse in the early afternoon for more mineral water and then settled down in front of the dining room portico to listen to a band play until two o'clock, when the large meal of the day was served. Dinner was always a crowded affair. The dining room consisted of twelve long tables, each seating as many as fifty people, and seating arrangements were organized by place cards bearing the names of individual guests. Lamb, beef, and chicken were supplied in abundance, and vegetables came directly from the garden. By all accounts, meals were nearly rowdy affairs, mainly because Americans were notorious for the speed with which they ate; epicurean sophistication was not a national trait, as visiting Europeans were startled to discover. John H.B. Latrobe offered this description in 1832: "Crowds collect around the doors of the dining room when the bell rings, and when they are opened every man, woman and child rushes to the seats assigned them and in an instant the viands are snatched and in another instant, almost, consumed." Historians say that fifteen to twenty minutes was considered plenty of time to eat a meal in the United States of the 1830s. The problem was aggravated at White Sulphur Springs because perhaps half of the visitors brought their own servants, and those servants went into the kitchen to collect and deliver meals directly to their employers. Thus, Latrobe gave the following advice: "When you eat, you must watch for the food immediately in front of you. If placed there for your own special use by your servant, it is your private property which will be snatched unless you look sharply to it. If you have no servant, you must bribe one of those attached to the place or you run the risk of getting little or nothing. Bribe high and you live high, avoid bribery and you starve. 'Look sharp—eat fast—and forget good manners,' this is the motto of the dinner room at the White Sulphur."

Once the midday meal was completed—which apparently was not very long after it started—visitors poured out from the dining room to pass a slow afternoon. The warmest part of the day at White Sulphur Springs was surely cooler than an afternoon in New Orleans, Richmond, Washington, D.C., or most other places in the South, but still the heat tended to make for lazy afternoons. Many visitors returned to their cottages to sit for a spell or to visit friends on their porches. Some took naps in preparation for the evening's activities, others played billiards or nine pins, while still others made their way to the store in Virginia Row, where the shelves were packed with buttons, laces, silks, shoes, perfumery, jewelry, baskets, stage whips and dry goods—"in short," one shopper noted, "everything which could be wanted or asked for."

In the early evening, once again, all made their pilgrimage to the Springhouse, then slowly the guests gathered in the dining room for a light evening meal. According to a writer with another of those unusual pen names, "Mark Pencil," this was a particularly lively time of day: "Til twilight the whole grounds are interspersed with company, promenading, laughing, chatting, and many anticipating the coming pleasures of the ball." Each night at eight the crowds met under the three brilliant chandeliers in the ballroom for the Virginia Reel until eleven. Looking out over the grounds at the end of the day's activities one writer evoked this dream-like scene from 1835: "We know of no scene more romantic and picturesque than that presented to a spectator from one of the cottages on the hill, after the lamps have been lighted for the night. The floods of light streaming among the trees and from every window, the throngs of the gay and fashionable crowding the walks for the evening's promenade, and the thrilling melody of the rich music from a fine German band throws quite a fairy-tale influence around this pleasant retreat among the mountains."

Going for a carriage ride through the mountain forests was always a pleasant diversion during a visit to White Sulphur Springs.

In the 1830s, several rather unique characters on the resort's staff invariably drew comments from guests. There was "Uncle Duncan," the Scotsman, who lived alone behind Alabama Row. Guests needing hot water, sulphur water, or firewood simply opened their back door and shouted his name. Then there was Charley, the butcher, who fascinated John H.B. Latrobe: "Were I a novelist he would be invaluable to me," Latrobe wrote.

accept or turn them away. Because of his authority, which appeared to be regulated mostly by whim, he was considered by some to be the most powerful man in the South. Getting past Major Anderson and into a room on the grounds could be a delicate task—another reason why it was a wise policy to own a private cottage. Peregrine Prolix (who never had any trouble with him) labeled Anderson "The Magnanimous, Mysterious, Mellifluent Metternich of the Mountains." Many guests never knew his real name, referring to him only as "Metternich," after the imperious Austrian statesman of the day. Everyone courted the Major because, as one British

An 1870 illustration from Every Saturday *magazine showing crowds gathered around the Springhouse.*

Charley could slaughter and dress a steer or sheep in a matter of minutes, all the while boasting of his feats of riding, shooting and fighting the British in the War of 1812. One could also bribe Charley for choice cuts of meat at the table. In addition, Charley served as the grave-digger, although "he often complains that his spade gets rusty," said Mark Pencil, "so few persons die here."

Every visitor had the rather nerve-racking opportunity to meet the "Minister Plenipotentiary and Envoy Extraordinary of the Calwells"—the legendary Mayor Baylis Anderson. He was sometimes called the manager, but his real function was to screen new arrivals and either

traveler explained, "his word is law and his fiat is immovable, and he presumes not a little upon his power." Tales of Anderson were legion and repeated from Baltimore to New Orleans as visitors prepared for their journey. "To him," a Richmond lady wrote, "senators bow, legislators, judges, professors are supplicants, flattering beaux and flattering belles sue for his high permission, without which all is lost."

Once inside the gates of White Sulphur Springs, however, guests might relax, and turn their attentions to more important matters; Colonel William Pope of Alabama, the master of ceremonies in the ballroom, made sure of that. Colonel Pope reigned in the ballroom

President Martin Van Buren's visit to White Sulphur Springs in 1838 made that one of the most memorable seasons of the antebellum era.

throughout the 1830s, where he took the disorganized gyrating that passed for dancing and perfected it into a system. His system was designed not only for smoother dancing, more importantly it established a proper means of introducing young people to the opposite sex, and was clearly a vehicle for arranging marriages. "Kind, good old man!" wrote an anonymous author who dedicated her book to him, "Few, like him, when they have passed the age of romance, retain sufficient recollection of their youth to excite an interest in the enjoyments of youth. But here he was promoting the happiness of all—causing sociability and hilarity where but for him stiffness and ceremony would have prevailed."

Colonel Pope was best known for the association he founded: The Billing, Wooing and Cooing Society. The constitution of this society was written on a long roll of pink paper and hung on the wall of the ballroom. Beneath the articles of the constitution were the signatures of all the members, no less than seventeen-hundred gentlemen from all parts of the United States. In order to make the acquaintance of a young lady, a gentleman had to known by at least one of the members. "He has fallen on an excellent plan," one matron wrote,

"for the protection of the dear sweet young ladies from villains and imposters who deceive them at the springs by an appearance of wealth." His plan was excellent indeed, for in 1835 Pope reported ten marriages, and of the fifty courtships then in progress he predicted at least twenty happy unions. Mrs. William Cabell, wife of a noted Richmond judge, published in the *Richmond Enquirer* an "Ode to White Sulphur Springs," and after verses celebrating the "limpid and cool" sulphur water and the "spruce beaux and belles," she ended her poem with these lines of tribute to Colonel William Pope:

> Yet ere I conclude, Lo! a paradox here
> Though Protestants all, yet obey we a Pope
> Whose mandates give pleasure, whene'er they
>   appear—
> That long may he reign most sincerely we hope.

Historian Perceval Reniers put Pope's organization into its larger context, "The Billing, Wooing and Cooing Society was the recognition of a fact, and the fact was that no other places in the South were the equal of the springs for the making of marriages . . . you took the waters or you took a mate or you took both, and with both it was the same—there was no knowing what the effect would be."

Though there were many legendary summers at White Sulphur Springs, the visit of President Martin Van Buren and his son in August of 1838 made that season more hectic and extravagant than usual. Van Buren, by the way, was not the first president to visit the resort. Andrew Jackson had stopped a few years earlier, though not for nearly as long. With Van Buren that season were the Governor and the ex-Governor of Virginia, the Secretary of War, the Spanish Minister to the United States, the Governor of Rhode Island and numerous members of Congress. The President was treated to one of the favorite pastimes at White Sulphur Springs, a picnic on the banks of the Greenbrier River, although his picnic was particularly bountiful. Pheasant, trout, chicken and turkey were served for appetizers; venison in the forms of roast, steak and stew for the main course; and apple and cherry pie for dessert.

One newspaper pointedly questioned President Van Buren's motives for his visit, writing, "Mr. Van Buren has gone there to try and make political friends and to convert the conservatives." And talk of politics must have been on the President's agenda because the Panic of 1837 had seriously shaken the nation's financial stability. In fact, the panic led to a severe depression, which stretched from 1839 until about 1845. Thus what they called the

"Flush Thirties" were followed by the "Hungry Forties," a world-wide depression, and that meant lean years for White Sulphur Springs too.

The season of 1838, then, turned out to be the apex—at least for a while—of the accumulating fame of the renowned resort. The widely-read English novelist, Captain Frederick Marryat, was at the resort that year and, with the perspective of a foreign visitor, was able to sum up the ambiance of White Sulphur Springs in its 1830s heyday: "Spa [the famous resort in Belgium], in its palmiest days when princes had to sleep in their carriages at the doors of the hotels, was not more in vogue than are these White Sulphur Springs with the *elite* of the United States. And it is here, and here only, in the States, that you do meet with what may be fairly considered as select society. Of course, all the celebrated belles of the different states are to be met with here, as well as all the large fortunes, nor is there a scarcity of pretty and wealthy widows. All the first old Virginian and Carolina families, many of them descendants of the old cavaliers, were at the spring when I arrived there; certainly I must say that I never was at any watering-place in England where the company was so good and so select."

THEY LIVED
in
PARADISE

. . . for $8 a week. In Paradise Row, we mean, the heaven of the brides and grooms
. . . Coaches from the heat-stricken South brought their families to the other Rows—Alabama, Louisiana, Carolina, Georgia, Florida, Baltimore.
. . . Today—now—you can recapture the essense of that colorful, patrician life
. . . in the same quaint Cottage Rows, completely adapted to modern family living.

The GREENBRIER and COTTAGES
WHITE SULPHUR SPRINGS • WEST VIRGINIA
L·R·JOHNSTON • GENERAL MANAGER·
High MEAN TEMPERATURE · JUNE TO SEPT · 73 · Cool

A 1932 advertisement featuring the tradition of honeymooning in Paradise Row.

This rather primitive 1842 drawing shows Baltimore Row in the back and Virginia Row in the front.

Visitors in the Springhouse practicing one of the daily rituals of White Sulphur Springs.

The Good Doctor and His Good Friends

In the midst of the commotion caused by President Van Buren's vacation at White Sulphur Springs, it was easy to overlook the laborious experiments being conducted by a young physician seeking to understand the mysterious curative powers of the sulphur water. Yet the work of Dr. John Jennings Moorman, begun in that summer of 1838, transformed the practice of taking the waters from an act of faith into a systematic method of health care. For the next forty-five years, Dr. Moorman's guidance was sought by thousands of visitors hoping for relief from a wide array of ills. In time, the Resident Physician at White Sulphur Springs became the nationally recognized authority on the uses and abuses of mineral water.

Today, the custom of drinking and bathing in sulphur water seems a dubious form of medical treatment, at best a mere antiquated curiosity. The practice, however, was followed by scores of divergent cultures. Ancient accounts in Egypt, Persia, India, and China prescribed spring water; Aristotle, Hannibal, Cicero, Emperor Hadrian, and Charlemagne all habitually resorted to mineral springs to preserve or enhance their health. Over two thousand years ago, Hippocrates studied the properties of mineral water, and later the Romans constructed hundreds of structures for public bathing. Since the early fifteenth century, Europe's most eminent scientists had analyzed and classified French, Swiss, Swedish, German and British waters. There is good reason why people have venerated mineral spring water throughout his-

tory—water is a basic element of life, without which humans cannot exist. Water containing chemical ingredients in solution, which leads to predictable results upon and within the body, has always been viewed as something near miraculous.

Dr. Moorman's lifelong pursuits in the field of sulphur water therapy must be set in the context of available medical options in nineteenth century America. When he began his studies, bloodletting was still a common antidote for almost all diseases, the existence of germs was unknown, and all kinds of herbal concoctions, forms of hypnotism, and age-old superstitions, remained the typical methods of fighting sickness. It followed that cynicism toward the medical professions was rampant: "Medicine slays its thousands and quackery its tens of thousands," warned *Godey's Lady's Book* in 1839.

James Calwell realized the urgent need for a Resident Physician at this growing resort and invited Dr. Moorman to establish that position. The thirty-six-year-old doctor had recently settled nearby, following two years of travel after his wife's death, and he took to his new position with great enthusiasm. "I at once turned pretty much my entire attention," he wrote in his memoir forty years later, "to the investigation of the chemical characters and the specific applicability of mineral waters generally; but primarily, these of the White Sulphur, which has long been regarded as the most highly medicated and efficient mineral water of its class in America, if not in the world."

Dr. John J. Moorman, the Resident Physician at White Sulphur Springs from 1838-1883.

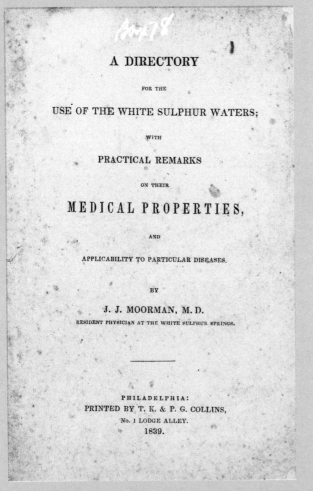

A DIRECTORY

FOR THE

USE OF THE WHITE SULPHUR WATERS;

WITH

PRACTICAL REMARKS

ON THEIR

MEDICAL PROPERTIES,

AND

APPLICABILITY TO PARTICULAR DISEASES.

BY

J. J. MOORMAN, M. D.

RESIDENT PHYSICIAN AT THE WHITE SULPHUR SPRINGS.

PHILADELPHIA:
PRINTED BY T. K. & P. G. COLLINS,
No. 1 LODGE ALLEY.
1839.

Dr. Moorman's first published treatise on uses of the mineral water.

Other doctors had visited the springs before Dr. Moorman, but their analyses were based upon brief examinations of the water and informal conversations with persons taking the water. A guest in 1791 remarked that "the towel I wiped with after bathing smelt so strong when I carried it to the fire that I could not bear it near me." The next year, a Dr. John Rouelle began performing rudimentary experiments at the spring. He first confirmed the existence of sulphur by placing a piece of silver in the water, and it immediately turned black. He then noted the odd fact that birds never flew directly over the spring, while vegetation grew quite well in the water. He speculated that the spring sat in the crater of an ancient volcano, and then recommended the water for diseases of the skin. His conclusion was that the sulphur water was "endowed with more powerful properties than any that I have analyzed when I traveled and lived in Europe." Dr. William Horner, of Philadelphia, also investigated the water at White Sulphur Springs. In 1833 he remarked that the waters, drunk at the rate of six to eight glasses per day, "impregnate the system so much that a sulphurous smell exhales from the skin." But he seemed baffled by the specific applications of the water, and was unable to distinguish which illnesses were actually eased by its use.

So the challenge for Dr. Moorman was to discover the precise diseases the water alleviated, and prescribe the proper methods of use. He took a very pragmatic approach, hoping that his observations might be beneficial "not by dazzling and futile theories, or by an attempt to create hopes that might end in sad disappointments, but by plain, practical facts in relation to the nature and use of our mineral waters." Moorman's first apprehension was the misuse of sulphur water, which sometimes led to painful consequences. His first published work in 1839 contained explicit directions for avoiding these problems; the essence of his message was that sulphur water is a strong medicine and like all medicines must be taken with caution. The most common error he found was the belief among visitors that "they are benefitted in proportion to the quantity which they drink." He was startled and alarmed at the enormous quantities of sulphur water that people drank. The diary of one sixteen year-old girl, for instance, recorded her daily intake, amounting to eighteen large glasses every day for five weeks. Dr. Moorman, on the other hand, recommended four to eight glasses per day at first, working up to ten or twelve glasses at most after two weeks. As a general rule, he believed that two weeks was the minimum period of time for the water to be effective, usually it benefits began to appear after three to six weeks.

What is in the sulphur water? (parts per million, except as noted) ■ *Temperature (degrees F) 62.5* ■ *Discharge (gpm) 25* ■ *Silica (SiO₂) 17* ■ *Calcium (Ca) 440* ■ *Sodium (Na) 22* ■ *Bicarbonate (HCO₃) 210* ■ *Chloride (Cl) 17* ■ *Dissolved Solids (calculated sum) 220* ■ *Iron (Fe) 1.1* ■ *Magnesium (Mg) 130* ■ *Potassium (K) 1.2* ■ *Sulfate (SO₄) 1400* ■ *Nitrate (NO₃) 0* ■ *Hydrogen Sulfide (H₂S) 13. (From* Springs of West Virginia, *West Virginia Geological and Economic Survey, 1986)*

"The sensible medicinal effects of this water," Dr. Moorman wrote, "are most obviously displayed in its action upon the bowels, liver, kidneys, and skin." He stressed that the water was not a panacea and therefore prescribed it for only a limited range of diseases, including dyspepsia (which he defined as a "derangement of functions in the organs of digestion"), chronic rheumatism, neuralgia, jaundice, scurvy and a few others. He found it of limited use, along with other treatments, for addiction to alcohol and opium. The sulphur water should not be used, he wrote, for acute diseases, cancerous infections, or heart problems.

Did the sulphur water indeed cure such diseases? To answer this question, Dr. Moorman, at least in the early years and following the practice of most physicians, printed testimonials in his published works from respected professors, prominent citizens and doctors. In later years he thought that such testimonials were no longer necessary, as the efficacy of the sulphur water had been clearly established through many years of use. Those who did write of their experiences ranged from individuals with very specific complaints that were relieved by use of the water, to more general benefits as noted in an 1849 letter: "We leave our lowland homes languid, listless and without appetite. In one week we feel comparatively strong, and eat beefsteak for breakfast."

Dr. Moorman did acknowledge that a cure, or at least relief, derived from a combination of drinking the water, (he thought that bathing in the water was useful only after drinking the water for a period of time) plus attention to a moderate diet, sensible clothing, daily exercise, abstaining from liquor and breathing the clean mountain air. Whether or not this regimen in fact "cured" people is difficult to ascertain, but water-drinkers did return year after year, decade after decade, and many reported that they felt much better when they left White Sulphur Springs than when they came.

Despite Moorman's attempts to promote intelligent use of the sulphur water, many skeptics wondered out loud about the remedy. This skepticism was fed by extravagant claims that a veritable fountain of youth poured forth from the White Sulphur Spring. One excited visitor wrote, "It cures ugliness itself, being a kind of elixir of eternal youth," and furthermore, it "restores physicians to health, causes sailors to forget, and lawyers to confess the truth." Writer Peregrine Prolix polled visitors' opinions and reported that according to popular belief it cured just about everything, "except chewing, smoking, spitting and swearing." He listed the standard chemical components in the sulphur water but included as one "a very strong infusion of fashion." Prolix supposed that this last ingredient was the key: "Its quantity cannot be precisely ascertained . . . but no doubt it contributes greatly to the efficacy of the water. When submitted to the ordeal of analysis, it vanishes into smoke."

Contemporaries described Dr. Moorman as a man who always dressed neatly, wore gold-rimmed glasses, and carried a gold-headed cane. He was a professor at Roanoke College, in Salem, Virginia, and at Washington University School of Medicine in Baltimore. In Salem, he owned a drug store and was president of a bank. He also served in the Virginia House of Delegates from 1833 to 1835. President Fillmore appointed him the U.S. Commissioner to the 1851 World's Fair held in the Crystal Room in Hyde Park, London, after which he visited some of the famous spas of Europe. For most of the nineteenth century, his name was closely linked to White Sulphur Springs, not only because he was a familiar figure at the resort each summer, but because of his writings on the use of mineral waters, the first of which was a slim, thirty-five page pamphlet entitled, *A Directory for the Use of the White Sulphur Waters*. This eventually grew into a much larger 1847 volume that included studies of the neighboring mineral springs of Virginia, and finally evolved into his major work, *Mineral Springs of North America* (1873), which provided descriptions and analyses of over one hundred thirty mineral springs from Mississippi to Canada.

White Sulphur Springs was one of about a dozen mineral spring resorts in the area, known collectively as "The Springs of Virginia." Although Moorman directed most of his attention to White Sulphur Springs, he also offered guidance to the use of the waters at those other watering places: Blue Sulphur Springs, twenty-two miles west of White Sulphur; Warm Springs, which—along with Sweet Springs—was in use as early as the 1760s; Sweet Chalybeate (then known as Red Sweet Springs), a source of iron water that Dr. Moorman used for his own ailments; Hot Springs, with its six baths ranging in temperature from ninety-six to one hundred six degrees; Salt Sulphur Springs, where a rare iodine spring was discovered in 1838; and Red Sulphur Springs, highly regarded as an antidote to "confirmed consumption" or tuberculosis. Travelers in this western region of Virginia frequently visited three or four resorts in one season, making what was called "The Springs Tour." These resorts straddled the continental divide and about seventy-five miles separated the most northern, Warm Springs, from the most southern, Red Sulphur Springs. Each was about one day's stagecoach ride from its neighbor, and all were connected by good turnpike roads. The mineral waters varied in their chemical components and temperatures, in fact in some cases invalids traveled with a physician's

A current photograph of one of the most famous of the old Springs of Virginia, Sweet Springs. About twenty miles south of The Greenbrier, this main building was, according to tradition, designed by Thomas Jefferson.

prescription to visit a number of springs in a strict sequence. Most of these resorts consisted of cottages surrounding a springhouse, and featured a lively social life; White Sulphur Springs was always the largest and also had the advantage of being located in the center of the springs region, so it was on almost everyone's itinerary.

Overshadowing motives of pleasure-seeking, fashion and poor health, however, was a much more ominous inducement to head for the mountains each summer. Dreaded epidemic diseases broke out with frightful regularity throughout the nineteenth century, at times fostered by conditions in the humid, swampy parts of the Southern coastal areas, or the lack of sanitation in the burgeoning cities. The first great epidemic in the United States was the 1832 outbreak of cholera, which spread from Europe, killing thousands of people. It is probably no accident, then, that 1832 seems to be the year White Sulphur Springs and the other springs resorts were discovered as good, healthful places to spend mid-July through mid-September. Yellow fever—known as the terrible "Yellow Jack"—was a constant threat, particularly in lowland Virginia, the Carolinas, and Louisiana; malaria, scarlet fever and measles were also incurable. As a consequence, physicians of the day advised people to leave those areas for as long as possible. Dr. James P.

Baker, the founder of The Greenbrier Clinic, studied the medical history of Virginia's mineral springs, and discovered that while fourteen springs resorts operated in 1830, the number more than doubled in the next thirty years, after epidemics caused devastating mortality rates. These springs prospered throughout the remainder of the century, but Dr. Baker observed that most went into a steady decline with the discovery of a cure for cholera in 1883, and Walter Reed's identification, in 1900, of the mosquito that carried yellow fever.

In the course of his professional duties, Dr. Moorman, more than any other individual in White Sulphur Springs' history—except James Calwell of course—became a representative figure associated with the resort. He was in a unique position for almost half a century, until the year before his death in 1885, to form personal acquaintances, and sometimes lasting friendships, with many of the prominent people who vacationed at White Sulphur Springs. Fortunately, near the end of his long tenure as the Resident Physician, Moorman recorded his impressions in a private memoir, and in it he repeated stories drawn from his experiences with clergymen, governors, philanthropists, generals, poets, biblical scholars and U.S. Presidents. His chronicle remains, even today, a fascinating guide to the human side of many of the great names in American history as well as an inside view of social interactions at White Sulphur Springs.

Dr. Moorman, of course, got to know Henry Clay quite well. Known the "The Great Commoner," Clay was described by Moorman as "tall of stature, full six feet, I think, in height; spare and erect; remarkable for a somewhat prominent nose, thin lips and an uncommonly large mouth. To his contemporaries I need not speak of this latter feature, however, for everyone knew very well that his mouth was fully capable of speaking for itself." Like other Americans who witnessed Clay's legendary rhetorical style, Moorman was in awe: "I have never seen a man of more easy, lofty and elegant volubility of tongue than Mr. Clay." But Clay's prowess was not limited to speaking to political crowds from podiums; his wit and manners extended to the kind of personal encounters expected at a social resort like White Sulphur Springs. Moorman observed Clay's "natural gallantry—and open, frank and manly expression of sentiments and, in his conversation with ladies, an irresistible tendency to say agreeable things." On one occasion, Dr. Moorman was approached by a woman who begged him to get a lock of Henry Clay's hair as a souvenir. Moorman duly delivered the request, and the next day saw Clay engaged in animated conversation with the woman. She was apologizing for the trouble she had caused, but Clay smiled, offered his then quite grey lock of hair, and said, "O Madam, don't mention it—it has been a very great pleasure to me—and I beg you to believe that not only a lock of my hair, but my heart and all I am are yours, except only my hand which is Mrs. Clay's."

In contrast, Henry Clay's attitude toward his political enemies was bold and defiant. In another incident Dr. Moorman recalled, a number of distinguished gentlemen had gathered in the Colonnade cottage of Clay's friend, Colonel Richard Singleton. The group included Andrew Stevenson, a congressman from Virginia and a former ambassador to Great Britain. Since Clay had strenuously attempted to block Stevenson's appointment as ambassador, the two were not on speaking terms. "Mr. Clay deferred an intended call upon Colonel and Mrs. Singleton," Moorman wrote, "until he knew that Mr. Stevenson and other of his enemies were in the Colonel's room—when he boldly walked in among them. Passing through the group without the slightest recognition of them, he approached Colonel and Mrs. Singleton with the greatest cordiality and volubility of speech, keeping up a lively conversation until all his enemies withdrew—leaving him just such a triumph as he desired, and which in the opinion of his friends then at the springs, he had sought

for." It is no wonder, then, that Dr. Moorman described Clay in admiring terms: "Henry Clay was for many years a central object of attention among the visitors at the White Sulphur . . . and when there, was always the most noted, honored and observed by all."

Besides Henry Clay, whenever historians cite the greatest political orators in ante-bellum America, two other names invariably top the list, John C. Calhoun and Daniel Webster. All three of these men frequented White Sulphur Springs in the 1840s (although it has been said that if they were not getting along with one another, they would schedule their visits so as not to overlap), and Dr. Moorman, of course, wrote at considerable length about each man and his impact on the resort. John C. Calhoun was the vice president under both John Quincy Adams and Andrew Jackson, held the posts of secretary of war and secretary of state, served as the senator from South Carolina, and was the most sophisticated political thinker in the South. He was also quite a talker. Moorman wrote that Calhoun "was always ready to engage in intellectual conversation, and to do all the talking himself if you desired." Nevertheless, he met stiff competition at these springs where agile public speaking was in abundant supply. Calhoun, Moorman recalled, "talked so well, so

Henry Clay (center) in front of the Colonnades Cottage. From William Grauer's murals in the President's Cottage Museum.

Upon the White Sulphur Springs, Virginia

Come all you, who thirst for the waters of life,
Whether father, or son, fair daughter, or wife;
Come, drink at this fount, and you'll certainly find
Relief for the body, as well as the mind.
For, the man who to-day, but totters along,
By using it freely will soon become strong;
The wife, who was losing her beauty, and charms,
Returns well again, to her husband's fond arms—
The pale cheek of the lass, once blooming, and red,
Will revive here again the rose that had fled—
And the sweet child, his father's dear boy,
Who no health from his birth could every enjoy,
Here begins like the lambkin, to sport and to play,
And chase from his mother, all sorrow away—
And thousands it's prov'd itself able to save
Whom the doctors had said, must go to the grave.
It confers all its blessings alike upon all,
Fits the old for their chat, and the young for the ball;
Where the lover may dance, with the girl of his heart,
And Hymen, will whisper, *they never shall part.*

This poem enumerating the wonderous results of using the sulphur water was published in a Richmond newspaper in 1833.

fluently, so sensibly, that ordinarily he had the lion's share of it, except perhaps when he met with such other talkers as Governor Tazewell or Governor Henry A. Wise [both from Virginia], neither of whom was ever known to yield the field of talk quietly for any length of time."

Daniel Webster was the defender of New England's interests in Congress and therefore viewed with suspicion by Virginians until his eloquent address to them in 1840. The speech was so impressive, Dr. Moorman thought, "that no one who heard it was likely to ever totally forget" Webster's words. At a party after the speech, where the wine flowed freely, Webster relaxed among his new friends and there Moorman overheard this remark to a Virginia military man: "I am told, General, that I am not popular in Virginia, and I cannot well account for it, for I am sure I am very Virginian in all my tastes and habits. I drink, I fail to pay my debts, and I am not overly scrupulous of my marital relations. Such qualities, I would think, ought to make me very popular with Virginians."

As White Sulphur Springs' fame spread, many European travelers included a visit to the resort on their "American Grand Tour." From England, Lord Morpeth, the Seventh Earl of Carlisle, arrived for a six-week stay in 1842, and he told Dr. Moorman that White Sulphur Springs was "the most beautiful watering place in the world." The Spanish Ambassador to the United States

also visited, but he received a less-than-dignified welcome from the imperious Major Baylis Anderson. Ambassador Decolderon was turned away from a cottage, according to Dr. Moorman, because he arrived "plainly dressed . . . looking more like a steady old valley farmer than a foreign minister." When Major Anderson was informed of his faux pas he exclaimed to Moorman, "the devil you say, I have made a mistake," and promptly assigned the ambassador an appropriate room in the Presidents' Cottage.

Perhaps the most interesting sections of Dr. Moorman's memoir are those giving his impressions of U.S. Presidents he met at White Sulphur Springs. His reactions, based on first-hand encounters, are more personal than those given in historical accounts. Dr. Moorman thought that Martin Van Buren "was a very nice gentleman, entirely unaggressive in manner and language, and reticent to a degree beyond any other public man I have known." Millard Fillmore, who visited for a week in 1852 with his Secretary of Interior, Alexander H.H. Stuart, struck Dr. Moorman as a "lusty farmer-like looking man of good manners and genial temper." Of the Mexican-war hero and twelfth President Zachary Taylor, Moorman wrote, "I have rarely seen anyone that looked less prepossessing or less at ease." John Tyler, of Virginia, visited White Sulphur Springs more often than any other

President, before his election to office, during his term (1841-1845) and frequently afterwards. The first President to be married in office, Tyler spent part of his 1844 honeymoon at White Sulphur Springs with his new bride, Julia Gardiner, of New York (which raised a few eyebrows because the widower President was fifty-four and Miss Gardiner was twenty-four). On one occasion, relates Dr. Moorman, ex-President Tyler was embarrassed by the unexpected arrival of his long-time political and personal enemy, none other than Henry Clay. Before Clay's appearance, Tyler was "literally the lion of the grounds," according to Moorman, but all attention soon turned to Henry Clay when he entered the grounds. "Mr. Tyler, evidently chagrined, stood this for a few days," Moorman explained, "and then having his baggage loaded upon a stagecoach at the very instant that a large crowd with a band of music was surrounding Mr. Clay's cottage, drove—unattended and as silent as a funeral procession—through the grounds to reach the highway of exit from the springs."

On the Fourth of July, 1854, President Franklin Pierce arrived with his wife at White Sulphur Springs in a Concord coach drawn by six white horses while the band on the lawn played "Hail Columbia." He was greeted by a delegation of twenty-four congressmen headed by ex-President John Tyler and escorted to his cottage. One newspaper reported, "Never before in the history of the country had a similar incident occurred, of an ex-President being called upon to address the actual President under such circumstances, and never did a more cordial feeling prevail." Dr. Moorman seemed strained to find something strongly positive to say about President Pierce. He was "what you might call a nice little gentleman, always nice and tidy in his dress, and nice in his manners. I think nice rather than elegant is the word for his manners. He made himself agreeable to his associates, and was always kindly attentive to all around him."

Summing up what he called his "Reminiscences of White Sulphur Habitues," Dr. Moorman concluded that he wanted "to notice hundreds of agreeable acquaintances I have formed in the summers I have passed at White Sulphur." He specifically mentioned three clergymen: the Reverend Dr. Dodd of Princeton, the Reverend Dr. Thornwell of South Carolina, and the Reverend Dr. John Hall of New York. "The latter gentleman," Moorman commented, "is the only clergyman I have ever known to be invited by the guests of the Springs, after hearing him on the Sabbath, to preach again during the week and at night, to the abandonment for the time of the usual gaieties of the ballroom." Dr. Moorman did not forget to acknowledge women at White Sulphur Springs: "I have not referred particularly to the distinguished ladies that have con-

President John Tyler spent part of his 1844 honeymoon at White Sulphur Springs.

stantly adorned society at the White Sulphur. Among such have been found those who have acquired distinction for their literary productions in poetry and prose; others that were distinguished for their marked intelligence, beauty, wealth, or peculiar elegance of manners." Citing the influence of numerous "high toned gentlemen" of South Carolina—specifically including Colonel Richard Singleton and Colonel Wade Hampton—Dr. Moorman captured the social flavor of the Springs in the decades before the Civil War: "together with many similar spirits from all the Southern States, all exercising their high and refined social qualities wherever they went, [they] were the main power in getting up a reputation for the White Sulphur (where they annually assembled) as the most fashionable and altogether the most refined place of public resort in America."

In the midst of this whirl of exclusive society, Dr. Moorman also found himself embroiled in an intense controversy over the proper applications of the sulphur water. Perhaps as a method of increasing revenues in the depressed years of the early 1840s, James Calwell initiated the sale of sulphur water in bottles and barrels for home use. The sales campaign began in 1841 with the publication of a brochure promoting home use, complete with testimonials of its effectiveness from editors, professors, legislators, doctors, pharmacists, merchants, lawyers, and Henry Clay. The marketing effort was so successful that in later years this branch of the resort's operations became a major source of income. However, the practice of bottling and transporting the sulphur water to apothecaries in major cities quickly drew Dr. Moorman into an unusually nasty dispute with the proprietor of a competing mineral spring resort. The medical argument began when William Burke, the owner of the Red Sulphur Springs, some forty-two miles south of White Sulphur Springs, questioned Moorman's motives in advising James Calwell to sell the water in this manner. Burke charged in an 1842 book that Dr. Moorman had concocted a theory "fraught with injury to the reputation of this justly popular water." The central point in this dispute was the source of the White Sulphur water's medicinal virtues: Did the water's curative power lie in its gaseous contents or in its solid salt contents?

The question had quite practical ramifications because in the bottling process the gases inevitably escaped. This was an unacceptable consequence for William Burke, who maintained that the water without its gases was worthless. He believed that the gases which gave the sulphur water its pungent odor were also the main ingredient curing invalids. Dr. Moorman disagreed. He advocated use of the water either fresh from the spring, with the gases intact, or after standing for some time, when the solid saline components alone performed the cure. Different diseases, Dr. Moorman explained, required different forms of sulphur water. As might be expected, Burke ridiculed this position and accused Moorman of fabricating a theory solely to justify the profitable sale of sulphur water. Burke's concluding attack on Moorman was couched in the strongest of terms: "His facts are without foundation in truth; his arguments puerile and shallow; his theories untenable; his absurdities ridiculous; his motives palpable and culpable; and his efforts to bolster up a selfish practice, a gross imposition."

Dr. Moorman was of course quick to defend his practice and reputation. He devoted forty-seven pages of his 1847 book, *The Virginia Springs*, to a detailed rebuttal of Burke's accusations. Mindful that Burke was charging that profit was the true source of his ideas, Moorman called attention to Burke's monetary interest in the matter: "He is the *proprietor* of a would-be rival watering place, we, the Resident Physician. Which, under the circumstances, we would ask, is likely to feel the deepest interest in the reputation of that water?" Moorman further

charged that Burke was simply trying to siphon off business to his own mineral spring resort. Although Moorman's retort was generally carried out in moderate and scientific language, he unleashed his sharpest comeback when he proposed the following as an appropriate subtitle to William Burke's book: "An Elaborate Puff of an Second-Rate Mineral Spring, by the Proprietor Thereof; With Brief, and Sometimes Disparaging Notices of Other Watering Places."

While there was no clear resolution of the conflict at the time, it should be noted that William Burke soon faded from the scene and Dr. Moorman's career blossomed. And the sale of water from White Sulphur Springs continued unabated; in 1880 it could be purchased from agents in Richmond, Baltimore, Washington, Philadelphia, New York, New Orleans and Charleston, South Carolina; in 1902 White Sulphur Water was available in almost any American drug store, at five dollars for a case of twenty-four quarts. In fact, the sale of bottled water—in concentrated form and billed as "America's Favorite Morning Laxative"—continued until as late as 1942, when the bottling equipment was dismantled.

1920s literature promoting the mineral waters.

William Grauer's portrait of the Old White Hotel in the President's Cottage Museum.

Summer Capital of the Old South

In August, 1845, a Virginia newspaper carried a brief notice from White Sulphur Springs, "a good crowd, the best since Van Buren's visit." This was very good news, much better than these brief words might seem to indicate, because it meant that the resort was regaining its popularity after seven years of a depressed national economy. But behind the scenes, all was not well; in November 1842 the Calwells had been forced to put their resort in trust to secure their debts, and for the next decade and a half, under-capitalization was a serious problem. Although the parcel of land had grown from Michael Bowyer's original nine hundred fifty acres to nearly seven thousand acres, (a size the resort has maintained ever since), cottage construction tapered off dramatically in the 1840s. One exception was the building of what would later be a cottage in South Carolina row, the private home of ex-Governor Joseph Manning of South Carolina. Colonnade cottage owner Wade Hampton wrote to his summertime neighbor, Richard Singleton, in 1842, "I regret extremely to learn that our old friend Mr. Calwell is in difficulty. I hope the extent of these difficulties are exaggerated." Referring to a detail in their cottage contracts, Hampton continued, "Whatever you do in this matter, pray avoid any measure calculated to injure the old gentleman's feelings. I would not want to add a feather to the weight he has to carry." The financial burdens of sixty-nine-year-old James Calwell had been made all the heavier, Hampton knew, by the recent death of his wife, Polly.

James Calwell died in 1851 and, although his son William took over the resort, the days of White Sulphur Springs as a sole proprietorship were numbered. For not only had William Calwell inherited a famous watering place, he had also inherited numerous creditors whose claims amounted to a staggering $400,000. So in 1853 the younger Calwell incorporated the business under the name "The White Sulphur Springs Company" and hired former Secretary of the Interior Alexander H.H. Stuart to sell the property. The sale took longer than William Calwell would have preferred, but in the end it led to vast improvements at White Sulphur Springs.

The general financial instability of the 1840s had also hampered improvements in transportation to Greenbrier County. The James River and Kanawha Turnpike was, in fact, the leading edge of a much more ambitious project, the building of a canal over the Allegheny Mountains from Richmond to the Ohio River. By 1840 the canal was finished from Richmond to Lynchburg and in the next decade pushed further to Buchanan, southwest of Lexington, Virginia. Work progressed on the third section to Covington, but was never completed due to increased competition from the railroads. On February 16, 1836, the Virginia Assembly chartered the Louisa Railroad, a very short line that eventually evolved into the Chesapeake and Ohio Railroad some thirty years later. The railroad expanded from Richmond to Charlottesville by 1850. At this point the Louisa Railroad's name changed to the Virginia Central, which was

William B. Calwell, the son of James and Polly Calwell, who managed the resort for almost sixty years in the nineteenth century.

James Calwell and members of his family are buried in a small cemetery near the Hilltop Tennis Courts.

thirty-four counties voted their support for the new railroad. Some work was completed on the Covington and Ohio in the years before the Civil War, including a complete survey of the railroad's route. That survey resulted in one very critical decision affecting the later history of White Sulphur Springs; a route through Greenbrier County was chosen which passed right by the resort, while a more southern route through Monroe County—past the Sweet Springs resort and the town of Union—was rejected.

Meanwhile, another intriguing idea was floated to take advantage of the renewed popularity of White Sulphur Springs in the late 1840s. A group of Virginia lawyers petitioned the General Assembly to move the Commonwealth's Western Court of Appeals from nearby Lewisburg to the resort property itself, reasoning that the healthful atmosphere at White Sulphur Springs would only increase the Court's efficiency and make their labors more bearable. These petitioners reported that James Calwell had offered accommodations for the lawyers and judges as well as security for the Court's documents, all free of charge. However, a group of outraged Greenbrier County citizens claimed that the proposal was a "mere freak of fancy" instigated by Richmond lawyers seeking recreation at the expense of their professional duties. As one opponent of the proposed move wrote, "It is idle to suppose that a few judges and lawyers will be absorbed in papers and books while everybody else is in the full enjoyment of relaxation and idleness." Apparently the General Assembly was equally suspicious of the lawyers' motives and the Court of Appeals remained in Lewisburg.

Despite the financial problems of the Calwell family and the slowness of improvements in transportation, summertime life for a visitor at White Sulphur Springs was again filled with excitement and pleasure throughout the 1850s. Prosperity returned to the nation, especially in the South, where in this decade the motto "Cotton is King" became a common rallying cry. The progress of industrialization, mostly in the North, added another motive for people to seek out summer mountain resorts: the increasingly large urban areas were notoriously hot, dusty and humid in July and August. And, of course, they were becoming crowded too. More and more Americans made their annual journey to the country simply to escape the crush of people in the cities. One Northerner, J. Milton Mackie, of Massachusetts, noted this aspect of White Sulphur's charm in the mid-1850s: "The manners of our Southern friends have a peculiar adaptation to the spas from the fact that their life at home

its name throughout the Civil War. The new Virginia Central railroad faced a harrowing challenge—building the necessary tunnels through the Blue Ridge Mountains. These four tunnels, a stunning engineering feat of the day, were designed by the French engineer Colonel Claudius Crozet. By 1854 the railroad reached Staunton in the middle of the Shenandoah Valley, and then proceed westward into the mountains to Jackson's River Station (now Clifton Forge) in 1857.

As it was clear by the 1850s that the railroad was the way to the future, the canal project languished, and in August of 1854 one of the first recorded conventions ever at White Sulphur Springs was called to discuss the prospects for a new line, the Covington and Ohio, to extend the Virginia Central to the Ohio River. This was a convention in the nineteenth century meaning of the word—a special meeting called to consider some single important issue—and three hundred delegates from

is mainly rural. This gives them an air of naturalness at these places and enables them also to pass their time pleasantly, without bringing thither the routine of morning calls and card leaving, the giving of balls and dinner with formal invitations, and refreshments sent by express from town." Indeed, Mackie seems to be the classic energetic Yankee seduced by the legendary slow pace of life in the South. On a summer day, he observed, the southern gentlemen "sit half the morning through in easy, wicker-bottom chairs under the trees conversing on the subject of politics, estimating the amount of the cotton and rice crops, smoking cigars, drinking juleps, commenting on a passing lady, a horse, or a stagecoach. Rarely does a Virginian propose a walk [whereas] an active, inquisitive Yankee will go out and explore a mountain or look at a neighboring farm and returning, find the Southerner in the seat where he left him." Mackie admitted it took some adjustment, but, "after a while all the visitors at these Springs learn more or less the art of getting through the summer day easily. One begins with taking no note of the hour of the day, then lets his watch run down, and finally forgets the day of the week and the month—all being alike save Sunday."

As always, it was the mix of people that made a visit to White Sulphur Springs memorable. J. Milton Mackie continued his review of the resort with complaints about the overcrowding, pandemonium in the dining room, the rain, the taste of the sulphur water, but concluded, "Still, one likes to be here at the fashionable Springs when the crowd is the greatest, here he desires to be in the midst of the grand movement. The more colonels, the better. The more pretty ladies, the better. He wants to talk upon politics with all the judges, attack or defend Sebastopol with all the generals, dance attendance on all the well-bred dames and waltz with all their daughters. Half the pleasure is in the excitement which proceeds from the great number of persons collected here . . . surely, the 'old families' of Virginia and South Carolina are no fable." Mackie was particularly enchanted by the young women at the resort. He saw in the daughters of the old

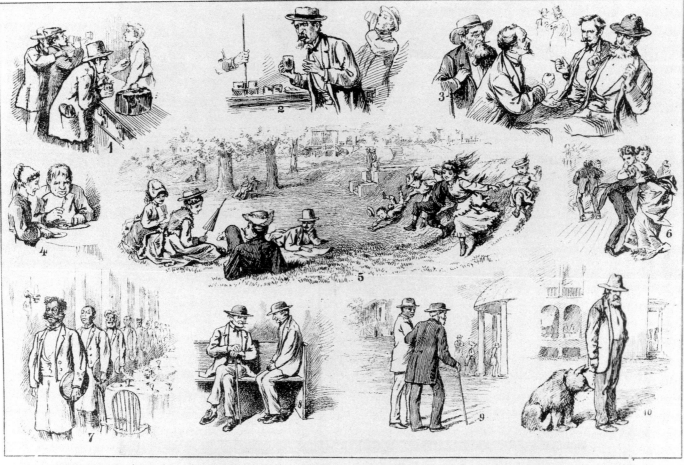

An illustration in the New York Daily Graphic depicted some 19th century scenes at White Sulphur Springs:
1. Ceremony on arrival. 2. First taste of the water. 3. Politics. 4. Business. 5. On the lawn. 6. The "Boston." 7. Perspective of the Commisary Department. 8. "Old Stagers." 9. Going for the morning's draught. 10. A couple of natives.

southern families "that high-born air, that easy grace, that feminine delicacy, which shows that their blood is gentle and, like oft-decanted wine, has been refined by being poured through the veins of at least three well-born generations." In short, Mackie wrote, "the accomplished belle of the White Sulphur had, to my eyes, the look of a lady who was never expecting admiration but who had been ever receiving it."

Certainly one of the most prolific promoters of White Sulphur Springs in the 1850s was Washington journalist Mary K. Windle, who published detailed accounts of her 1856 and 1857 visits. She was enthralled by the natural beauty of the resort—"Never did our imagination conceive a distinct idea of the Garden of Eden 'til we beheld the environs of this enchanting spot"—but her reports were filled mostly with accounts of the people gathered, their clothes, habits, backgrounds, etc. In that more

modest era she utilized the common technique of never printing full names, rather she referred only to, for example, "Miss S _____, South Carolina" or "Judge K _____ of Louisiana," although the personages were well-known enough to be recognizable to readers of the day. She did give a wide-ranging general description of the types of characters she observed: handsome, gentlemanly planters; wild young men; "spruce well-brushed dandies"; experienced travelers; mysterious European royalty figures; wealthy philanthropists; French-speaking children from New Orleans; "fossil specimens of the sterner sex"; conventional married couples; and, in one of her better phrases, "very wealthy families moving through life on easy chairs with golden castors." Her fervor for the attractions of White Sulphur Springs came close to that of a modern day public relations writer. The following lines appeared in advertising

The finest painting of The Greenbrier property in the early 19th century is this 1853 panorama by Edward Beyer now hanging in the Presidents' Cottage Museum. The Springhouse is visible at the far left. Today, The Greenbrier Hotel stands off to the right of this scene. The view is from about the location of today's Hilltop Tennis Courts.

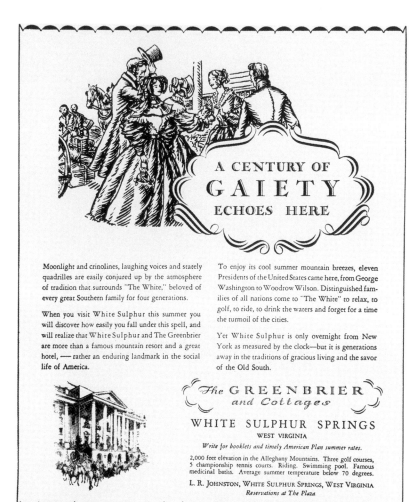

Themes of the resort's 19th century history carried into The Greenbrier's advertising in the 1930s.

Off to the Hunt with the Hounds. *From William Grauer's murals in the Virginia Room.*

Edmund Ruffin, the man who stirred up political controversy at White Sulphur Springs on the eve of the Civil War.

White Sulphur Springs, Va., _____ Sept 17 , 185 6 .

M. _____ Rich W. Kings 8

TO WHITE SULPHUR SPRINGS, DR.

To 4 days Board, Win Out ⌐c	$	9 50
Lady		9 50
Miss Batho		9 50
Mrs Lewis		9 50
	$	38.00

Received Payment, B. W. Eakle clk

In 1856, this bill for four persons for four days totaled $38.00.

copy from The Greenbrier in the 1930s, although Windle was actually describing the resort in 1856: "Has society palled upon you, dear reader? Have the week-day struggles of the world made you wish for some short Sabbath of repose? Are you fretted in the harness of the working-day life? Are you tired of the city's infected air? Do your chafed lungs require the soothing of balmily breathing breezes? If so, bend your steps to the White Sulphur."

One of the characters at the springs that Windle did mention by name was Francis W. Pickens, a planter and Congressman from South Carolina. At White Sulphur Springs Pickens met Lucy Holcome, of Tennessee, in the summer of 1857, and they were married the next year. Pickens went on to become the Minister to Russia upon President Fillmore's appointment and later the Governor of South Carolina. In 1862, pictures of Lucy Holcombe Pickens appeared on two issues of Confederate currency. F.W. Pickens' letter to Lucy's father asking for her hand in marriage is a classic, the kind not seen for many a decade, and illustrates that summertime romances at White Sulphur Springs did lead to respectable marriages. On the 27th of August of 1857, Pickens wrote from White Sulphur:

My dear Sir,

With your daughter's permission, I write to say, that, in the uncalculating impulses of my heart, I have offered her all that I am and all that I hope to be this side of the grave, as far as the affections and sympathies of life are involved.

She has accepted my offer, and if I can only know that it will finally meet with your sanction, it will be to me the dearest happiness of my life to minister in tender affection to the sensibilities of her high and delicate nature.

Yet for the country as a whole, all was not well. The decade of the 1850s was a time of impending disaster, as cultural, economic, and ideological forces steadily pushed the states into a Civil War. Though thousands of travelers still made their annual pilgrimage to White Sulphur Springs with no sense that war was imminent, even at this most peaceful resort an increasing tension between North and South loomed all too ominously over the grand and fashionable crowds. Inevitably, as the decade wore on, White Sulphur Springs became embroiled in the national quarrels that preceded the outbreak of war in 1861.

During the restless years before the tragic confrontation, many Southern newspaper and magazine editors urged their readers to avoid Northern travel by vacationing close to home. In 1850, the South's most important novelist, William Gilmore Sims, loudly denounced those he termed "softheads" who rejected their native Southern soil for visits to the popular Northern resorts at Newport, Cape May and Saratoga Springs. Other writers, in contrast, viewed White Sulphur Springs as an ideal place for conciliatory meetings between the antagonistic regions. One Northern visitor wrote after her 1851 stay, "Few better opportunities can be offered than it presents for dispelling prejudices and reconciling sectional differences. I wish more Northern travelers would come here . . . let them come, and meeting visitors from the South as at a sort of half-way house, forget that South and North were ever at variance, and learn that friendships need not have the boundaries of states."

By 1859 the sectional tensions were well beyond the aid of a quiet spell of companionship at a summer resort, as illustrated by the visit of a man who was recognized as the foremost agricultural reformer in the South, but notorious as a political extremist and militant defender of slavery—Edmund Ruffin. Wherever he went, Ruffin always seemed to be in the midst of controversy and that year's stay at White Sulphur Springs was no exception. The influential crowd he met that season during his visit was open to his brand of agitation. In his diary, Ruffin mentioned meeting such notables as Governor Manning of South Carolina, Judge Guyanne of Louisiana, John A. Winston the ex-Governor of Alabama, Judge John Robertson of the Supreme Court of Appeals in Richmond, the Secretary of Interior, Jacob Thompson of Mississippi, the entire membership of the Board of Public Works of Virginia and numerous Southern congressmen, bankers and ministers. His political views, however, were too extreme even in this crowd, "I find myself alone," he wrote, "as an avowed dis-unionist *per se*, and I avow that opinion upon every occasion."

Ruffin proceeded to focus his attention upon a disturbing fact concerning the new Methodist Church being built upon the resort property. When the proprietors originally offered to sell the land, they were unaware that the National Methodist Church had split into hostile factions over the issue of slavery. The Northern faction, known as the Baltimore Conference, claimed jurisdiction over the new church building, but many White Sulphur guests donated money assuming that they were supporting the Southern arm of the Church. Ruffin took it upon himself to explain to these guests that they were in fact "aiding to strengthen an abolitionist religious association," and he accused the owners of trying to conceal these facts. A committee of prominent guests brought their complaints to the proprietors who, Ruffin reported, were "alarmed" that word of this situation might reach the press. Ruffin, the political agitator, saw a fine opportunity to further his staunch pro-slavery crusade: "I have tried to excite and to keep up the ferment and have allowed them to expect that I will expose the facts to the newspapers." White Sulphur's owners were trapped in a dilemma—it was impossible to go back on their land offer to the Methodist Church, yet they certainly did not want to offend the opinions of their predominantly Southern clientele. Finally, a compromise was reached when, on Ruffin's suggestion, a clause was added to the Church deed directing that "no minister is to be excluded from preaching in it because he may be a slaveholder." This wording gave equal rights to both factions of the Church and prevented exclusive use by the Northern group.

While signs of friction mounted across the nation, White Sulphur Springs underwent a financial renewal and a massive physical rebuilding. As mentioned, William Calwell had put the resort on the market in 1853 and quietly sent his agent, Alexander H.H. Stuart, to New York, Philadelphia, Washington and Richmond in hopes of closing a deal. Calwell ordered Stuart to ask one million dollars for the property since anything less, he thought, would lower the public's esteem of the resort, but he was prepared to accept $750,000. The next few years were anxious ones for William Calwell. Prosperity had returned to the nation, the crowds were increasing and he was having difficulty finalizing a sale. Contacts were extended to London, it was rumored that President Van Buren's son was interested, and in 1855 Calwell apparently felt that a sale might be made to W.W. Corcoran, a wealthy Washington, D.C., banker, but that did not materialize. Between 1854 and 1857, Allen T. Caperton, who owned a splendid mansion and vast plantation twenty-five miles south of White Sulphur Springs, provided major financial support for the resort.

Finally, on May 1, 1857, the sale was completed when eight prominent Virginians formed a joint stock company and agreed to pay $600,000. The new "White Sulphur Springs Company" delivered $200,000 in cash and Calwell's creditors received a new set of promissory notes for their $400,000 in claims. Seven thousand acres of land changed hands in the transaction, along with an inventory of nine hundred mattresses, four hundred fifty-seven bedsteads, one thousand pillows, one thousand towels, one thousand eleven sheets, three hundred two mirrors, three hundred seventy-one chamberpots, fifteen hundred chairs, hundreds of pieces of kitchen and household equipment, and two pianos. The new owners were all

The front of the Old White Hotel. The emblem at the upper left, from stationery of the 1880s, gives the official name of the building: the Grand Central Hotel.

The Dining Room of the Old White Hotel (Courtesy Valentine Museum, Richmond, Virginia).

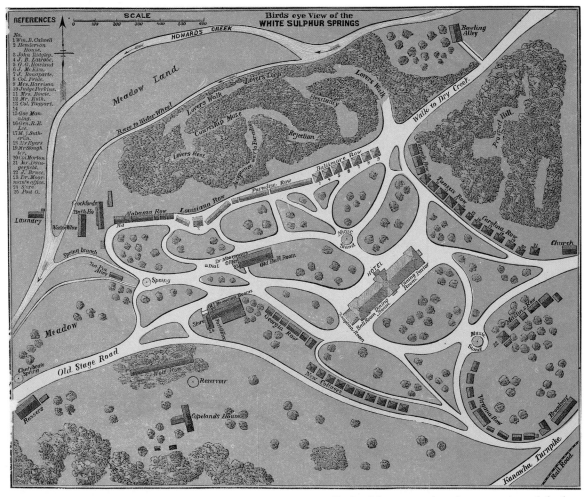

The layout of the resort's grounds did not change substantially for fifty years after the expansion of the late 1850s. This map is from about 1880.

well-known gentlemen with connections throughout the Commonwealth of Virginia. Jeremiah Morton of Orange County, the newly elected President of the company, had recently served as a representative in Congress and held extensive business interests in Virginia and Texas. Allen Caperton remained the largest stockholder, with twenty percent of the stock. Caperton's plantation home, "Elmwood," in Monroe County, faced another huge plantation "Walnut Grove," whose owner, Oliver Bierne, was a major investor in the rival Sweet Springs resort.

In two years the new company poured almost $300,000 into new construction, repairs, improvements, furniture and farm stock. The largest portion, $120,000, was devoted to the building of a huge new hotel in the center of the grounds, a structure that came to be known throughout the nation as the Old White Hotel. The new hotel—begun in the summer of 1857—was, by the standards of the mid-nineteenth century, a gigantic affair. It was over four hundred feet across the front facade, which was lined with wide arched porches for promenading, and built entirely of bricks made on the grounds. There were two hundred twenty-eight guest rooms on the two upper floors, and on the first floor, a dining room, parlors, several reception rooms and the ballroom. The broad steps of the main entrance faced more or less north, looking out at a fountain about halfway between the hotel and Paradise Row. At the eastern end of the building was the elegant parlor, which the company's brochures boasted was "half again as large as the celebrated East Room of the White House"; a ballroom of equal size graced the other end of the hotel. But the most stupendous room, the one that caused guests to gasp in awe, was the dining room, which took up almost three hundred feet of the first floor. This was the largest dining room in the United States. Twelve hundred guests were comfortably seated three times each day at the five long rows of round tables. A legend grew from those days that the dining room was so enormous that the waiters were required to serve meals on horseback.

Oddly enough, the new hotel known universally as the "Old White" was never officially given that name. When it opened its doors in 1858, the new owners christened it "The Grand Central Hotel" and for the remainder of the century the resort's stationery carried that name. But visitors familiar with the resort did not use that term; instead they called the hotel "The White" after its gleaming white paint and its location at White Sulphur Springs. In 1910, when the property was purchased by new owners, they bowed to this affectionate name and formally renamed the hotel "The White," but by then the guests, in deference to its age, had informally renamed it "The Old White."

The layout of the grounds changed dramatically in the area around the new hotel. The location of the hotel necessitated moving eleven cottages—those of Virginia Row and the large boarding house known as Broadway—to a new site near the James River and Kanawha Turnpike. Many more cottages were added. The six cottages of Tansas Row were erected next to the Colonnades (they received this unusual name because the owners of the first two units were from Tensas Parish in northern Louisiana). South Carolina Row was completed, and four of these cottages were immediately sold to families from Louisiana, Mississippi, and Virginia, and company President Jeremiah Morton took another. Ten new cottages south of the hotel were also added. These eventually became known as Florida Row. The old dining room in the center of the grounds was torn down, opening up new walkways across the property. William Calwell remained with the new company as its supervisor and he built a handsome new cottage at the end of Alabama Row with a pleasantly terraced fruit and flower garden in the rear.

Finally, to incorporate the romantic traditions of White Sulphur Springs into the physical design of the property, the wooded area stretching across the hills behind Baltimore, Paradise and Alabama Rows was transformed into a series of walkways for the resort's annual population of sweethearts. The walkway began at the last cottage of Baltimore Row, where it was called Lover's Walk. Before the woods got too dark and isolated, one pathway veered off to the left—this was Hesitancy Row, obviously prepared for those who were not quite ready to continue their stroll. Hesitancy Row,

FLIRTATION ON THE LAWN.

Pausing to chat during a stroll along Lovers' Walk.

The Old White Hotel as seen from Baltimore Row.

needless to say, led to a dead end. The next obstacle was Lovers Leap, a point overlooking a steep cliff, which may have given pause to a number of individuals, but there is no record of anyone actually taking that plunge. Couples moved along Lovers Walk until they came to a sharp turn which led into Courtship Maze, a spot that was the source of endless tales for generations. At the end of Courtship Maze came a crucial juncture: to the left was Rejection Row, which petered out into the woods; but to the right, the larger and more inviting walkway was Acceptance Way to Paradise. This path led to Paradise Row, which seems to confirm the legend that these cottages were reserved for honeymooning couples.

With all these improvements, the developed area almost doubled in size. The grounds of the resort extended from the Turnpike (today's Route 60) all the way to Howard's Creek, with the new hotel occupying the center surrounded by cottages. The capacity of White Sulphur Springs also doubled: through the early 1850s a complete crowd was six or seven hundred people; by 1859 numbers of twelve to fourteen hundred were

reported, and in 1860 Edmund Ruffin found "an immense crowd here—1600 in all."

When the new hotel opened its doors in 1858, fifty years had passed since Michael Bowyer built the first permanent tavern. Now the resort was at its nineteenth century apex; for the remainder of the century the grounds changed relatively little.

The grandness of the expanded resort represented more than money invested and structures built, because by a stroke of fate, ground was broken for the new work in the very month—June of 1857—that another financial panic struck the United States. Not as severe as the Panic of 1837, this one threatened the bankers and merchants of the North, but left Southerners almost unscathed. As historian Perceval Reniers commented on the new hotel at White Sulphur Springs, "Sprawling there in unprecedented length, financed by Southern energy at a time

Lovers Leap, part of Lovers Walk, from an 1878 magazine.

no one predominates. At the springs of the Old Dominion everybody and everything is generally Southern and specially Virginian." The Northern resorts consisted of many hotels in one location offering a range of accommodations at different rates, therefore the crowds were more diverse, perhaps more cosmopolitan. At White Sulphur Springs not only were most visitors from the same region and the same social class, everyone paid the same rate, which in 1860 stood at two dollars per day for a fortnight or more, two dollars and fifty cents per day for a shorter visit.

No one captured the connection between White Sulphur Springs and the larger social structure of the South better than William Alexander MacCorkle, a former West Virginia Governor, in his 1916 essay on the resort: "It is difficult for one not a part of the old South to understand the relation that the White Sulphur held to the people on the lower side of Mason and Dixon's line. The members of the governing families of the South had intermarried and were largely interrelated throughout the Southern country. I would say that the ruling families of the South did not number more than four hundred, and these were bound together in many instances by ties of close relationship. Hence a member of a well-known family in the South was welcome where there was one member of the family. So, if a member of that family came from under the shade of the hanging moss of South Carolina, from the cotton fields of middle Georgia, from the hemp lands of Missouri, or the corn and wheat plantations of Virginia, he was not a stranger, but was known and taken into one or another of the circles of this great resort. This assisted in making the White Sulphur one great family gathering-place for the whole of the Southern people."

MacCorkle's sentiments are an accurate description of White Sulphur Springs throughout the nineteenth century, but especially in those last years of the 1850s. It is no small irony, then, that the culmination of a half-century of development at the resort was achieved just a few brief years before Southern civilization as it had been known was washed away in the forceful currents of war.

when building and enterprise in the North stood still, was it not further evidence that the South could get along very well by itself, that it had no need for the North at all?" That is, White Sulphur Springs played a direct role in reinforcing a sense of the South as a distinct and separate region. As Daniel Boorstin has remarked, "Hotels were both the creatures and creators of community,"—and this is even more true of resorts than hotels.

The community at White Sulphur Springs displayed a uniformity, stability and simplicity not found elsewhere. One Northern journalist noted this aspect of the social life during his August, 1860, visit: "The visitors are so generally natives of the South, the springs partake more of the sectional characteristics than the Northern watering-places. At Saratoga and Newport every element of character, habit and impulse is to be found, and

Edward Beyer's 1858 print of the White Sulphur Springs from his famous Album of Virginia, *a collection of scenes throughout the Commonwealth in the decade before the Civil War. This view is an updating of his earlier painting (see pp. 46-47) to include the Old White Hotel. (Courtesy Virginia State Library and Archives.)*

Mural in the President's Cottage Museum showing Robert E. Lee and his family on the porch of their Baltimore Row Cottage.

Confederate Troops, Confederate Memories

At 4:30 a.m. on April 12, 1861, a cannon shell, ignited by none other than Edmund Ruffin, arched out over the harbor of Charleston, South Carolina, and exploded upon the federal troops holding Fort Sumter. The War for Southern Independence had begun. Because White Sulphur Springs was located on the turnpike connecting the Kanawha Valley to the west with the strategically important Shenandoah Valley to the east, both sides fought vigorously for control of the area, especially in the early months of the war. In fact, shortly after the declaration of war, Union General George McClellan, recognizing that the Shenandoah Valley was a natural alleyway for moving troops deep into Virginia (as well as a plentiful source of supplies such as wheat and cattle), launched the first land invasion into Southern soil, crossing the Ohio River into what is now West Virginia. The critical target was the Virginia Central Railroad with its terminus about twenty miles east of White Sulphur Springs. Control of those tracks would provide a direct rail link to Richmond.

Although McClellan was pushing down through the mountains in June of 1861, White Sulphur Springs opened for business as usual that month. Confederate General (and former Virginia Governor) Henry Wise was locked in combat to the west until early July, when he retreated from the Kanawha Valley, moved eastward along the turnpike, and eventually brought his troops to White Sulphur Springs. Here indeed was incongruity: fashionable visitors signed the resort's register per custom, only their names were now interspersed with the signatures and ranks of the troops of "Wise's Legion." The register for the season of 1861 broke off abruptly on August 22nd, normally the absolute zenith of the season.

On August 6, Confederate troops under the command of another ex-Virginia Governor, John Floyd, also camped at White Sulphur Springs, and the two rebel generals huddled together to plan a defense of the region. Floyd and Wise were longtime political enemies, and amidst the oaks, cottages and porches of the South's premier resort, the two men continued their bitter disputes, this time over military rather than political matters. Their bickering had tragic results, for as the days and weeks went by, Federal troops consolidated their control of the Kanawha Valley, and the Baltimore and Ohio Railroad to the North.

For more than a month Floyd and Wise traded charges and counter-charges, unnecessarily delaying Confederate military operations in the area. As a result, Robert E. Lee was ordered into the theatre to coordinate the strategies and movements of the various commanders. This was General Lee's first field duty of the war. Lee found chaos, sickness, rain, rain, and more rain. Fever and measles broke out among the green troops and there were few and crude hospital facilities. Moreover, in a politically disputed area such as this one, nobody was ever sure of the sentiments of the local citizens, and therefore all information was subject to doubt. More miserable conditions could hardly be imagined. Yet,

upon entering the mountains, Lee was reminded of his earlier trip in 1840, when he had spent three days at White Sulphur Springs, and he wrote to his wife: "If anyone had told me then that the next time I traveled that road would have been on my present errand, I should have supposed him insane."

The two-month operation in the area, a contest for the mountain passes and the roads that wound through them was, at best, a draw and, at worst, a complete failure for the Confederacy. After all, a major section of Virginia fell into Federal hands and remained so for the duration of the war. Indeed, without the results of this campaign the State of West Virginia might never have been formed. It was a somber Robert E. Lee who rode down out of the mountains in October, but before he departed he stopped at White Sulphur Springs to visit the wounded and sick soldiers. For two years, until the summer of 1863, the resort served both as a military headquarters and as a hospital for the Confederacy. The great hotel became the hospital, accommodating as many as sixteen hundred patients; its grand parlor and enormous dining room were filled with rows of cots bearing the wounded. In the National Archives is a list of one hundred ninety-two Confederate soldiers who died at White Sulphur Springs, the majority of them in the months of October, November, and December, 1861. Most of the young men were Virginians, although the list includes a large number from North Carolina and Georgia, and a few from Tennessee and Mississippi.

There is one side story to Lee's months in the mountains of western Virginia. During this period Lee first saw the horse he rode through the heat and danger of battle and later in the last years of his life. The horse, born about twenty miles west of White Sulphur Springs, was originally named "Greenbrier." A year later the owner, Major Thomas Broun, met Lee in South Carolina, remembered how much the General admired the horse, and offered it to him as a gift. Lee turned down the kind offer of a gift, paid $200 for the horse, and re-named him "Traveller."

The summer of 1861 also marked the beginning of serious agitation for a new anti-slavery state, aligned with the North, to be formed from the western counties of Virginia. Long at odds with the parent state over economic and political issues, these counties—especially those along the Pennsylvania border and Ohio River—now opposed Virginia's secession from the Union. The matter of West Virginia statehood created desperate division of opinions south of the Kanawha River and in Greenbrier County. The debate raged for two years, and

not a small part of that debate was exactly which counties should be absorbed into the new state. The inclusion of Greenbrier County in West Virginia, as well as a number of other counties that now border Virginia, was a controversial issue at the statehood conventions in Wheeling. Political and military considerations affected the final decision, of course, so despite the large number of Confederate sympathizers in the area, Greenbrier County was included. Consequently, White Sulphur Springs, where Virginians had hosted the rest of the

To the Patriots
—OF—
NorthWestern
VIRGINIA!!

WHEREAS—a Convention is to be held in Wheeling on the 11th. of this month, for the avowed purpose of effecting a division of the State, and attaching a portion thereof, as a miserable appendage, to one of the Republican states, or else forming the same into a new, and insignificant Free State: And believing that either change would be ruinous to our property and our social happiness:—We therefore earnestly call upon the people of North-Western Virginia, in their several counties, who still remain loyal to the "Old Dominion," and are opposed to being tacked on to the "TAIL END" of the BLACK REPUBLICAN DESPOTISM! to send Delegates to a convention to be held at Lewisburg, on the first Monday in July next, to enter their solemn PROTEST against this wicked and treasonable scheme; and also to take such action as may then be thought proper, after knowing the result of the Wheeling Convention. If a convention, gotten up as the one to be held at Wheeling has been, has the power to divide the State; then, upon the same supposition, we, in convention, by the same right and power, can annul their acts, or SEPARATE AGAIN FROM THEM!!

Lewisburg, Va. June, 1st. 1861.

Clearly some residents of Greenbrier County vehemently opposed the creation of the new, pro-union, state of West Virginia, as indicated by this 1861 broadside.

Col. George Patton, leader of the Confederate forces at the Battle of White Sulphur Springs.

William Averell, commander of the Union troops at the Battle of White Sulphur Springs.

South for generations, was ultimately scooped up in the pro-union state of West Virginia created by President Lincoln's proclamation on June 20, 1863.

After the early battles, or near-battles, in the summer and fall of 1861, the war in western Virginia settled into a stalemate for two years as dreadful fighting continued to the west and east. Confederate troops stubbornly held onto their position at White Sulphur Springs, an unusual encampment one Union officer enviously described as "comfortable, even elegant quarters." The lull was shattered in August of 1863, when thirteen hundred Union troops raided the area, seeking to capture the Virginia State Law Library in Lewisburg. Union commanders reasoned that these valuable law texts were now the rightful property of the new state of West Virginia and so General William W. Averell marched his troops west from Warm Springs into one of the most unusual en-

counters of the war, "The Battle for the Law Books." Colonel George S. Patton, grandfather of the World War II general of the same name, commanded the two thousand Confederate troops ordered to intercept Averell and protect the law books. The two armies met two miles east of the resort, at the present intersection of state routes 60 and 92, on the morning of August 26, 1863. From nine in the morning until darkness fell, Northerners and Southerners charged against each other's barricades across the broad valley. Throughout the long day neither side made any substantial advances and when ammunition ran dangerously low, fierce hand-to-hand combat ensued.

That night the units rested fitfully in their frozen positions as commanders poured over maps working out the next day's strategy. The Union troops were prepared for a possible retreat, while the Confederates strengthened their resolve to hold the law library and the hospital at White Sulphur Springs. At daybreak fighting began anew, Federal troops again attempted to smash through the Confederate defenses, but with no success. A Confederate countercharge finally drove the Union troops from the field, and General Averell ordered his soldiers to leave the ground in the hands of Colonel Patton's units. Casualties were heavy, a total of 218 Northern dead, wounded, and missing; 162 for the Confederacy. More than three hundred wounded soldiers, both Union and Confederate, were removed for care to the White Sulphur Springs hotel-turned-hospital.

For a few months after the Battle of White Sulphur Springs, the Confederates controlled the Greenbrier Valley, but in November of 1863, General Averell's Union troops inflicted a disastrous defeat upon the Confederacy at the Battle of Droop Mountain, some forty miles north of White Sulphur Springs. This battle was the last major conflict in the area and for the remaining two years of the Civil War combat degenerated into brief raids and numerous scuffles with ambushers.

A year after he was driven from the field attempting to capture the Law Library, General Averell did reach White Sulphur Springs, this time under an army commanded by General David Hunter. The tired and hungry Union troops straggled onto the resort property on June 24, 1864, in retreat from their defeat at the hands of Jubal Early at Lynchburg. Before arriving, the army had burned and looted the Virginia Military Institute, in Lexington, and was in dire need of rest and supplies. One Massachusetts private wrote in his diary about the march from Lexington through the mountains: "I could endure this marching no longer and, live or die, rest I must have. The guerillas and bushwackers are very plentiful about here." He then went on to describe in graphic detail the scraping of flour boxes, barrels and the gristmill at White Sulphur Springs for the makings of a meager meal. Another soldier in the Union unit was the popular writer David Hunter Strother ("Porte Crayon" was his pen name) and he described a wartime scene in stark contrast to the one he had seen during his 1855 visit: "We arrived at the White Sulphur about sunset, and in spite of its handsome buildings and extensive improvements it has a desolate and forlorn appearance. The new mammoth hotel was entirely dismantled and has been for some time used as a hospital for the Confederates. There was a good deal of waste and decay visible. I went to the famous spring, but could not bring myself to quench my thirst with the mineral water. Yet there was none other to be found."

During this June, 1864, occupation the famed resort came perilously close to total destruction at the hands of the Union troops. It was saved from the torch only by the quick thinking of a later U.S. Senator, Henry A. DuPont, of Delaware. Some sixty years later DuPont recalled that as the troops rested at White Sulphur Springs a rumor passed among them that General Hunter had ordered the burning of the entire complex. DuPont was taken aback at the news: "It seemed to me," he wrote, "that the burning of the buildings would be a clear violation not only of the rules of civilized warfare but of the specific instructions of the United States government." Aware that there was no organized resistance in the area, DuPont spent the night devising an argument to convince the tough General Hunter to alter his plans. The next morning they met for breakfast on the lawn and DuPont asked Hunter if the rumors of impending destruction were indeed true. "Yes, I intend to burn them all down," the commander replied, gazing at the hotel and rows of cottages. After a short pause DuPont said, "Don't you think, General, that the burning of these structures would be a military mistake?" He felt a pang of fear when Hunter countered, "What do you mean, Captain, by that inquiry?" DuPont summoned all his courage and answered, "I mean this General—if we have later to occupy and hold this country, the White Sulphur will be the natural point for our principal stations, as so many roads converge here. Such being the case, the buildings as they stand would furnish excellent winter

Mass grave of Confederates on The Greenbrier property, near the Hilltop Tennis Courts. "The Battle of Dry Creek" and "The Battle of White Sulphur Springs" are two names for the same encounter.

Gen. David Hunter, in command of the Union troops occupying White Sulphur Springs in 1864.

Capt. H.A. DuPont, whose persuasive arguments saved the resort from the torch in 1864.

quarters." There was a long silent spell as the general pondered this plan, for DuPont knew that only a practical, military reason would influence Hunter's decision. Finally, General Hunter called for his adjutant-general and said at once, "Colonel, I have changed my mind about burning the buildings here. Don't issue that order." DuPont immediately excused himself, departing "with the satisfaction of knowing that I had been the means of averting a wrong and unjustifiable act." It has been said that many years later, when the DuPonts visited The Greenbrier, they were always accorded special treatment in gratitude for Henry DuPont's rescue of the resort that June day during the war.

It is difficult to ascertain precisely how often White Sulphur Springs was used as a military headquarters during the war, but it seems that for many months during the war the buildings sat abandoned. On April 9, 1865, General Robert E. Lee surrendered his Army of Northern Virginia to Ulysses S. Grant at Appomatox Court House, and the War Between the States was finally over. A few months later in Amelia, Virginia, not far from White Sulphur Springs, the man who, on the eve of the war, had whipped up the fighting sentiments of Southern leaders at the resort now weighed the awful consequences of defeat. Edmund Ruffin calmly sat down, turned a loaded rifle to his head, and ended his cherished dream of a Southern Confederacy.

The owners of White Sulphur Springs returned to their property soon after the war's end to survey the damage to their investment and found the place a shambles. Fortunately, most of the buildings had withstood permanent structural harm, but the process of repairing steps, replacing furniture, fixing leaks and cleaning up the grounds was extensive. The buxom statue of Hygeia atop the Springhouse was gone, and though no document records precisely what happened to her, for years the story circulated locally that callous Yankee soldiers shot her down and used her wooden limbs for firewood. Financially, the war was a calamity for the White Sulphur Springs Company. The Confederate Government had paid rent and reimbursed the Company for damages to the property while the buildings were used as a hospital; to meet earlier liens on the property the owners had sold off much of the furniture and supplies. This rent and sale income was placed entirely in Confederate bonds, and with the war's outcome those bonds proved worthless. All of the company's records were lost in the fires that raged across Richmond when the city fell in April of 1865. William B. Calwell, the president of the White Sulphur Springs Company after the war, reported to stockholders in 1870 that their debt had swollen from $400,000 when the resort was purchased to almost $1,200,000. For thirty years after the Civil War the Company's officers were enmeshed in legal disputes— for many years all lease decisions were subject to approval from the Federal District Court—and some of these suits eventually reached the United States Supreme Court.

It took two full years to restore the property. White Sulphur Springs finally opened to the public when the firm of George L. Peyton and Company of Staunton agreed to lease the resort. The Richmond *Dispatch* was not optimistic about the prospects that summer of 1867: "We cannot expect to see there the society that once gave life and gayety and grace to that incomparably delightful summer resort. The remembrance of the past days must sadden the feelings of many visitors the present year." But the newspaper greatly underestimated both the determination and the fond memories of White Sulphur's clientele. Even for the defeated Southern states, life was not all politics and war. With amazing resilience old patrons returned again to their favorite spot, bringing in tow a whole new generation of young visitors filled with bright stories of glorious seasons before the war. It is surely an indication of how integral the resort was to the rhythms of Southern social life that visitors came back in great numbers just a few years after bitter defeat.

In 1936, a few months after the publication of her astonishingly successful book *Gone With The Wind*, Margaret Mitchell wrote a letter to The Greenbrier's General Manager which reveals her personal sense of the role of White Sulphur Springs after the war:

I have never been to White Sulphur but have always thought of it as a lovely and a romantic spot. When I was a small child listening to old ladies' conversations, so much was said about White Sulphur. So many of their romances had begun there. So many honeymoons had been spent there before the war, and time and again I have heard them tell of how much they missed their annual trip there in the hard days of Reconstruction, and the great excitement when finally times were prosperous enough for them to go back and spend the summer! I even remember how the old ladies described, in loving detail, the dresses they made to wear there, not so fine, not so numerous as they packed in their trunks before the war, but I like to think that they looked even prettier in these dresses, which they wore with great pride, than in the satin and laces of their great prosperity.

The original statue of Hygeia atop the Springhouse (see page 26) was lost during the Civil War. The current statue of Hebe, the goddess of youth, was added in the mid-1870s. This is a rare photograph of the Springhouse during the brief period when there was no statue at the peak of the structure.

This 1872 photograph, taken on the front porch of the Old White, shows the rather somber dress of the postwar seasons.

On July 24, 1867, General and Mrs. Robert E. Lee, with their daughter, Agnes, and son, Custis, arrived at White Sulphur Springs for their summer vacation. In October, 1865, General Lee had begun his work as President of Washington College (today's Washington and Lee University) in Lexington, Virginia, and this was to be his first vacation; Mrs. Lee specifically requested that they travel to White Sulphur Springs to seek aid for her chronic rheumatism. The Lee family was assigned to the last cottage in Baltimore Row, probably through the request of its owner George Harrison, a cousin of Lee's, and they soon found themselves surrounded by many of their oldest and closest friends. General Lee's three consecutive vacations at White Sulphur Springs allowed him to forget, for a while at least, the terrible memories of war that constantly haunted him. At this happy place in the mountains he re-discovered the joys of sociability. Douglas Southall Freeman, Lee's foremost biographer, wrote of these visits, "The social impulse of the General was always strong and now, in renewed contact with long-separated friends, it asserted itself vigorously."

The most complete description of Lee's 1867 visit to White Sulphur Springs is the memoir of Christiana Bond, then a young Baltimore girl who stayed in a cot-

tage near the Lee family that summer. She was enthralled at the renewal of life at the resort she shared with Lee. "It was a beautiful life at the 'White' in those old days," she wrote in 1926, "much of the charm of the kindly, simple customs of the ante-bellum days still lingered . . . regard for others, attentions to little amenities, remembrance of the stranger, respect for the aged, were the rules of life." To Miss Bond, General Lee's presence suffused White Sulphur Springs that summer: "It was General Lee who was the embodiment of the distinctive beauty in the social atmosphere. Day by day he lived amongst us, his influence impressed itself deeply. We saw his carriage erect and noble, his face grave, gentle, resolute and tender, his manner dignified, modest, unobtrusively courteous; we saw, moreover, his absolute loyalty to the allegiance he had sworn when he laid down his arms."

Lee participated fully in the Southern traditions conscientiously maintained by the old habitues, marching along in the evening promenade up and down the great shining pine wood floor in the parlor, meeting old friends and introducing strangers. The general's son, Robert E. Lee, Jr., recalled the family's reports from White Sulphur Springs and wrote that his father's old friends "could not sufficiently testify their pleasure in this renewal of intercourse. Whenever he appeared in the parlor or ballroom, he was the center of attraction and, in vain, the young men tried to engage the attention of the young ladies when General Lee was present." Christiana Bond also noticed that Lee seemed to be most comfortable in the company of young women: "Apparently he felt among the maidens a safety from intrusion which he could not have among those to whom his personality, and the great issue which he represented, were uppermost thoughts. He avoided all conversation on the war and its outcome."

General Lee was particularly upset to see former Union army officers and the small number of Northern visitors left standing somewhat apart from the merriment because resentful and defensive Southerners refused to include them in their company. He strove to break down the intangible barriers of suspicion between the groups, even though, in Miss Bond's words, "the manner of the Northern group was not inviting of courtesy." One Northern party included Andrew G. Curtin, the wartime Governor of Pennsylvania, and this group was so forbidding in manners that none of Lee's friends had even attempted to approach them. "I have tried in vain," Lee said to Miss Bond and her friends, "to find any lady who had made the acquaintance with the party and is able to present me. I shall now introduce myself, and shall be glad to present any of you who will accompany me." Only Christiana Bond dared volunteer: " 'I will go, General Lee, under your orders,' I said, and proudly arose to accompany him." And so the General and the young girl from Baltimore started out across the great ballroom and paused under the brilliant crystal chandelier. There, she wrote, "He told me of the grief with which he found a spirit of unreasoning resentment and bitterness in the young people of the South." But Miss Bond could not resist an impulsive question, "General Lee, did you never feel resentment towards the North?" He replied in low, earnest tones, "I believe I may say, looking into my own heart, and speaking as in the presence of God, that I have never known one moment of bitterness or resentment." After a thoughtful pause he added, "When you go home, I want you to take a message to your young friends. Tell them from me that it is unworthy of them . . . to cherish feelings of resentment against the North . . . It grieves me inexpressibly to know that such a state of things exists, and I implore them to do their part to heal our country's wounds."

Miss Bond and General Lee finally reached the formidable Northern group, accepted seats at their table, and chatted politely for a short while. Inspired by Lee's genuine expression of courtesy, the bonds of restraint loosened ever so slightly, and Northerners and Southerners at least spoke to one another at White Sulphur Springs.

A few days later a rumor swept the resort that a visit to White Sulphur by Lee's former adversary, Ulysses S. Grant, was imminent. Upon hearing the news, one young girl excitedly ran up to Lee, exclaiming "Well, General Lee, they say General Grant is coming here next week, what will you do then?" Christiana Bond witnessed this outburst and was properly mortified: "Some of us would gladly have slain her on the spot, but she evidently failed to comprehend the covert slab of her thoughtless words." A faraway look came across Lee's eyes, and overlooking the poor taste of the question, he responded, "If General Grant comes I shall welcome him to my home, show him all the courtesy which is due from one gentleman to another, and try to do everything in my power to make his stay here agreeable." General Grant did not arrive that summer (although he did visit seven years later), and Miss Bond sighed, "We missed a sight for men and angels."

While Christiana Bond delighted in the continuation of ante-bellum Southern customs at White Sulphur Springs, not all of the guests there were intent on simply re-creating the aura of those bygone days. A reporter from Wheeling, West Virginia, with decidedly Northern sympathies, found many signs of America's discontents at the resort that season. He was shocked to discover the class of nouveau riche Southerners, enriched by their wartime business dealings, whose wives and daughters paraded about in "silk dresses gorgeously trimmed in famous laces." He was disturbed by the "shameless abuse" he overheard heaped upon Congressional legislation and stunned by the machinations of disreputable politicians. But the writer did locate one bright spot: "Different is the manly, quiet behavior of General R.E. Lee, who is here with his family, but who positively refuses to be made a lion or fool of . . . Would that the example of General Lee be followed by others."

The Wheeling reporter thought that Lee might help the nation pass through the trials of Reconstruction by rallying Southern support for Federal programs. A similar idea, but for different reasons, occurred to William S. Rosecrans, the former Union General who had faced Lee in the fall of 1861 on Sewell Mountain, to the west of White Sulphur Springs. In 1868, Rosecrans was active in the presidential campaign, working for Horatio Seymour's bid against the Republican candidate Ulysses S. Grant. While Lee was vacationing a second summer at White Sulphur Springs, Rosecrans traveled from New York to enlist his support for the Democratic candidate. But Lee, who had vowed never to become involved in public debates, demurred at Rosecrans' proposal. Furthermore, Lee felt (in Douglas Southall Freeman's words) he "could not speak for the South . . . if Rosecrans wishes to know the feelings of the former Confederacy, he could inquire of the public men who were at the springs." Lee sincerely wanted to further better understanding between North and South, thus he invited a number of prominent Southern leaders to his Baltimore Row cottage to hear Rosecrans' appeal.

All these leaders gave Rosecrans their verbal support, but to him this was not satisfactory. So Rosecrans addressed a letter to Lee asking for a written statement from the men he had met at White Sulphur Springs. Lee hesitated once again, but turned for advice to Alexander H.H. Stuart, the Virginia lawyer who had acted as the agent for the sale of the resort ten years earlier. Stuart persuaded Lee that a written response would be appropriate, that such a move would in fact aid national unity, and Stuart drafted an answer. The reply that General Lee and thirty-one other leading Southerners at the springs signed was later named "The White Sulphur Manifesto." It read, in part:

Whatever opinions may have prevailed in the past with regard to African slavery or the right of a state to secede from the Union, we believe we express the almost unanimous judgement of the Southern people when we declare that they consider these questions were decided by the war, and that it is their intention in good faith to abide by that decision . . .

In conclusion, the agreed-upon message declared:

. . . Above all, the people would appeal to their countrymen for the re-establishment, in the Southern states, of that which has been justly regarded as the birth-right of every American, the right to self-government. Establish these on a firm basis, and we can safely promise, on behalf of the Southern people, that they will faithfully obey the Constitution and laws of the United States, treat the Negro populations with kindness and humanity and fulfill every duty incumbent on peaceful citizens, loyal to the Constitution of their country.

"The White Sulphur Manifesto" was widely reprinted in newspapers across the country and created a favorable image for the Democratic candidate, but Rosecrans pressed for further commitments. Lee adamantly refused to make more exceptions to his public silence on political matters: "When I united with the gentlemen at the White

Sulphur Springs," he told Rosecrans, "I went as far as I thought it was proper for me to do under the circumstances of the case, and did not intend to connect myself with the political questions of the country." General Lee's action at White Sulphur Springs that summer of 1868 remained the single instance he ever allowed his name to be used in political debate.

Despite the political pressures that season, General Lee enjoyed the companionship during his stay at White Sulphur Springs. As usual, he reserved his private moments away from the crowds, spending hours riding on Traveller through the surrounding countryside, yet there was much to make him happy when he chose a more social life. As he wrote to his son on August 28: "The place looks beautiful—the belles very handsome, and the beaux very happy. All are gay . . . there was a grand fancy masked ball last night. The room was overflowing, the music good, and as much spring in the boards as the conversation, and the German [a popular dance of the day] continued till two o'clock this morning."

Washington College (Washington and Lee University today) in Lexington, Virginia during the period when Robert E. Lee was the president of the school.

General Lee visited White Sulphur Springs a third and final time the next year, and the season of 1869 was long remembered as one of the most brilliant of the entire nineteenth century. W.W. Corcoran, the Washington, D.C., banker who founded the Corcoran Gallery of Art and owned one of the Colonnades cottages, was spending the summer. His guest was George Peabody, the Massachusetts philanthropist who had donated millions of dollars to support the far-reaching Fund for Southern Education. Ex-Virginia Governor Henry Wise mingled among the crowd, strolling the grounds where he had camped with his troops eight years earlier. Commodore Matthew Fontaine Maury could be heard discussing his

B. F. Eakle served as the Superintendent of White Sulphur Springs for twenty-five years after the Civil War.

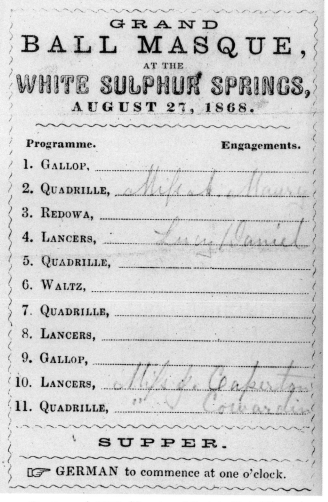

Dance card, 1868. (Courtesy Virginia State Library)

recent offer from the French government to build new waterways in that country. From the ranks of ex-Confederate officers, there were Generals MacGruder of Virginia, Beauregard of Louisiana, Brent of Maryland, Lawton of Georgia, and Connor of South Carolina. George Pickett, whose name will always be fused with the famous uphill charge at Gettysburg in July, 1863, was also in attendance with his wife, as were former Confederates Johnston, MacCausland, Pegram, Hood, Loring and Mosby. Indeed, there were so many former Southern officers at the resort that the Khedive of Egypt sent agents to White Sulphur Springs to recruit military leaders for his army.

An enormous crowd of two thousand visitors overflowed accommodations meant for twelve hundred at the peak of the 1869 season. Journalist Charles Pilsbury witnessed the teeming crowds and gave this account of the pandemonium: "During the rush of visitors, men, women and children slept on the parlor floor, and ladies, total strangers to each other, were stowed away five or six together in a small room, two in a bed, and others on mattresses on the floor. Husbands were often separated from their wives, and ludicrous scenes resulted from the confusion attending the arrival of two or three hundred guests late at night." In general, he continued, "What with the slamming of doors, the rattling of locks, the dragging or luggage through the halls, the squeaking of boots, and the vociferous shouts of the servants, the hotel was for some days a perfect bedlam." Large crowds were nothing new at White Sulphur Springs, and the visitors coped that year the same way they had done in the past. "For the most part," Pilsbury wrote, "good humor and a disposition to make the best of everything prevailed."

Among the many luminaries at the resort, George Peabody held a special place. His generous gift of over $3 million to create a Fund for Southern Education—usually called the Peabody Education Fund—had touched the hearts of Southerners alarmed by the devastation of the Civil War. Peabody was in the United States (he was then living in London) to make arrangements with leading Southern educators for the distribution of the Fund; in fact during his visit to White Sulphur

This is the most famous photograph ever taken at White Sulphur Springs. Taken in August, 1869, it is the only photograph of Robert E. Lee and a group of former Confederate generals. Lee is second from left in front row. The generals, standing behind him, are, left to right: James Conner of South Carolina, Martin Gary of South Carolina, J. Bankhead Magruder of Virginia, Robert Lilley of Virginia, P.G.T. Beauregard of Louisiana, Alexander Lawton of Georgia, Henry Wise of Virginia, Joseph Brent of Maryland. Seated in the front row are, left to right: Blacque Bey, Turkish Minister to the U.S.; Lee; philanthropist George Peabody; banker W.W. Corcoran; Judge James Lyons.

Springs he donated $60,000 to General Lee's Washington College. With Peabody that season was Dr. Barnas Sears, the former President of Brown University, who was the General Agent of the Peabody Fund. As Sears described the visit: "Mr. P. is delighted with the establishment and with the gentlemen he has met. More attention and respect he could not wish, and yet they are very delicate in their attentions and do not weary him. Everything is as you desire. The people have received him as their benefactor."

The climax of that 1869 season was an elaborate fancy dress ball held in honor of George Peabody, an expres-

sion of gratitude by the Southerners for his gifts. At White Sulphur Springs, a ball was the natural form of celebration, for as Charles Pilsbury explained, "One word tells what people do at the White Sulphur; and that is—Dance!" The Richmond *Whig* deliriously reported the event in the next day's issue: "Never has there been brought together a crowd of fair women and brave men which represented more largely the refined beauty, grace, worth, and intellect of our country than that which last night did honor to Mr. Peabody." In loving detail the newspaper described the most handsome costumes of the evening: Miss Mary Thomas of Baltimore—

"dress of satin, striped downward with blue, red and white, crimson satin coat, canteen swung gracefully around the shoulder and wearing a jaunty military cap"; Mrs. James Lyons of Richmond—"ball dress of pearl colored silk, white and pink wreath of flowers and a collar of costliest lace"; Mrs. Captain Conner of Louisiana—"pink silk shirt over dress of green satin, made in the Watteau style, satin pearl necklace." The grand Peabody Ball was so large that the hotel's enormous dining room was temporarily converted into a ballroom for two thousand revellers.

The honor and respect shown George Peabody at White Sulphur Springs was elaborate and magnanimous; that shown to Robert E. Lee, in contrast, was quiet and subdued. Lee was hesitant to vacation at the White when he learned of the vast crowds. He feared his presence might create a disturbance among ex-Confederates. Since the war, Lee's every step had been dogged by admirers, ex-soldiers, journalists, and curious onlookers, yet in the end he decided to travel with his daughters, Mildred and Agnes, to the resort. He first appeared at the springs that season in the hotel's grand dining room. John S. Wise vividly described that scene in his novel, *The Lion's Skin*: "The vast dining room, so long that people could not recognize each other from one end of it to the other, was filling rapidly. The noise and babble of a meal was something indescribable. The rush and hurry of hundreds of waiters bearing trays of viands, the brilliant costumes and gems that sparkled as far as the eye could reach, the varied types of men and women from the dark Creole of the Teche to the florid Kentuckian and Virginian—all these combined to make a never-to-be-forgotten scene." The most respected families from South Carolina, Georgia, North Carolina, Alabama, Maryland, Kentucky, Louisiana, and above all, from Virginia were represented in the dining room that evening. "The gathering had no political significance whatever," the novelist wrote, "It was simply the coming together of a great throng of long-tried friends, weary of years of anxiety, sadness, death and defeat, resolved (for a while at least) to try to forget pain and to search for health and surcease of sorrow."

General Lee climbed the steps to the hotel porch and moved into the dining room, Wise continued, "dressed in a suit of spotless white duck and bore in his hand a panama hat with a deep mourning band. There were deep lines of care upon his face and an expression of sadness which neither his smiles nor his imposing dignity concealed." Within the bustling dining room the meal's clatter went on: "Suddenly, apparently without a sound from anyone, a hush fell on the company. Conversation stopped and there was a silence as if the bands had been slipped from the wheels in some great noisy machine-

shop. The waiters desisted from their labours and stood still in their places. All eyes were turned to a doorway opening into the great reception-room. The doors were thrown open and a tall, white-bearded man advanced. 'General Lee has come!' flashed the message across the breadth of the room. As if by military command, twelve hundred chairs were pushed back and twelve hundred men and women, half of whom had never laid eyes on him before, rose up spontaneously to do him homage. His table was far down the room, and his progress was slow. He had evidently expected no such ovation. His first look when he saw the movement was one of surprise and regret that he was being made conspicuous; but if he felt it he had no time to indulge it, as on either side he saw and recognized friends who were bowing and to whom he bowed smilingly in return. There was no noisy demonstration. It was not the sort of crowd that cheers; nor was there anything in his appearance to bring forth a cheer."

Tears welled in the eyes of those who had been in battle with him, the story relates, because the great leader looked much older, much changed. But respect dictated that these emotions be kept in check. "With the same

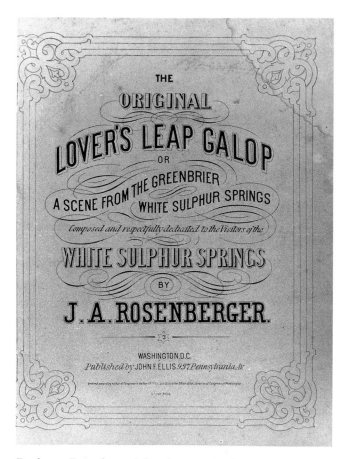

Professor Rosenberger's band entertained resort visitors for a decade after the Civil War. He composed this music in 1871.

Brochure cover after Civil War, showing the resort's location in the new state of West Virginia.

Included in this late 1860s group are former Confederate Gen. Joseph Johnston (standing right of tree) and Robert E. Lee's son Custis (seated at right).

decorum which had marked its rising," the novelist concluded, "the company was seated, after General Lee, and the merry hum of conversation was resumed." For an hour or more after the meal Lee sat at an informal reception in the parlor, greeting hundreds of friends in a characteristic air of simplicity. For the remainder of his visit Lee was treated as a friend and companion and, with the exception of ladies seeking his autograph on their costly Japanese fans, he was not subject to any ostentatious demonstrations of affection.

In 1870, George Peyton, again leasing the resort, invited Lee to vacation at White Sulphur Springs, noting that Jefferson Davis—the former President of the Confederacy—had arrived. In early August Lee replied, "It would give me great pleasure to see Mr. Davis as well as the other friends now at the White Sulphur, among whom I always number yourselves. I will, therefore, if nothing prevents, be there about the middle of next week." On August 8th Peyton wrote back to inform Lee that Davis had left unexpectedly early and Lee postponed his visit, but answered, "If I can accomplish a visit after trying the baths [at Hot Springs and Warm Springs] it will give me pleasure to do so, for I always enjoy the White Sulphur very much."

But the visit never took place. Biographer Douglas Southall Freeman drew this portrait of General Lee in the summer of 1870: "His hair was entirely white now and his gait was slow. Once the most erect of men, he was beginning to stoop in the shoulders. The nervous strain of the war and the difficult exercise of a stern self-control during Reconstruction had proved too much for even his stout system. Although he was only sixty-three, he was an old man." A serious illness set in during September and, just after daybreak on October 12, 1870, Mrs. Lee sat down and held the hand of the dying General. About 9:30 A.M., Lee's final, distinct words broke through his delirium: "Strike the tent," he said, and spoke no more.

One of the last photographs of Robert E. Lee, taken in Spring, 1870.

An especially well-designed 1883 poster clearly announces the resort's location on the C&O Railway.

Railroading the Belles
to the Ball

While the season of 1869 was long remembered for the galaxy of prominent Americans who gathered at White Sulphur Springs, that summer another event occurred which profoundly altered the course of the resort's history. On June 29th, Collis P. Huntington, one of the greatest of America's railroad magnates, crossed the mountains to White Sulphur Springs by means other than stagecoach; he traveled over the Chesapeake and Ohio Railroad's temporary tracks on the first passenger train to reach the legendary resort. On this maiden journey, Huntington was making a tour of the railroad to determine whether the line's advantages justified not only a substantial investment of his capital, but also his time, since he would be managing the railroad's affairs. Like George Washington, who almost one hundred years earlier had extolled the vast potential of this "Great Connection" between the Chesapeake Bay and the Ohio River, Huntington was favorably impressed with the commercial possibilities of the route. Subsequently, he agreed to commit his considerable skill, experience and influence to the completion of the new railroad.

For many years the proprietors at White Sulphur Springs had anxiously awaited the completion of the railroad, but the Civil War left the tracks of the Virginia Central Railroad in ruin. At the end of the war, only twenty-two of the line's one hundred seventy miles of track were serviceable. Conferences were called at The White in July of 1867 and August of 1868 to discuss extending the line to the Ohio River. "It did not just 'hap-

pen' that they met at White Sulphur Springs," wrote historian Perceval Reniers, "it was not chance or design. It was simply the inevitable rendezvous." The railroad backers were all long-time habitues of the resort, and they realized that its visitors would provide a major portion of the anticipated passenger revenue. At the 1868 meeting, commissioners from Virginia and West Virginia signed a contract for the construction of a new railroad, combining the old Virginia Central with the Covington and Ohio. A new name was adopted for the new railroad, one that proclaimed the impressive scope of its iron tentacles: the Chesapeake and Ohio Railroad. Ten years later, after a reorganization, the name was changed slightly to the C&O Railway.

The arrival of that first train was a triumphant day for the grand old Southern watering place. Passenger service by rail guaranteed the resort's survival. In fact, White Sulphur Springs was the only resort among the Springs of Virginia that could boast of service directly to its main gate. 1869 was, then, one of those watershed years in the history of the place. That season the past and present merged, as travelers from the north and west sped on iron wheels drawn by steaming locomotives to mingle with an older generation of southerners. Robert E. Lee, "the embodiment of the Lost Cause" in Christiana Bond's phrase, reigned on the porch of the Old White hotel while the railroad train, the physical expression of the North's industrial power, rumbled up to the station a few hundred yards away. This scene was not only a watershed moment in the resort's history, it was also a highly symbolic moment in American history.

On July 1, 1869, three days after Collis P. Huntington's maiden run, regularly scheduled trains began arriving at the Springs from Richmond; a new era had begun. Via the railroad, the act of traveling—not just to White Sulphur but to other points—was actually pleasurable for the first time. Travelers coming from Washington, D.C., for instance, now reached the resort in fifteen hours whereas in the past the same trip had taken four or five days.

With the postwar renewal of social life at White Sulphur Springs, the resort was irresistibly attractive to writers curious about the social interactions among this new mix of visitors: Would expanding railroad connections spell an end to the resort's legendary Southern atmosphere? Could visitors from sections of the country recently at war blend together in peace? Was romance still the uppermost thought on the minds of the newer guests? Did the rise of new industrial wealth mean a nouveau riche class would push aside the customs of the old Southern planters? And finally, how would White Sulphur Springs survive the competition from newer resorts appearing across the country?

Having arrived by train, a group of visitors poses on the porch of The Old White, 1872.

The first thing that impressed writers about White Sulphur Springs was the resort's splendid history. Even in the 1870s it was considered an historic landmark which drew visitors from around the nation because of its heritage. Travel accounts invariably included at least a few paragraphs about its celebrated history and repeated the long list of influential visitors who frequented the watering hole before the war. Ante-bellum accounts had depicted a resort with all the necessary ingredients for a compelling myth—miraculous mineral water, light-hearted courtships, sophisticated guests, refined conversation, and difficult access. The White did, in fact, remain one of the few public places in America where the customs and manners of the Old South lived on. Without railroad service, most of the neighboring Virginia Springs never fully recovered from the war's devastation. White Sulphur Springs, on the other hand, was able to advertise itself for decades as "The Representative Resort of the South."

Still, financial problems plagued both the resort and the fortunes of its regular patrons, slowing the progress of post-war restoration. In the 1870s there were some ragged edges a visitor could see. In 1872, Mary B. Dodge wrote in *Lippincott's Magazine*: "We find the grass unmowed except by tramping feet, the gravel paths unweeded, steps leading to once-favored summer houses falling into decay, everything evincing taste in the original design, but unkempt as a beggar child's profuse and ringleted hair." In spite of such shabby conditions, Mary Dodge perceived another, more intangible force that was working in favor of the White: "Nobody talks of the discomfort, nobody appears to feel it. Has not fashion lifted each and all above the meanness of a comment upon such petty details? Ah! Fashion is kind or cruel as she wantonly pleases, and she pleases to be mad-

ly in love with the White Sulphur."

Writers continually compared the attractions of White Sulphur Springs to those of Northern resorts. In the September, 1877 issue of *The Nation*, an unmistakably Northern magazine, one article noted the friendliness and joviality at White Sulphur Springs, and furthermore, "one of the marked characteristics of Southern life, namely, the extent to which nearly all Southern men and women associate comfort not with the trimness and order of Northern or English homes, but with an abundance of service. Well-to-do Northerners used to be surprised, in fact, at the amount of what they would consider discomfort in the way of rude or unfinished surroundings, hard beds, poor fare, want of order of all sorts, which even Southerners in easy circumstances were willing to put up with; but the explanation lay in the fact that Southerners placed their comfort in having plenty of service at command." The writer offered an interesting perception regarding the different qualities of

An early C&O Railroad Meal Ticket.

resorts North and South: the traditions at White Sulphur Springs "are unquestionably a better basis for good hotel-keeping than anything we have at the North. The first condition of excellence in all places of entertainment is exactingness on the part of the public. To be well cared for, you must expect it and be used to it, and this condition the Southerners fulfill in a much higher degree than we do. They look for more attention, and they therefore get it."

In 1878, one of America's best-known writers, John Esten Cooke, published in *Harper's New Monthly Magazine* one of the most extensive descriptions of White Sulphur Springs ever written, and perhaps the most informative. Cooke was delighted by the natural beauty of the resort's setting: "All around are mountains—mountains—mountains; the near slopes clothed in deep green pines, oaks, maples, laurels, and rhododendrons; the distant ranges rolling away like (there is no other comparison) blue waves of the ocean. There is no doubt that this landscape beauty enlivens the spirits and freshens the faculties of enjoyment." The social scene inside the gates of the resort caused him to muse, "If, as Pope wrote, the proper study of mankind is man, the White Sulphur is an excellent place to pursue that study. If you please to consider it, it is a gay comedy which is played before you, with a large and varied company, whose individual members you admire or laugh at as the case may be, the only trouble being that you are not always certain whether they are acting their real characters or only playing a part."

Cooke was pleased to report that the new infusion of guests had not diminished the refined social customs so long associated with summers at the White. "You find here the same air of high-breeding and rational relaxation for the sake of relaxation," he wrote, "which characterized the White Sulphur during the ancient *regime*, before the modern spirit of democracy had leveled everything to so distressingly a uniformity." The writer paused to explain his comparison between old and new: "Let us not be misunderstood. Democracy has many desirable results, and that ancient *regime* was by no means altogether lovely; but there was a grace in social intercourse, a freedom from self-assertion, and a natural, unpretending ease, springing from true simplicity and refinement, which made society delightful, especially amid the informal and agreeable surroundings of a summer resort. The 'White' was, and still is, the chosen point of reunion for this class of persons. It is probable that it will remain to the last the chosen resort of the really 'best society' of the whole country."

This concern about the social standing of new visitors to White Sulphur Springs was summed up in a tale that circulated among resort guests for many years. The anecdote epitomized the subtle tension between the old Southern economy and the newer industrial wealth. It seems that on one occasion a Mrs. Beverly Dandridge Tucker was politely introduced to a group of ladies relaxing on the porch of the Old White, and conversation soon turned to the subject of their fathers' occupations. The first woman reported that her father was the president of a Pittsburgh steel company, another was the daughter of a Western copper company president, while the third woman's father was the head of a Chicago meat-packing plant. When Mrs. Tucker was asked what her father did, she replied simply, "He's a farmer." As she left the other ladies immediately began to cluck, "A farmer's daughter? What on earth is the White coming to?" The woman who had made the introductions interrupted, "I do not think my friend told you the name of her farm." The other ladies shook their heads, trying to maintain the appearance of some degree of interest, and the speaker smiled as she dropped the name. Mrs. Tucker was the former Anna Marie Washington, she explained, the daughter of the owner of the farm called Mount Vernon.

There was some difference of opinion regarding the smooth mixture of guests coming from formerly antagonistic regions, however. John Esten Cooke wrote in his "Harper's" article that North and South were getting along quite well at White Sulphur Springs. He pointed to the 1874 visit by President Ulysses S. Grant as evidence: "General Grant paid a visit to the 'White' and was received with courtesy and respect," he wrote; "a singular commingling one would say . . . the General-in-Chief of the North and some of the hardiest fighters of the South, the men who but yesterday sworn foes, and today familiar associates." This depiction of sectional harmony was contradicted by the observations of Colonel James B. Walton of Lousiana in a letter to his daughter. "I thought the war was over until my experience at the White," Colonel Walton wrote in 1883. "The Northern were 'Yankees' and the Southern were 'forward,' 'pert,' 'bold,' and 'overdressed,' such were the epithets applied on either side. No love between them. The war is not over!"

These tales of social one-upmanship and regional bickering were, for the most part, exceptions to the rules of social discourse at White Sulphur Springs. Besides, there was one overriding concern that knit the company together: fashion. Northerners and Southerners, old wealth and new, shared one common attribute, and that was a desire to parade their finery at the elaborate balls held two or three times each week. This ongoing sartorial

Poster announcing the largest ball of the 1873 season. One of the managers of the event was Jefferson Davis, former President of the Confederacy.

Exotic costumes added flair to one of the grand balls of the 1880s.

Dancers at an evening German pose for the photographer about 1890.

display climaxed at the Annual Grand Fancy and Full Dress Ball staged at the peak of the season, the last two weeks of August. All visitors routinely participated in the merry spectacle of changing outfits three to five times per day—a different suit or dress was worn for breakfast, dinner, supper, lawn parties, riding, etc.—however, the finest attire was always reserved for dancing in the ballroom of the Old White. The beginning of train service in 1869 had a particularly dramatic effect on this aspect of life at White Sulphur Springs, because travelers arrived with more and larger trunks of clothing than in the old stagecoach days. With the assistance of baggage cars, the norm for a single family was eight to ten trunks for the season, and more if the family included daughters. (Indeed, arriving with less than this number of trunks could cause something of a scandal among the elderly ladies ensconced on the porch of the Old White.) Every young girl brought what she called her "August trunk," which held her prettiest clothes and was opened only in that month and only for dances at White Sulphur Springs.

The gowns were a source of delight for most visitors, though others were startled by some of the dresses and accompanying jewelry. A gentleman from Louisiana described the following scene in a letter: 'There was grand dressing such as displays by Baltimore and Louisville, Atlanta and Norfolk, a little of New York and much of Richmond. Where all the diamonds came from, if they were *all* diamonds, was to me a marvel. If all true, some of the ladies at the evening soirees were ablaze: ten to twenty thousand dollars of gems adorning some of the young girls was not at all exceptional." Some men saw in this lavish display the doom of civilization, including one New Orleans editor who wrote after the Peabody Ball in 1869: "The overdressing is awful, and may well alarm the political and social economists of the South for the future of our section. What a terror to aspiring bachelors to contemplate the potent agencies of bankruptcy which flutter and glitter around them!"

There was a new factor to consider in the ballroom dressing of the 1880s and 1890s, and that was the presence of the press. Newspapers in Richmond, Washington, Baltimore, Norfolk and other cities printed lengthy columns each week describing the social events at White Sulphur Springs and the dresses worn to the evening dances. One member of the press repeated this conversation to the Virginia writer Edward A. Pollard:

Reporter. 'Miss _____, have the kindness to describe your costume to me.

Miss _____. (Shocked and blushing at the idea of being put into the paper.) 'Oh, indeed, don't put my name in. It's a horrid way. Now, really, you mustn't.

Reporter. 'Oh certainly, Miss _____, of course not, as you wish otherwise.

Miss _____. (Startled and turning pale at the idea of *not being put in the paper*.) 'Well—but—at any rate—if you should, say that I wore,' etc.

And there followed a catalogue a half page long.

Taking a break from an 1890s lawn party, visitors pose on the lawn in front of Paradise Row.

Dancing out on the lawn around the turn of the century.

A photographer adjusting his camera for a photo in the 1870s. (Courtesy Valentine Museum, Richmond, Virginia)

A ladies' tea about 1900.

COTILLON

Miss Howard.

GREENBRIER
WHITE SULPHUR
SPRINGS.

SATURDAY,
AUGUST 13.
1898.

'96

GRAND

BALL

The Old White.

LAWN PARTY AND COTILLION
GREENBRIER, WHITE SULPHUR SPRINGS, W. VA.
WEDNESDAY AFTERNOON, AUGUST 11th, 1915.

COLONEL JO. LANE STERN	DR. JOHN FREELAND
MR. JOHN W. GRANT	MR. JAMES R. BRANCH
DR. J. A. WHITE	MR. F. W. HANEWINCKEL
MR. HENRY L. CABELL	MR. EDWARD H. INMAN
DR. LEROY CHILDS	MR. GARRET B. WALL
MR. JOHN CURRIE	MR. DE SOTO FITZGERALD
MR. ELMORE D. HOTCHKISS JR.	MR. THOMAS B. SCOTT
MR. THOMAS B. PAINE	

Cotillon ribbons, which a gentleman wore on his lapel during the dance. These ribbons were used as invitations and saved as souvenirs.

The scene of the morning German, from Harpers Weekly magazine, August 1886.

The new post-war crowd at White Sulphur Springs was somewhat younger and attuned to a faster, more modern, style of enjoyment, which was a source of surprise to some of the older guests, especially in the less-than-formal dancing that swept into the ballroom. Charles Bruce, the owner of one of the best cottages on the grounds, was plainly shocked by the newer dances. "All my ideas of decency and propriety are so completely upset that I feel as if I had caught a glimpse of pandemonium," Bruce wrote to his wife in 1875. "If our cousin Adelaine had been present, I am sure she would have had an attack of hysterics, or been carried out in a fainting fit." What, precisely, the dancers may have been doing Bruce did not report, but what probably made it so shocking was its contrast to the vastly more popular dance, the German.

In the last two decades of the nineteenth century, the German was constantly performed at White Sulphur Springs. It was an elite dance—that is, since it required formal training in the various "figures," it was known in those social classes with the leisure to perfect such maneuvers—and it was a so-called parlor dance, which is to say that it was done best in small groups. After the Civil War, German Clubs were established throughout the United States. The Richmond German was founded in 1870, and a participant in the first gathering described the dance this way: "The etiquette was to be strictly ordered . . . white gloves were obligatory, for no gentleman would have dreamed of taking a lady's hand or enclosing her 18-inch waist with bare hands. At least a foot of daylight must come between the partners as they whirled, swooped, reversed and stepped to a polka, a schottische, or a Stauss waltz." Germans were so popular that they were held not only in the evening, but during the day. Around the turn of the century, outdoor daylight dancing became a national craze. At White Sulphur Springs, daytime Germans began at eleven in the morning. The twirling took place on the lawn around the bandstand that stood in front of the Old White Hotel.

If there was concern in various quarters that tradition might be under siege at White Sulphur Springs—specifically, that it had lost its distinctive Southern atmosphere—those notions were confounded by the splendid Lee Monument Ball of August 15, 1877. The ball was held to raise funds for an equestrian statue of Robert E. Lee to be erected on a prominent site in Richmond. It was the first of four consecutive fund raisers at The White, though the one that drew the largest and most brilliant crowd to the Springs. By the time the day arrived, sixteen hundred guests had gathered in the hotel and cottages to show their affection for General Lee. For one Richmond newspaper, the Ball was evidence that the days of bitter sectionalism were over: "This ball has shown to the

politicians here that there is 'No North, No South.' Now the ex-Confederate General danced with the belle of New York, while the brave Union General was foremost in the dance with his fair Southern partner."

As at the Peabody Ball eight years earlier, the Old White's ballroom was not large enough to contain all the guests, so the enormous dining room was opened to the crowds. "Pretty ladies and good-looking gents skipping the light fantastic beneath the glare of two locomotive headlights and a hundred lamps was a decidedly attractive spectacle to look upon," reported one newspaper. The Lee Monument Ball was led by a Captain Jo Lane Stern of Richmond, who became another of those representative personalities about White Sulphur Springs from the 1870s until his death in 1932. A Confederate veteran, a student of Lee's at Washington College, and a well-known Richmond attorney, Captain—and eventually General—Jo Lane Stern's arrival at White Sulphur Springs each season marked for more than fifty years, the definitive moment when the society of the Old South reached the peak of its annual assembly at the Springs.

Jo Lane Stern of Richmond.

The Lee Monument Ball attracted correspondents from newspapers across the country, but the most memorable account of the event was the one submitted by a woman from the Richmond *Whig*. Her witty description of fashions at the Ball departed sharply from the reporting conventions of the time. She observed that most stories about balls focused solely on the ladies' toilets, each more or less the same insofar as they dwelt at length on the gowns, gems, lips, teeth, hair, and eyes of the women. A gross injustice had been perpetrated on the gentlemen at the Lee Monument Ball, she felt. "Never before in the annals of the White Sulphur did men look better," she wrote. "These gentlemen have rights. They have an eye to matrimony as well as the beautiful belles. They have been ignored cruelly." To correct this one-sided perspective, the Richmond writer published a satirical portrait of the neglected male fashions.

"The scene was beautiful and exhilarating," read her newspaper story, "on every side manly forms could be seen. Beautiful blondes predominated and were the recipients of much attention from the ladies. Well-polished boots gleamed in the lamplights like stars on the black sea, and unique swallowtails danced backwards and forwards with graceful irregularity, suggestive of a wheel within a wheel, while diamond pins sprung boldly out on a glossy lake of white shirt-bosoms, and added more brightness to the picture." Her story was a perfect parody of the style of writing that regularly appeared in society columns. With the eye of a practiced observer, she noted details: "A blonde from Texas wore a pair of shoes that were made by an old shoe-maker who once half-soled a pair of shoes for General U.S. Grant." "The wealth of striped socks has never been rivalled . . . a member of Congress wore a pair, black and white, that cost one dollar a pair and were made by Worth of Paris."

Regardless of costume, either male or female, the Lee Monument Ball and those that followed were financial successes. Money raised from those events contributed significantly to the $90,000 expended for the Lee statue by Jean Antonin Mercie, which was unveiled in 1890 and still graces Monument Avenue in Richmond.

Although social activity at the White rebounded quickly from the effects of the Civil War, the resort's owners were still hard pressed to steady its shaky financial foundations. Throughout the 1870s and well into the 1880s, the proprietors had difficulty meeting the interest on the loans by Colonel Richard Singleton and others back in the 1830s, plus their account books were under constant scrutiny by a Federal judge in Charleston, West Virginia. The catastrophe of war had increased the number of debts, and tedious legal battles dragged on in court as creditors demanded their due. Unfortunately, many of the much-needed improvements to the property had to be neglected until these problems were ironed out. In addition, The Panic of 1873 threw the nation into an eight-year-long depression, further drying up sources of capital. And in 1877, as the Company began building a new hotel adjacent to the railroad station, the unfinished structure burned to the ground (in the only major fire ever on the property) before it even opened. Henry M. Mathews, of Lewisburg, the court-appointed Commissioner of the property, was in charge of leasing the property and collecting rents until 1876, when the resort was quietly put on the market. In his final report Mathews wrote: "The improvements upon the property, not withstanding the wise efforts of the court to keep them in repair, are steadily deteriorating. In their present condition it is impossible for any lessee to entertain guests with comfort or to give satisfaction to the visiting public."

Nothing seemed to be going right. Then on March 31,

The management of The Greenbrier White Sulphur Springs Company in 1880. Owner W.A. Stuart is seated at the far left.

A poster from the 1880s showing the new wing added to the right of the original section of the Old White, plus various scenes on the resort property.

1880, William A. Stuart, a wealthy salt manufacturer and cattle baron from nearby Russell County, Virginia, purchased the resort for $340,000. Stuart subsequently joined with three other gentlemen to form the "Greenbrier White Sulphur Springs Company." This was the first time the word "Greenbrier" was officially used in the resort's title. In the years since the Civil War other resorts had developed which also bore the name "White Sulphur Springs." Therefore, the new owners added the county name to distinguish their established resort from its newer competitors.

W.A. Stuart brought a wide variety of business experience to his new investment. He owned and operated the famous Exchange Hotel in Richmond. His herd of short-horn cattle was said to be the most valuable in the world. And his salt manufacturing company (one of the largest in the country) had been almost the sole source of salt to the Confederate forces in the last two years of the war. It was perhaps no coincidence that he had also worked closely with Dr. Moorman during the war, when the White Sulphur Springs physician served as Virginia's Salt Commissioner. In addition, Stuart, whose family had come to the Commonwealth in 1726, had solid connections: his father was Alexander H.H. Stuart, the man who drafted the "White Sulphur Manifesto" for General Lee's signature in 1868, and had acted as William Calwell's agent in the 1857 sale of the resort; his mother was a cousin of Governor Letcher of Virginia; and his brother was the famous Confederate cavalry commander, J.E.B. Stuart.

Under Stuart's guidance the Springs property received the complete face-lifting it deserved. It had been over twenty years since the massive rebuilding of the late 1850s. During that period the resort had survived four years of war followed by years of low economic fortunes. The first and most dramatic change Stuart made was the construction of a new four-story frame wing which extended from the western end of the hotel to form a large "L" shaped structure. The wing contained office space, ladies' reception rooms, reading rooms, a telegraph office and private dining rooms. A new $10,000 kitchen boasted the most modern culinary equipment. Inside the original section of the hotel, a grand staircase was added, all the public rooms were painted—and in some cases frescoed—and on the upper two floors a number of guest rooms were eliminated creating large, well-ventilated hallways that served as cool places to sit during the summer's heat. There were other important improvements—a large steam laundry was built, gas and electric power were added to light the hotel and grounds, a new sewerage system was installed, as were baggage elevators. The hotel's exterior and all the cottages received fresh coats of white paint, and new furniture and bedding were bought for each of the guest rooms. Quite pleased with these improvements, the Company issued brochures calling White Sulphur Springs "the Athens and Paris of America." Rates in the early 1880s stood at $3.50 per day, $21.00 per week, $75.00 per month.

As America entered the first golden age of the grand resort hotel, which was the result of an astonishing expansion of railroad lines, the refurbished White Sulphur Springs was a major resort on par with the most elaborate competitors springing up across the United States. No longer was it seen simply as one of the Springs of Virginia. The railroad boom of the post-Civil War era not only made far-flung resorts accessible to wealthy patrons but to more middle-class travelers too. Many more people were traveling each summer, though they were visiting more resorts, each for a shorter period of time.

A good example of the hectic pace of rail travel was Charles Dudley Warner's 1886 novel *Their Pilgrimage*. The itinerary of Warner's characters indicated that by the 1880s it was no longer necessary to vacation at one resort for the whole summer. Their summer began at Fortress Monroe on the Virginia coast, they moved north by train to Cape May and Atlantic City, in New Jersey, then on to New York's Catskill Mountains. Next they traveled east to the famous resort town of Newport, Rhode Island, and out to the island of Martha's Vineyard, in Massachusetts. Then the group spontaneously headed south once again, to White Sulphur Springs and Sweet Springs, before backtracking to Long Branch, Saratoga Springs, Niagra Falls, the Thousand Islands in the St. Lawrence River, and finally to the White Mountains of New Hampshire. If White Sulphur Springs was to vie with these other locations, it had to change with the times.

However, the old watering place offered two things that none of the newer resorts could buy with mere money: a deep-rooted historical environment and, perhaps the more crucial feature, scores of classic Southern belles. The legendary belles of White Sulphur Springs alone made a trip to the mountains of West Virginia a unique adventure. Though the age of the Southern belle's reign at White Sulphur Springs dated back to Colonel Pope's Billing, Wooing and Cooing Society of the 1830s, the height of her domain (when being a belle was both an art and a science) was reached roughly between 1875 and the end of the century. There was something almost divine about belledom at the White, as conveyed in the popular saying reported by a Massachusetts writer in 1889: "The Lord made the White Sulphur Springs and then the Southern girl, and rested, satisfied with his work."

Mary Triplett

Lena Jackson

IRISH CLUB.

DEJEUNER.

Complimentary to
MISS LENA JACKSON.

Melons Canteloups en glace,
Bouillon Clarife en demi tasse,
Sheepshead grille a la Tartare,
Amontillado.
Pommes Julienne.
Chablis.
Cotelettes de Mouton a l'Anglaise,
Croquettes de mais de Turquie,
Cliequot, Y. L.
Jeune Canard a la Rothschild,
Timbale de Macaroni,
Tomates Frits,
Sorbet au Rhum.
Pluvier sur croustade aux cressons,
Celeri a la Francaise,
Gelee a l'Oporto.
Fromage a l'Anana.
Fruits Assortis.

Cafe.

White Sulphur Springs,
August 17th 1886.

The Irish Club, one of the social organizations of the day, prepared this menu in honor of Lena Jackson, a belle of 1886.

Some of the belles of White Sulphur Springs gather for a photograph in the 1890s.

May Handy.

Mattie Ould.

Irene Langhorne.

To be considered a belle at The White, a young woman needed to dance well, dress with taste and style, conduct herself gracefully, and most important, not be married. For this last reason, a belle's reign was usually quite short—in fact something was wrong with the system if it went on too long. The intense desire to be a Springs belle was illustrated in the letter sent to W.W. Corcoran, who was by then a familiar figure at the resort: "Dear Mr. Corcoran," wrote one young woman, who wasted no time getting to the point, "What are one hundred dollars to you? Nothing. And yet they represent to me everything that is beautiful and delightful. With one hundred dollars I could go to White Sulphur. I could get muslin dresses, pretty sashes, a leghorn hat just loaded with flowers. And oh, I could get a Nile green silk ball gown and a white parasol and everything I would need to make me a belle. My grandmother and my mother have been belles there, and I do believe if I could just get there, I could be a belle, too. But how can I go without an outfit? Please, dear, good, Mr. Corcoran, send me this small sum and I will bless you all my life." Mr. Corcoran sent the check, the girl made it to White Sulphur Springs, became a belle, and, in the phrase of the day, "made a conquest."

The exploits of individual belles were retold for years among the resort's guests, and many tales were published in books and magazine articles so that their names became synonymous with joyful summers at White Sulphur Springs. Perhaps the most appealing of the belles of the 1870s was Mattie Ould—pronounced "old"—the daughter of a Richmond judge. Miss Ould was never celebrated for her beauty, rather it was her quick wit that kept visitors clustered within earshot. Her classic retort to an undesirable advance, gleefully passed down for generations, was prompted when a certain elderly admirer named Mr. Page noticed that Mattie had dropped her glove. Leaping at this opportunity to start a conversation with her, Mr. Page retrieved the glove, bowed to Mattie, and presented it to her with the following words:

If from your glove you take the letter "g,"
Your glove is love and that I bear for thee.

To which Mattie Ould, without pausing a second, responded:

If from your name you take the letter "p,"
Your Page is age, that will not do for me.

Mary Triplett, also from Richmond, was Mattie Ould's chief rival, but Miss Triplett was blessed with extraordinary beauty. Indeed, she was generally considered one of the most beautiful women in the South. Their rivalry was a friendly one, as demonstrated by the gracious toast Mattie offered to Mary at a dinner in their honor; "Here's to beauty, grace and wit," said Mattie as she raised her glass, "which united make a Triplett." Mary Triplett was wooed by a journalist, or rather, by two journalists, a romantic dilemma that resulted in her suitors meeting in the last pistol duel ever fought in the Virginias. Mary's engagement to Alfred Mordecai, though never officially announced, was known to just about everyone at White Sulphur Springs. Nevertheless, a persistent Page McCarthy managed to dance once with Mary, yet she refused to pay him any further attention. Slighted by the rejection, McCarthy published brazen verses in a Richmond newspaper where all her friends could read:

When Mary's queenly form I press
In Strauss' latest waltz
I would I could those lips caress
Although those lips be false

Upon seeing these shocking sentiments openly printed, Mary's fiance, Alfred Mordecai, immediately challenged McCarthy to a duel. The outcome was tragic for all involved. Mordecai was fatally shot, McCarthy never fully recovered from the trauma of taking another man's life, and Mary Triplett, who was blamed for the tragedy, could never escape the cloud of sorrow that haunted her after the duel.

Besides Mattie Ould and Mary Triplett, there were other equally renowned belles at The White: Page Aylett, the great-great-great-granddaughter of Patrick Henry, "dazzlingly beautiful with a fair complexion and dark glowing eyes"; Lizzie Cabell, aunt of the famous Virginia writer James Branch Cabell and mother of Maryland Governor James Richie; and May Handy, Mattie Ould's half-sister. It was said that when Richmond taxi drivers were asked the fare from the railroad station to their hotel, they responded, "One dollar to the hotel, but two dollars to go by Franklin Street where you just might see May Handy on her porch."

When a belle's behavior neared the scandalous, the social world could be rocked. Bettina Padelford caused a sensation by the rather unorthodox use of her evening slipper. As the story goes, one night, during a private dinner at White Sulphur Springs, Bettina was sitting at a table where talk turned to the old Polish wedding custom of drinking wine from the bride's slipper. One man loudly made it known that he would under no circumstances drink from any woman's shoe, while another, George Morris of Charlottesville, mused that it depended on the woman. This was all Bettina Padelford needed to hear, and off came her slipper with the words, "Here is your challenge." Morris quickly responded by filling it with

One of the classic images of a lazy summer afternoon at White Sulphur Springs, this illustration of a honeymoon couple on their cottage porch appeared in Harper's Weekly *in August, 1888.*

Virginia State Bar Association's 1st Annual Meeting, White Sulphur Springs, July 24-25, 1889.

SACRED CONCERT.

WHITE SULPHUR SPRINGS, W. VA.
SUNDAY, JULY 10TH, 1898.
8.00 O'clock, P. M.

DREXEL'S CONCERT BAND,
of READING, PENN.
HAROLD V. DREXEL, Director.

SOLOISTS: { ELAM C. JENKINS, HAROLD V. DREXEL.

PROGRAMME:

1. Funeral March, ... F. Chopin.
   (In memory of heroes of the " Maine."
2. "Gloria," from 12th Mass, ... Mozart.
3. Cornet Solo—"Alice, Where Art Thou?" .... White.
4. GRAND SELECTION—
   Cavalleria Rusticana .... Mascagni.
5. Pilgrim Chorus from Tannhauser.......................... R. Wagner.
6. Song—"Hearts and Flowers." .... T. Tobani.
7. "Peer Gynt Suite".. E. Greig.
   A—"The Morning."
   B—"Ase's Death."
8. Trombone Solo—"Romance." .... Bennet.
9. "Largo" .... G. F. Handel.
   10. Star Spangled Banner.

Drexel's Concert Band performed for afternoon concerts and evening dances during the 1898 season.

champagne and drinking heartily, and within weeks slipper-drinking was on its way to becoming a national fad. Such goings-on were considered by some to be a severe breech of traditional decorum at The White, causing one visitor to remark, "The moral and social structure of the famous resort was almost demolished." For Bettina Padelford, however, the resulting publicity launched her successful twenty-year career on the stage and in vaudeville.

Despite such shenanigans, enduring fame came to those belles who possessed all the classic ingredients, and there was one belle in particular—a woman whose face was well-known to every American from the 1890s through the first World War—about whom The White's patrons could boast. On a July night in 1889, this young girl was sitting on a windowsill at the hotel when a Philadelphia beau spotted her and asked her age—"sixteen," she replied—to which the young man declared, "Well, then, it is time you were out." With that, Irene Langhorne was whisked off to the ballroom and the greatest of all White Sulphur Springs belles made her informal debut. In fact, so great was Miss Langhorne's fame, some social historians date the end of belledom in America by her 1895 engagement. But if belledom did indeed die on that occasion, a new era also began, for Irene Langhorne subsequently married the struggling artist Charles Dana Gibson and through him achieved international celebrity as the stunning model for his world famous "Gibson Girl" drawings.

Irene Langhorne was one of five daughters in a family that annually summered at White Sulphur Springs. Her father was an official of the Chesapeake and Ohio Railway. Her sister, Nancy, later became known to the world as Lady Astor, a staunch feminist and Member of Parliament in England. Nancy wrote of her sister, "Irene wasn't only beautiful. She had wonderful charm. When she came in, it was like the sun streaming into the room." Irene herself spoke fondly of her youthful days at White Sulphur Springs in an interview with society chronicler Cleveland Amory in the 1950s: "I loved it, loved it, loved it. I never wore a speck of make-up of any kind—not even powder—and I ate everything. Big breakfasts, big dinners, big suppers." Somehow, Irene maintained her twenty-inch waist. "The beaux were supposed to be able to put their hands around it," she recalled, "but my father never let them." She received sixty-two marriage proposals before she fell in love with Charles Dana Gibson, the man her father called "that damned charcoal artist." Even today Irene Langhorne's face in the instantly recognizable drawings by her husband conjure up vivid images of all that was gay about the Gay Nineties.

With belles such as these at the center of the social life at White Sulphur Springs, the resort easily maintained its longstanding reputation as fertile grounds for romantic match-making. Here, in 1875, Miss Alva Smith, of Mobile, Alabama, consented to William K. Vanderbilt's proposal of marriage, and together they took their portion of the $200 million Vanderbilt fortune, sailed the seas in the world's largest yacht, and built the luxurious resort cottage, "Marble House," at Newport. But lack of wealth was no reason to miss the romantic possibilities at The White. It was a common practice for Southern families with fine lineages, but reduced assets (or in some cases for entire small towns), to pool together their limited resources and send a promising young woman off to the springs hoping she might meet a man of more substantial means. Of course that meant that Lover's Walk, the maze of walkways behind the cottages, was a very busy place. Notorious for the love affairs that began on its rambling paths, there were "legends enough about it to fill a book," one writer noted, adding that "there is not a southern woman living who has not been engaged there at least once." Or, as another journalist commented, "It has been poetically said that [at the White] the fire flies that brighten the nights of summer are all the love words that have been breathed by generations of happy lovers."

Lover's Walk was strictly for daylight strolling as custom forbade unchaperoned mixing of the sexes after sunset. Therefore evening flirtation had to be carried on in the midst of a lively dance ceremony called the Treadmill, an institution peculiar to White Sulphur Springs. Actually, it wasn't really a dance at all, but a form of stately marching, which was regularly performed after the evening meal and before the ball. Though its heyday

Virginia Row was torn down in 1930; this 1895 photograph shows one of the more interesting cottages in that row as a backdrop for a lawn party.

coincided with the height of belledom at The White (roughly the last two or three decades of the nineteenth century), legend dates the Treadmill's origin back to one night long before the Civil War, when Henry Clay offered his arm to the wife of a doubtful political supporter and began a slow march around the center of the old ballroom. John C. Calhoun, John Marshall, John Tyler, and Winfield Scott immediately followed Clay's lead, and so a tradition was born. In many ways the Treadmill came to embody the fundamental spirit of the resort: it was dignified and at the same time lighthearted; it was a place for the exhibition of sumptuous gowns, handsome figures and beautiful faces; and it was the occasion when couples formed during daytime strolls could wordlessly announce their new romance. It was also an opportunity to see the great names of the political, social and literary world on parade; and, of course, it was a marvelous political conduit, since politicians could spread messages to other politicians via their wives.

In Charles Dudley Warner's *Their Pilgrimage* the main character, a Northerner named Stanhope King, was fascinated and puzzled by the Treadmill. "But for the seriousness of this frank display and the unflagging interest of the spectators," Warner wrote, "there would have been an element of high comedy about it." For a Northerner like King, it was quite an education to sit among the onlookers and listen to the constant evaluation and criticism of dress styles and physical charms. At one point, Stanhope King turned to a Southern friend and remarked on this continual round of comment in the gallery, to which she replied, "Well, I suppose beauty is worshipped in the South—we worship what we have, we haven't much money now, you know."

Their Pilgrimage captured White Sulphur Springs at the peak of its post-Civil War glory. Though fiction, Warner's tale gave an accurate picture of life at the resort and its attractions to a new generation of travelers. For one thing, Warner reported the particulars of a typical day at White Sulphur Springs, that is, an account of the daily "order of proceedings." The most conscientious visitors took their glasses of sulphur water the first thing in the morning, and then joined the crowd at the post office before a late breakfast. The remainder of the morning hours were filled with lounging and gossiping in the Old White's parlor, flirting on the lawn, organizing champagne and watermelon parties in the shade of the oaks, or visiting friends in their cottages. "The bar-room," Warner reported, was "not absolutely deserted and cheerless at any hour, day or night." (Indeed it was in this bar in the basement of the Old White hotel, according to legend, that the Governor of North Carolina greeted the Governor of South Carolina with that famous invitation "It's a long time between drinks.") The afternoon passed with dinner from two until four, followed by riding parties or strolls on Lover's Walk. Supper was served at eight. Each evening a dance was staged in the hotel ballroom, with perhaps a private supper and party afterwards that went on to the early hours of the morning. Gambling continued throughout the night in a remote cottage participants called "The Tiger" (thus the sport was known as "chasing the tiger"). In other words, it is clear from Warner's description that the daily routine of life at White Sulphur Springs had not changed very much since the days of Richard Singleton and Henry Clay a half century earlier.

The irony of White Sulphur Springs' nineteenth century history is that no owners, from James Calwell to W.A. Stuart, were ever able to make the resort financially solvent, at least for any length of time. Stuart's Greenbrier White Sulphur Springs Company collapsed in the late 1880s, and for a few years ownership of the resort remained in limbo. In 1892, a group of Virginia business leaders proposed purchasing the property through a public sale of ten thousand shares of stock at $100 each. Their idea was to sell all of the buildings—each cottage was to bring $100, the Old White Hotel, which had capacity for seven hundred fifty guests and was fully furnished, was to produce $5,000—plus one thousand unimproved lots. A street railway from the C&O depot would then tie all the individual parcels together. This plan never materialized, presumably because the Panic of 1893 substantially reduced the number of potential investors. Instead, in 1894 the property was sold to three attorneys acting as trustees for the Dulany family of Middleburg, Virginia.

Henry Grafton (Hal) Dulany was a well-known social figure in Washington, D.C., and White Sulphur Springs in the 1880s. It was rumored, in fact, that he was the wealthiest man in Washington due to the rather sizable annual income he received from his mother's old English family. By 1889, Hal Dulany had loaned W.A. Stuart some $250,000 to keep White Sulphur Springs afloat. Dulany died in 1890; Stuart died in 1892; and through the 1894 purchase, control of the resort passed to Dulany's heirs. Though the social seasons continued merrily for the next fifteen years, court documents indicate that the operation became an increasing drain on the family's resources. Between 1896 and 1909, the resort only showed a profit for two years (1900 and 1901). In the remaining years it broke even or lost money. Then in 1910 the fate of the legendary watering place was inexorably changed when the Chesapeake and Ohio Railway purchased the resort from the Dulany family. Perhaps it was only fitting that the railroad that had transported guests to White Sulphur Springs for forty years, should now become the agent responsible for the resort's twentieth century renaissance.

A children's costume party in 1902. The little boy directly in the center of the front row (with the big black hat) is Edward R. Stettinius, Jr., later the secretary of state under President Franklin D. Roosevelt.

In perfect period style, this artwork from about 1914 shows afternoon tea at the south end of the newly opened Greenbrier Hotel.

A New Palace and a New Sport

By the early years of the new century, White Sulphur Springs was beginning to show its age. The ancient cottages were sadly in need of repair, and in some cases the wallpaper was hanging loose in the guest rooms of the main hotel. It was reported that in order to raise enough money to pay the taxes, the owners were negotiating with a local lumber dealer to sell the gigantic oaks on the lawn. In the words of one writer: "Naught was left but the broken buildings, the life-giving springs, the green of the grass, the majestic trees, the translucency of the brilliant air, the witchery of the sunlight, and the memories of the old days. The old place was in its decadence."

What was really needed was a massive infusion of new capital. How the Chesapeake and Ohio became that desperately needed source of new capital is an intriguing story best told by its key player, former West Virginia Governor William A. MacCorkle, who related the tale in his book, *Recollections of Fifty Years*. As the story goes, Governor MacCorkle, who loved the White for its wealth of Southern traditions, was approached one day by Frank Enslow, a prominent lawyer from Huntington, West Virginia, and George Stevens, the President of the C&O, with the idea that the railway should purchase and rejuvenate the old place. Though Governor Mac-Corkle immediately agreed with the proposal, there was one major obstacle. First they would have to convince Edwin Hawley of New York—who controlled a significant portion of the C&O's stock—that preserving the

resort was a good investment.

MacCorkle knew that his act of persuasion would be no easy task because Hawley was primarily interested in handsome dividends. Moreover, Hawley was neither sentimental about Southern traditions, nor lured by the glamour of fashionable social life. The financier Bernard Baruch, who was associated with Edwin Hawley in a number of railroad purchases, wrote that Hawley "was one of the few men I knew who had a natural poker face. It was pale and cameolike, and when he talked he hardly opened his lips." Despite Hawley's formidable nature, MacCorkle, Enslow and Stevens proceeded with their scheme by arranging inspections of the railroad line that carefully included frequent stops at White Sulphur Springs. During these visits the three conspirators subtly educated Hawley about the charms of Southern society and explained the vital role of the White in Southern history. Yet they never mentioned the possibility of a C&O purchase for fear of scaring off their prey.

After months of shrewd maneuvering, MacCorkle sensed that the time was right for the hard sell, so he hosted an elegant dinner in Hawley's honor in a private dining room of the Old White. "It was in the summertime," MacCorkle recalled, "with the cool nights and bright moonlight and perfume of the flowers, and the whippoorwills singing all the night long." A group of sixty attended the dinner, a deliberately selected gathering of beautiful Southern women and stately Southern gentlemen. With great care a splendid meal was served, be-

William Howard Taft (in chair) visited White Sulphur Springs during his successful campaign for the presidency in 1908.

ginning with mint juleps—"the mint [was] eight inches high," MacCorkle remembered precisely. The dinner started with "a dainty dish of terrapin just from the Chesapeake Bay, prepared with a dash of old sherry, served along with Madeira sixty years in the wood." This was followed by what MacCorkle called the "piece de resistance—half a canvas back duck for each plate cut by a cleaver directly in two, and served with heaping plates of hot Virginia corn dodgers and vegetables fresh from the Company's gardens, while the whole was crowned with golden champagne."

Governor MacCorkle kept a close eye on Hawley throughout the meal until he saw that the railroad magnate's face was flushed "not with champagne, but with the exhilaration of the occasion." Seizing the moment, MacCorkle delivered a long toast celebrating the wonders of Southern civilization and the history of White Sulphur Springs. Finally, he turned to Hawley and concluded, "There is one among us today, from the North it is true, who is moved with the sweetness and beauty and romance of the cavaliers and the beautiful women of the old place, and," here MacCorkle paused

before his fateful final line, "he proposes to touch with his golden wand the old 'White' and to bring it back its wonderful life." All the guests rose from their seats with glasses in hand, many with tears in their eyes, and saluted Mr. Hawley. MacCorkle, Enslow and Stevens later agreed that when they saw Hawley rise and bow to the guests' ovation they knew the victory was theirs.

The next morning Hawley and MacCorkle walked the old paths of Lover's Walk and the financier mentioned, as if it was all a part of the day's work, that he intended to buy the property and turn it over to the Chesapeake and Ohio Railway. Thus on February 1, 1910, the newly-formed White Sulphur Springs, Inc., wholly-owned subsidiary of the C&O, purchased the resort. The terms of the sale, which Edwin Hawley surely appreciated, were quite attractive to a railroad in a period of sustained growth—$50,000 down in cash, followed by two further installments of $50,000 each. Even by 1910 standards, $150,000 for seven thousand acres of land on the railroad's main line, all the resort's historic buildings, and the magnetic name "White Sulphur Springs" was quite a bargain.

The Chesapeake and Ohio Railway immediately turned its attention and considerable funds towards restoring the declining resort. For twenty years the railway had been enjoying tremendous economic success, partly due to extensive coal mining throughout southern West Virginia, and partly because of the vast expansion of America's industrial output. Not only was the C&O the major link between the Southern coalfields and the factories of the Northeast and Midwest, its financial stability was further insured by the backing of the powerful J.P. Morgan and Vanderbilt interests. In addition to coal, the railroad carried tremendous quantities of livestock, agricultural products, timber, and iron. And passenger traffic had grown as well, swelling from one million in 1890 to two million in 1900 and then leaping to five million in 1910. The acquisition of White Sulphur Springs only further complemented the railroad's passenger marketing strategy—it was virtually impossible to get to the resort except by rail, and the only railroad that carried visitors there was the C&O.

Within two months of the railway's takeover of the resort, President George Stevens was regularly visiting the property to oversee the army of workmen refurbishing the buildings and grounds for the upcoming season. A local newspaper happily announced "the improvements on the Springs grounds has brought plenty of work for everyone." The Old White Hotel received a new coat of paint—it took five hundred gallons just to cover the roof—the cottages were restored and painted, a new kitchen was built, bathrooms and supplementary sewer lines were added, as were electric lights and telephones. Tennis courts were built (these original courts stood where today's guest parking lots are located), a small nine-hole golf course was laid out (about where the first nine holes of the Lakeside Course now are played) and a clubhouse was constructed (at the site of today's outdoor pool). The 1910 brochure noted that "a dairy will be maintained with a fine herd of selected Jersey cows. Parents may be assured of having the best quality of fresh milk everyday for their children." The same brochure struck a prophetic note: "New ownership, new management and new features insure a successful future."

Eventually, the Chesapeake and Ohio Railway developed much grander plans for White Sulphur Springs. Construction began in 1911 on a new Bath Wing, designed by the Philadelphia architectural firm of Harris & Richards, and it opened the next year. Promoted as "the most complete and luxurious in its appointments of any institution of its kind in America" the new Bath Wing demonstrated the railroad's commitment to maintaining

Before the roads in the area were paved in the late twenties, virtually all guests arrived at White Sulphur Springs on the C&O. This photo from about 1920 shows a brass band meeting dignitaries at the train station directly across from the front gate to The Greenbrier. (Courtesy The Chesapeake and Ohio Historical Society)

A postcard view of the indoor pool about 1915.

Construction of the Bath Wing, begun in 1911, which houses today's indoor swimming pool.

Better than Europe!

Take the Cure at White Sulphur

the reputation of White Sulphur Springs as the nation's pre-eminent health resort. Before the wing opened, a team of medical experts traveled to many of the famous spas of Europe—Bath in England, Baden-Baden and Weisbaden in Germany, Marienbad in Austria—to insure that the therapy and equipment offered at White Sulphur Springs matched the finest in the world. In fact, the next year the Company's brochures proclaimed The White "A European Cure in America." As it turned out, the slogan was an accurate premonition. With the outbreak of World War I, Americans who had annually crossed the ocean to visit the spas were obliged to break the habit, not only because of fighting on the continent, but also the danger of travel by sea. Instead, they rode the Chesapeake and Ohio to White Sulphur Springs.

The Bath Wing featured a huge and handsome indoor pool on the first floor, which one 1914 writer described as "a bathing-pool which might have been the pride of Rome." Measuring one hundred feet by forty-two feet, the indoor pool was, at the time, one of the largest of its kind in the world. "One of the prettiest parts" of the resort, commented a travel writer in 1916, "is beyond question the pool in the bathhouse. A large rectangle of crystal-clear water, enclosed and bottomed with mosaic tile, it is set under a high glass dome and encircled by broad walks on which palms, hot-house plants, and comfortable chairs have been placed." This writer noted that "the pool was the favored congregating point for the ladies who gathered there each morning to sew and discuss problems of feminine statecraft." The second floor of the Bath Wing was the Men's Department and the third floor was the Women's Department. The hydrotherapy practiced on these floors included mud baths with, according to a brochure, "an excellent quality of mud obtained from the bed of sulphur springs in the vicinity" used in the treatment of gout, rheumatism and neuritis; the Vichy Bath, a massage under a spray of water at moderate temperature; and an Inhalation Room with "apparatus for the inhalation of the volitile properties of the mineral water" useful for treating the nose, throat, lungs and certain types of asthma. Great importance was placed upon diet and exercise. A special diet kitchen was maintained as part of the overall "cure," and active or passive exercise was encouraged in the "mechanico-theraputic institute" on strange-looking pieces of equipment known as the Zander apparatus.

One visitor, upon inspecting the Bath Wing, reported, "The management has expended prodigious sums of money to bring into the bath establishment all those features and treatments which have made various European places famous, and it seems to have been successful in securing every variation of the normal means of using water that has been invented since good old Noah used it for boating on."

The Greenbrier Hotel as it looked when it opened in 1913.

Before the Bath Wing was completed, the C&O hired the British architect Frederick Junius Sterner to design a new hotel, one that would be open year-round and fire-proof (an important quality in the days of so many older, wooden hotels). Sterner had established an outstanding reputation in Colorado, where he planned some of the most impressive hotels, private residences, clubs and office buildings in the Denver and Pike's Peak areas. He designed the six-story, two-hundred-fifty-room structure, christened The Greenbrier, that forms the central section of today's building. Georgian in architectural style, the unit that Sterner designed includes the area from the Cameo Ballroom to the Colonnades Dining Room. The Greenbrier was officially scheduled to open on October 1, 1913. But due to pressure from guests, it actually began receiving guests a week early, and the first person to sign the guest register on September 25, 1913, was none other than Frederick Sterner.

The interior of The Greenbrier was designed by the architect's sister, Maude Sterner. The main lobby featured putty-colored enameled wood panels lighted by fifteen eighteenth-century crystal chandeliers, and massive fireplaces modeled after French museum pieces at either end. In the original design, guests entered and registered in the main lobby (today's entry to the lower lobby was not created until after World War II). Opposite the entrance, where the musicians now play at tea each afternoon, was the Wisteria Room, which was separated from the main lobby by dark-green iron latticework. Near the ballroom were parlors with exposed red brick walls; one featured great stone Italian fountains containing lily ponds and goldfish. The ballroom, especially the grand plaster ceiling, appeared much as it does today, only it was painted in three tones of French gray and lacked the central chandelier. Downstairs there were shops, a billiard room, a card room, and a separate dining room for children, nurses and chauffeurs. The guest rooms upstairs were furnished, according to one writer, "in the delightful home-like style which is generally known as English. The furniture and woodwork of the rooms are painted in soft tones of French gray, Queen Anne green and Italian yellow. Chintzes and printed linens are profusely used for hangings, bed-spreads and bureau tops."

For the hotel's opening, the President of the C&O, George Stevens, hosted private dinner parties nightly in the main dining room, which was decorated with a railroad carload of long-stemmed American Beauty roses. The first event was a dinner for the press. When guests strolled over from the Old White, the first sight of the new Greenbrier caused one journalist to see the building as "a new and gorgeous hostelry which to my

The menu for the first meal served in The Greenbrier Hotel.

The original main entrance of The Greenbrier Hotel.

The Springroom where guests might stop to drink sulphur water inside the hotel.

One of the lobbies in The Greenbrier. The interior decor remained much the same from 1913-1931.

The Wisteria Room of The Greenbrier in the teens. Today, this is where the musicians perform at afternoon tea.

The front porch of The Greenbrier in 1913. This area is now enclosed and is the walkway alongside the main dining rooms.

A room along the upper lobby in the 1913-31 period.

The Cameo Ballroom before World War II.

mind was like a fairy palace set amid the lights and shadows of the Allegheny hills." Another guest remarked upon entering the expansive main lobby, "It was like a Roman palazzo made entirely habitable." The first president of White Sulphur Springs, Inc. was Decatur Axtell, who served as first vice-president and director of the C&O and had been, since 1890, second-in-command in the leadership of the railroad. Frederick Sterry of New York was appointed the managing director of The Greenbrier. Sterry, one of the most highly regarded hotelmen of the era, was noted for his role in opening the Plaza Hotel in New York.City in 1907, which he continued to direct in conjunction with The Greenbrier. It was through his influence that many of the most prominent families in New York eventually found their way to White Sulphur Springs. In fact, in the years immediately following The Greenbrier's 1913 opening, both The Plaza and The Greenbrier advertised their plush accommodations and facilities in a single brochure.

During this period two new cottages were added, both for C&O Railway officials. Two of the three Colonnades cottages, the old summer homes of Richard Singleton and Wade Hampton, were removed, and in their place a house for Edwin Hawley was built. Ironically, Hawley died February 1, 1912—two years to the day after the railroad purchased the resort—thus was never able to use the cottage, which was completed later that year. The house has borne his name ever since, however. The second cottage, which was sited on a hill above Florida Row, was built in 1912. This one was the private summer home of George Stevens. For years it was known simply as the Stevens Cottage, but after the C&O President's death in 1920, it was renamed Top Notch Cottage.

The third major improvement to the White Sulphur Springs property (besides the hotel and Bath Wing) was the one without which The Greenbrier would be unrecognizable today—golf. Though a rough course had been hacked out across some pastures around 1910, first-class golf arrived at the resort in late 1913 with the completion of an eighteen-hole course. Undoubtedly, C&O officials had surveyed both the soil and the layout in the wide-open area between the Springhouse and the foot of Greenbrier Mountain before their purchase and found it quite suitable for a fine course. Before 1910 this land had been mostly pastures, although building the course meant removing the old brickyards and slaughterhouse. The course, known for years as the Number One Course and later renamed the Old White Course, was designed by Charles Blair McDonald, the greatest authority on golf architecture in America in the early twentieth cen-

tury. McDonald was best known for his design, a few years earlier, of the National Golf Links at Southampton, Long Island. The 6,250 yard course he created at The Greenbrier was described in *Town and Country* magazine as "beyond a doubt one of the finest courses in the country, and probably the very best south of Philadelphia." Besides the essential ingredients of good soil, challenging topography and a well thought-out design, the new course possessed one other important asset—spectacular scenery. For a century, visitors had been traveling to White Sulphur Springs to enjoy the splendid mountain views, and with this course they

The medal awarded to the winner of the annual tournament at the Oakhurst Club, a few miles from The Greenbrier.

could now pursue the sport of kings surrounded on all sides by the dramatic Alleghenies. As one writer commented in 1916: "The golf course here is a jewel in the midst of the most exquisite setting."

Before golf came to the resort grounds proper, many visitors traveled a few miles to the six-hole course on the private estate of Russell Montague called "Oakhurst." In 1884, Montague, an American, and four friends from Scotland established what has been recognized as the first golf club in the United States. Although the Oakhurst Club was informal, and disbanded after a decade, the members met annually, whacked at billiard-ball hard "guttie" balls with solid brass-headed clubs, and presented an attractive Challenge Medal to the winners of the matches. Golf was a strange sight in the 1880s and many guests at the White rode over to Oakhurst in their carriages to stare in amazement at what appeared to be grown men playing a variation of marbles. Indeed the

Golf at The Greenbrier in the 1920s.

This fashionable fivesome appeared in Town and Country *magazine in 1929.*

Driving over Howard's Creek from the first tee of the Old White Course.

Out on the Old White course in the 1920s.

GREENBRIER

AIRPORT

GREENBRIER

NUMBER

CHESAPEAKE AND

KATE'S

Aviation Country Club 1931

Hangars and Service Station

MIDLAND

NUMBER ONE

VALLEY

Greenbrier Lake

NUMBER TWO GOLF COURSE

Chalybeate Sp

THREE GOLF COURSE

Forest Drive

Stables

OHIO RAILWAY

MOUNTAIN

The
GREENBRIER
and Cottages
White Sulphur Springs
West Virginia
1931

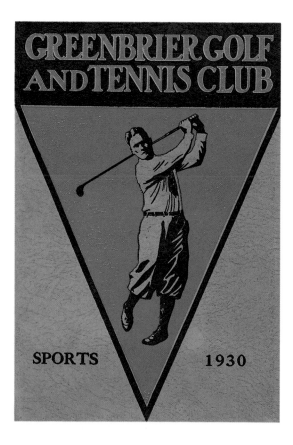

game was so unusual that one of the Oakhurst members was stopped by customs officials in New York when he tried to bring his clubs in from Scotland, and accused of trying to conceal "implements of murder." However, by the second decade of the twentieth century, resort and country club golf was spreading rapidly across the nation. The Greenbrier was at the forefront of a craze that would eventually sweep the country.

There was one more practical problem to be solved in order to blend all of these facilities into an efficient operation, and that was a dependable water supply. Since 1901, the resort's drinking water had been obtained from the Alvon Spring, located about twelve miles north of White Sulphur Springs, and then delivered by rail in huge cases of half-gallon jugs. But in 1912 the people of West Virginia voted in favor of Prohibition, and local moonshiners found those half-gallon jugs perfect for the bottling of their considerably more potent concoction. Thus the jugs disappeared at an alarming rate, making railroad transportation impossible. The next year, the C&O purchased the Alvon Springs and began building a pipeline made of cedar wood slats bound with steel bands and covered with sawdust and tar. The Alvon Springs have supplied the drinking water to The Greenbrier ever since, albeit in more modern pipes.

By June of 1914, the Chesapeake and Ohio Railway had spent $2.5 million on improvements at White Sulphur Springs. Building and furnishing The Green-brier Hotel cost just over $1 million, the Bath Wing $200,000, and the eighteen-hole golf course $60,000. In August of 1913, while the golf course was under construction, the old stables burned to the ground, killing thirty horses. The next year the management decided to build a new golf clubhouse (also designed by Frederick Sterner) on that site, and five tennis courts. That 1915 clubhouse has expanded over the years, the first time in 1930 and then in 1975, and was known to all as the Casino (the word then was used in its more general sense as a building intended for social amusements—any gambling that went on was of the friendly, informal type).

In 1914, for the first time, the resort was open year-round. And it operated under a new name: The Greenbrier and Cottages (in 1909 the adjacent town had incorporated and taken the name White Sulphur Springs—a change from "the village of Dry Creek"—and the resort adopted the county name; after World War II, the resort dropped the "and Cottages" to become simply The Greenbrier). It was immediately discovered by families listed in the social registers in the large cities of the Northeast and Midwest. By 1914 as many visitors were coming from New York, Philadelphia, Chicago and Cleveland as from Richmond, Washington, Baltimore and Charleston, West Virginia. Though the high season had always been summer, the newer guests now set a different pattern, preferring the spring and autumn months.

The porch of the Golf Clubhouse in the twenties.

By 1915 automobiles appeared in front of the Baltimore Row cottages where Robert E. Lee strolled half a century earlier.

President Woodrow Wilson was among the first golfers to play the Old White Course during his April, 1914, visit. The President and his first wife, Ellen Louise Axson, arrived for Easter; he returned to Washington for a few days, and then traveled back to The Greenbrier again the next weekend. With each arrival, throngs of local citizens, as well as members of the vacationing cafe society, came out to meet him in his private railroad car, the "Philadelphia." Over the Easter holiday, the President was entertained by the Princeton Glee Club, which for over twenty-five years became a constant feature of Easter entertainment at The Greenbrier.

Mrs. Wilson died in August of 1914, and in December of the next year the President married Edith Bolling Galt of Wytheville, Virginia. The newlywed couple spent part of their honeymoon at The Greenbrier, but their trip was cut short when word was received that a British passenger liner sunk by a German submarine had precipitated an international crisis.

Mr. and Mrs. Joseph P. Kennedy arrived at The Greenbrier on October 11, 1914,—four days after their wedding in Boston—for a two-week honeymoon. They were assigned room #145, directly above the main entrance. The signatures of the Kennedys and many other prominent guests are recorded in a brief run of hotel registers that survive from the time. For instance, on November 12, 1914, Mr. and Mrs. Cornelius Vanderbilt, II registered with their two children, a nurse, two governors, maid and valet, and occupied twelve rooms. The story has often been repeated that Mrs. Vanderbilt arrived each year in her private railroad car, and while it was parked at the station a servant was sent to see that she was not only assigned her regular room, but that the furnishings were exactly the same as they were on her last visit. When this was verified, she would disembark and check in. The hotel registers also contain the names

TENNIS
at
White Sulphur
1930

GREENBRIER GOLF
AND TENNIS CLUB
White Sulphur Springs
West Virginia

Pulitzer, Armour, Guggenheim, Bloomingdale, Carnegie, Gimbel, Auchincloss, Rockefeller, Flagler. On August 10, 1915, Miss Wallis Warfield of Baltimore signed in; she of course later became the famed Duchess of Windsor. Indeed, on November 7, 1916, Mr. and Mrs. E. Winfield Spencer registered—this in fact was Wallis Warfield's honeymoon with her first husband. Other guests in the teens included Virginia writer James Branch Cabell; actress Ethel Barrymore; the publisher of *Vogue*, Conde Nast, and his editor, Frank Crowninshield; the Ambassador to France, Hugh C. Wallace; composer Irving Berlin; General Motors chief Alfred Sloan; golfer Bobby Jones; Secretary of the Treasury (and son-in-law of President Wilson), William Gibbs McAdoo; members of the Valentine family of Richmond; and the Commander of Allied Forces in World War I, General John J. Pershing (who, incidentally, completed his memoirs in Top Notch cottage).

But the most famous of all the visitors to The Greenbrier during this era was the Prince of Wales, later King Edward VIII of England, until his dramatic abdication from the throne in 1936 to marry Wallis Warfield Simpson. In November, 1919, the twenty-five-year-old Prince made his first visit to the United States and was greeted by wildly enthusiastic crowds in New York and Washington. His three-day trip to White Sulphur Springs was planned as a respite from the throngs of well-wishers, the constant press coverage, and the endless formalities. All attempts were made to keep the visit secret—the Prince traveled incognito in a special railroad car—but still word got out. A large Union Jack flag fluttered across the front of The Greenbrier and the hotel porch was filled with a small, but lustily cheering crowd. The Prince took full advantage of The Greenbrier's facilities, going for brisk walks in the countryside, displaying quite athletic somersaults off the diving board at the indoor pool, playing thirty-six holes of golf one day and eighteen the other two, and dancing an accomplished foxtrot in the Ballroom. The heir to the British throne took it all in stride, "I'm having a good time just like any other chap," he remarked. With his party of thirty-five, the Prince of Wales occupied the entire third floor of the hotel. The Prince himself stayed in the same room President Wilson had used four years earlier. According to one newspaper account, the Prince enjoyed his visit so much that he danced in the Cameo Ballroom until three minutes before his train left for New York.

After a brief post-World War I depression, the American economy shot off in the twenties on a decade-long boom that brought about a splurge of free-spending and

The Prince of Wales standing inside the Springhouse during his November, 1919 visit.

One of the all-time tennis greats, Bill Tilden, on the courts in front of the Golf Clubhouse in the 1930s.

a remarkable growth in industrial productivity. This economic upsurge greatly affected the fortunes of The Greenbrier, its success exceeded all expectations. The twenties were also a "Golden Age of Sports" as Americans tried to forget the misery and disillusionment of World War I. In the first major golf tournament held at The Greenbrier, the 1922 United States Women's Championship, nineteen-year-old Glenna Collet won the first of her record six national championships. Miss Collet shot an impressive seventy-five in a warm-up round two days before the championship matches, and to preserve her good luck she superstitiously continued her previous night's menu throughout the competition—lamb chops, string beans and creamed potatoes. Although she laughed at herself for this behavior, she not only repeated the same meals, but stuck with the hat, skirt and sweater she wore in that warm-up round. With her resounding victory at White Sulphur Springs the attractive Glenna Collet immediately became the darling of the sports world and was quickly nicknamed "the female Bobby Jones."

The incomparable Bobby Jones himself was one of the first golfers to play the second eighteen-hole course when it opened in 1924. Once again Charles Blair McDonald and his engineer Seth Raynor teamed up to design and build the Number Three Course (later renamed The Greenbrier Course), which drew acclaim from professional golfers as one of the best resort layouts in the nation. In 1927, famed golfers Walter Hagen and Gene Sarazen met at White Sulphur Springs in one of their frequent exhibition matches. Sarazen defeated Hagen (for the fourth time) but only after an honorable show of sportsmanship—although Sarazen had arrived early to practice on the new course, when he learned that Hagen had not played the course, Sarazen refused to even look over the links.

In the twenties numerous sports stars gathered at The Greenbrier. In 1925 tennis sensation Bill Tilden played his first matches on the courts in front of the golf clubhouse. That next month boxer Gene Tunney was photographed jogging about the grounds preparing for an upcoming challenge. Johnny Weismuller and Buster Crabbe brought their traveling swimming exhibitions to the indoor pool. And in March of 1924, the same month that the famous sports writer Grantland Rice shot a par seventy-two on the Old White Course, legendary golfing great Francis Ouimet was also a visitor. The indoor pool drew curious onlookers because there Charles Norelius, the swimming instructor and former champion in his native Sweden, daily trained his young daughter Martha,

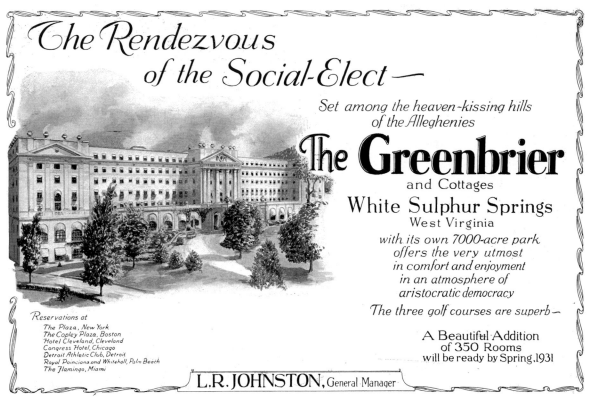

The Rendezvous of the Social-Elect—

Set among the heaven-kissing hills
of the Alleghenies

The **Greenbrier**
and Cottages

White Sulphur Springs
West Virginia

with its own 7000-acre park
offers the very utmost
in comfort and enjoyment
in an atmosphere of
aristocratic democracy

The three golf courses are superb—

A Beautiful Addition
of 350 Rooms
will be ready by Spring, 1931

Reservations at
The Plaza, New York
The Copley Plaza, Boston
Hotel Cleveland, Cleveland
Congress Hotel, Chicago
Detroit Athletic Club, Detroit
Royal Poinciana and Whitehall, Palm Beach
The Flamingo, Miami

L. R. JOHNSTON, General Manager

A magazine advertisement from July, 1930.

who later became one of the greatest swimmers of the day. Martha Norelius won gold medals at both the 1924 and 1928 Paris Olympics in the 400-meter event; and by 1929 she was regarded as the strongest female swimmer in the world. When her father retired, Martha Norelius assumed his position as The Greenbrier's swimming instructor. Occasionally, however, the pool was put to other uses. Golfer Babe Didrikson caused quite a stir one New Year's Eve when, tired of the festivities, she decided to take a midnight swim in the pool. She was promptly followed by scores of guests in full evening dress who watched her impromptu performance.

Throughout the twenties, The Greenbrier proved itself a gold mine of information for the ever-inquisitive society columnists who tracked the movements of the country's prominent. Besides social leaders, financiers, lawyers, industrialists, movie stars and railroad presidents, the resort was a particular favorite of American and foreign diplomats, as well as Senators and Cabinet members, seeking a pleasant retreat from Washington. For those who made up what was variously called the "Smart Set" or "Cafe Society," The Greenbrier provided a natural spring and autumn interlude since most traveled by rail between winter homes in Palm Beach, Florida, and summer homes at Newport, Southampton, or Bar Harbor.

With such illustrious crowds at the resort, society page editors could not resist printing tidbits about, for example, the annual golf outings of Charles Schwab, the man who personified "Big Steel" in America; the arrival of Mrs. Lawrence Armour of Chicago, with her ten thousand dollar German Shepard, "Astor"; seeing Harry Payne Whitney and his wife Gertrude Vanderbilt in their private railroad car; the informal gatherings of the J.P. Morgan firm; Mrs. William K. Vanderbilt and Mrs. Joseph Harriman strolling on their way to the clubhouse; Mr. and Mrs. Joseph Kennedy at a spring luncheon they were giving; seeing the daughter of Mark Twain, the son of Henry Ford, the granddaughter of Alfred DuPont, and on it went. Indeed, The Greenbrier provided a grand opportunity for increasing one's facility at name-dropping after meeting (or at least seeing) other such notables as General Billy Mitchell, architect Cass Gilbert, playwright Noel Coward, New York society figure William Rhinelander Stewart, former Treasury Secretary Ogden Mills, financier Walter Salmon, writer Booth Tarkington, automaker Walter Chrysler, and so on.

Easter was very much the time to be seen at The Greenbrier. As society writer Cholly Knickerbocker noted in 1926, "the Easter parade on Fifth Avenue is becoming obsolete to society as fashion dictates leaving town. . . . It is 'the thing' to pass Easter-tide at The

Greenbrier." *Town and Country* magazine reported in 1927, "On the Casino lawns and verandas any morning in April may be seen bankers and brokers of Wall Street fame, railroad presidents, motor car magnates, government officials from Washington, besides leaders of society in Newport and all our large cities, and multimillionaires aristocratic and otherwise from the North and Middle West by the dozen. Many representatives of the older and more conservative families of the country are here too, who have come up from Augusta, Aiken, Jekyll Island, Nassau and the Bahamas."

With this kind of clientele, it was inevitable that numerous stories and anecdotes arose about "the life" at The Greenbrier. According to one tale, if someone telephoned and asked for the King's Suite, the operator invariably answered, "Which King?" A Texas newspaper correspondent wrote, "When The Greenbrier serves you an egg for breakfast, they also serve you the registration papers of the hen that layed it." When Charles Ingersoll of Pennsylvania had a slight misadventure in the stock market that called for some belt-tightening around the house, he found that he needed to dismiss the family's pageboy, although he was able to retain the three gardeners, a chauffeur, a cook, two maids and a butler. Distressed to see his family suffer, he sent them all off to The Greenbrier for an extended holiday while he got together the means to hire a new pageboy. The importance of a trip to White Sulphur Springs for Virginians had not slackened either, even if one could not afford it. One frequently practiced strategy was to hop a train from Richmond headed for The Greenbrier, get off at the first station out of town, sneak back into town, and while hiding out for a week or two carefully read the society columns in the newspapers. Then one could triumphantly reappear in the midst of friends, filled with detailed knowledge of the social goings-on at White Sulphur Springs.

Conde Nast, publisher of Vogue *magazine, at the Golf Clubhouse in October, 1933.*

The patrons of the Greenbrier are respectfully requested not to ask any employee to perform any service in violation of the prohibition law.

A sign of the times in the 1920s.

New York Yankee Lou Gehrig traded his baseball bat for a golf club at a 1932 Greenbrier outing.

Despite all the change of society at the resort following the C&O purchase, White Sulphur Springs still remained the rendezvous of Southern society in the summertime. The social correspondent for *Town and Country* magazine wrote in 1926: "The lure of White Sulphur Springs in August is proverbial. During this month the social life of the resort takes on a peculiarly Southern aspect. Filled with Southern people, in whose families a season at The White is traditional, the old regime lives again for a few brief weeks." Throughout the teens, features of summer social life were the morning cotillion in the ballroom of the Old White, which began promptly at high noon, and gatherings on the lawn at five in the afternoon for tea and dancing around the bandstand.

In the thirties, The Greenbrier honored this annual migration of Southern families by instituting Robert E. Lee Week, scheduled for the last week in August. The festivities centered about dancing of course; traditional figures, reels and promenades were held every evening in The Greenbrier's ballroom, highlighted by a revival of the "White Sulphur Riley," a round dance of the 1860s that was one of General Lee's favorites. From 1932 through 1941 the annual Lee Week generated more news-

paper coverage of activities at The Greenbrier than any other event. Those activities included lectures by Douglas Southall Freeman, Lee's biographer, and Francis P. Gaines, the President of Washington and Lee University, plus watermelon fetes on the lawn, costume parties, and trips to Lexington, Virginia, to visit the Lee Chapel.

One permanent legacy of the 1932 Lee Week was the creation of the Presidents' Cottage Museum. The stately two-story cottage—built in 1835 for Louisiana sugar planter Stephen Henderson and later used by five presidents—had not been a guest accommodation after the Civil War, but had served instead as the headquarters for a social organization of Southern gentlemen called "The Presidents' Cottage Club." Restoration of the building took over a year. Cleveland artist William C. Grauer was commissioned to paint murals for two rooms that depicted General Lee at White Sulphur Springs and views of the grounds at the time of his visits. The management of The Greenbrier conducted an exhaustive campaign to recover historical letters, photographs, books and memorabilia. Much of this material, it turned out, was donated by long-time patrons who had searched through treasured family possessions and heirlooms for appropriate items. On August 22, 1932, the Presidents' Cottage Museum was officially opened and dedicated in a ceremony graciously led by Mrs. Woodrow Wilson, the President's widow, and Henry Waters Taft, the brother of President Taft and a New York attorney who was a regular Greenbrier visitor.

Of course the most tangible link to the old Southern watering place was the Old White Hotel itself. Ten years before the opening of the Presidents' Cottage Museum, on August 16, 1922, a very nostalgic cotillion was held in the ballroom of the Old White. It was to be the last dance in the sixty-four-year-old building. That night two hundred fifty guests of Thomas Paine, an Atlanta banker who had been visiting the resort for fifty years, gathered to follow General Jo Lane Stern, the leader of cotillions at White Sulphur Springs since the 1877 Lee Monument Ball. Though the Old White had been used to house summer guests after The Greenbrier Hotel opened, the building failed to pass West Virginia's fire inspection code in 1922, and was reluctantly torn down in November of that year.

The removal of the Old White meant the loss of accommodations for hundreds of guests, and though a small wing was added to The Greenbrier in 1920, the hotel and cottages simply did not provide the required number of rooms. Throughout the twenties, especially during the Easter and Labor Day holidays, the resort was often filled to capacity. It also became apparent that a 250-room hotel, even with the space in the cottages, was not large enough to generate the income necessary to

Clare Boothe Luce wrote the first draft of her most enduring play, The Women, *during a three-day stay at The Greenbrier in 1936.*

Lee Monument Ball
×
Friday, August 30th, 1935
×
the Greenbrier
WHITE SULPHUR SPRINGS

*Dancing the "White Sulphur Riley" during Robert E.
Lee Week in the 1930s.*

Mrs. Woodrow Wilson and Henry Waters Taft at the opening of the Presidents' Cottage Museum on August 22, 1932.

road boosters traveled to the Springs in the summers before the Civil War. These nineteenth century meetings were usually called in response to a particular crisis, or to organize the promotion of a single event, or were simply the result of a seemingly natural gravitation of certain people to White Sulphur Springs. For instance, in the post-Civil War era, it was understood that an informal meeting of Southern governors occurred each summer at the resort because everyone knew that the governors spent August there. The new twentieth century organizations, in contrast, were more durable and created continuing programs. (Also, the decorum of modern meetings had improved considerably since the convention of cotton brokers in 1875, where guests noted with some alarm that the members sat down to cards with pistols in their pockets.) In the twenties, The Greenbrier found itself in the unhappy position of turning away the new kind of organized group business due to the relatively small size of the hotel.

Beginning in the late twenties then, complex plans were drawn for a dramatic expansion of The Greenbrier to meet the demands of large crowds in the fashionable spring and autumn months and the swelling number of

maintain the entire operation. And there was one further factor that made expansion plans imperative: it was clear that a larger hotel was needed if The Greenbrier was to successfully respond to the profound restructuring of American business and professional life taking place. Since the late nineteenth century, a widespread "managerial revolution" had moved control of business policy and decision-making from the founders and owners of ever-larger corporations to a new generation of executives. In addition, attorneys, physicians, skilled workers, administrators and other professionals had become increasingly aware of their mutual interest. The result of these and other causes was a fantastic growth of business and professional associations held together by what one historian called "the forces of occupational cohesion." With the spread and diversification of these associations came a need for suitable locations to hold annual meetings of their members; The Greenbrier offered an ideal setting.

Meetings of businessmen, politicians and professionals at White Sulphur Springs were nothing new, however. In a more informal and less structured way such meetings had convened at the resort since the days when cotton planters, congressmen, merchants and rail-

These two young women obviously selected their most fashionable outfits for their 1931 trip to The Greenbrier.

ALTERATIONS & ADDITIONS TO
GREENBRIER HOTEL,
WHITE SULPHUR SPRINGS, WEST VA.
PHILIP L. SMALL, INC., ARCHT'S.,
THE JOHN W. COWPER CO., INC., GEN'L. CONT

JUL 3 1 1930

The Greenbrier Hotel was virtually rebuilt and doubled in size in 1930. This photograph shows the construction of the North Wing pictured on the cover of this book.

association members. Architect Phillip Small of Cleveland was hired to design new additions to the original hotel, which would carefully extend yet preserve the existing harmony of The Greenbrier's Georgian style. After months of discussing various options, Mr. Small and The Greenbrier's newly-appointed General Manager, Loren Johnston, settled on a plan in 1928 to add large wings to each side of the building. To the south the dining room was expanded, creating the present 650-person capacity, and the two-story Virginia Wing was built (the wing received that name because the cottages of Virginia Row were removed to make way for it.) Beyond the ballroom, at the north end of the hotel, a massive six-story addition was erected, connecting the main hotel to the Bath Wing. In designing this wing, Phillip Small created a facade that echoed, on an enlarged scale, the arched galleries and towering columns of The Old White Hotel. Construction on these and other improvements began in 1929, and in order to build the two major wings The Greenbrier closed entirely from November 1930 until early March 1931. When guests arrived for the traditional Easter stay in 1931, The Greenbrier's capacity had more than doubled to 580 rooms.

Since transportation to White Sulphur Springs had al-

ways been a crucial factor in the resort's success, The Greenbrier included in this expansion a new garage built over the site of The Old White to house the automobiles of the increasing number of motoring guests. Also, a one-hundred-seventy-five-acre parcel of land was purchased from former Company President Thornton Lewis to construct an airport. The Greenbrier became one of the first resorts in the nation to offer its guests private landing facilities.

The great majority of guests still arrived by train, however. For this reason the Chesapeake and Ohio Railway took particular care in designing a new railroad station across from the hotel's main gate. In keeping with the railroad's advertising slogan—"the Route to Historyland"—the station was built in the same Georgian style as the hotel. Many of the trains arrived quite early in the morning, and The Greenbrier advertised itself as "just overnight" from most of the major Eastern and Midwestern cities. Cars bound for the resort were dropped off at a siding, where hotel guests could sleep as long as

A brochure from the 1930s describing The Greenbrier's new airport. This airport was closed in 1986.

A limousine met William K. Vanderbilt's airplane in October, 1938.

they pleased until they were ready to check in. In addition to the C&O's regular service, private railroad cars frequently carried patrons to the station, and in the twenties and thirties it was not uncommon to see twenty cars parked in the sidings at any given time.

The Greenbrier's 1929-1931 face-lifting was not confined solely to new construction. All of the cottages were restored, including Alabama Row, which became the studios of an art school under the direction of William and Natalie Grauer. The hotel's interior was completely redecorated by the Cleveland firm of Rorimer-Brooks and featured French telephones (a dazzling new fashion), chrome bathroom fixtures, and numerous luxurious suites. One room in the new Virginia Wing was set aside for murals by William Grauer which illustrated the history of White Sulphur Springs from its humble beginnings to its status by 1930 as one of the premier resorts in America.

Unfortunately, between the planning of The Greenbrier's expansion and its execution, the stock market took the spectacular crash of October, 1929. In hindsight, the $3 million investment in upgrading the resort was at best ill-timed. To be sure, the Crash was a major blow, as General Manager Loren Johnston recognized in a 1931 letter, "Financial readjustments throughout the country," he wrote, "have permanently destroyed a certain percentage of our past patronage which must be replaced with new business." But, as Johnston continued, "We are confident that with a return of normal activities we shall be able to secure this business within a reasonable time." In other words, the grim duration of the Depression did not seem at all inevitable, the sentiment of the time was that better times were just ahead. Certainly, maintaining The Greenbrier during the thirties was a struggle, though there were a few factors that helped the resort make it through these hard times. For one, only a percentage of the past patronage was lost, not all lost their entire fortune. (Incidentally, from 1931 to 1941, rates remained fairly constant—in the peak months of spring and autumn, rooms rented from $12 to $20, European Plan, plus $6 per day for three meals. These rates were not significantly higher than in the twenties.) New business was sought—for the first time—through the marketing technique of direct mail, which involved sending personalized letters to 25,000 individuals. In addition, the Chesapeake and Ohio Railway, unlike most American businesses or other railroads, continued to increase profits through the worst years of the Depression. In fact, in the thirties the C&O introduced two of the finest trains in its history, The

For a century, from the 1860s to the 1960s, The Greenbrier was one of the classic railroad resorts in America. These photographs capture rail passenger service at its peak in the 1930s. Left: Boarding the George Washington in 1932. Bottom: Huge Pacific F-19 steam locomotives pulled trains to the mountain resort.

One of The Greenbrier's more elaborate promotional brochures of the thirties shows the hotel as expanded in 1930-31 and the various activities at the resort.

The Greenbrier's new fire truck posed proudly with the North Entrance as a backdrop.

Sportsman from the Mid-west and The George Washington from the Northeast, both of which carried passengers to White Sulphur Springs.

But above all, the established reputation of the place was responsible for its continuing success. The Detroit *Free Press*, for example, examined a number of resorts across the country and concluded, "When money, brains, good taste and the proper standards have created the form [of a resort], only the life that then takes possession of it and uses it for its own aims and purposes can infuse it with warmth and color. Only when manifold conditions have been fulfilled—and years must go into the accomplishment—can a resort truly be said to have achieved distinction . . . White Sulphur Springs is one of the few resorts that have received this stamp of personality." That The Greenbrier's personality remained intact, in spite of the Crash and subsequent collapse of the national economy, is reflected in the thoughts of a writer for the Cincinnati *Post* in the mid-thirties: "Much of the grandeur of the pre-crash days has been lost. Many large estates have been closed because the owners cannot afford their upkeep. Luxurious ocean liners cross the seas with only a few passengers, and many expensive establishments have gone completely on the rocks. Because of this White Sulphur Springs seems particularly glamorous, since it is one of the few resorts that has not

been affected by hard times. The proverbial Rolls-Royce and other cars of foreign make may still be seen sweeping up the curving drive. Some of the guests still come by rail in their private cars that are run onto the spur track. European ambassadors, titled nobility and American heiresses are among the guests."

In the 1930s, just as had been the case a century before, it was the people and their activities that breathed life into White Sulphur Springs. According to newspaper accounts, many of the same business and social leaders who vacationed at The Greenbrier in the twenties continued their journeys to the resort, joined by some newer visitors such as David Sarnoff of RCA; Henry Luce, the publisher of *Life* magazine; Ham Fisher, the creator of "Joe Palooka"; New York Yankee Lou Gehrig; the "King of Jazz," Paul Whiteman; illustrator James Montgomery Flagg; Federal Relief Administrator Harry Hopkins; actress Mary Pickford; Babe Ruth, in his role as President of the Left-Handed Golfers Association; U.S. Steel President Thomas Girdler; Eleanor Roosevelt; actor Edward G. Robinson; President of General Motors, William Knudsen; and singer Bing Crosby.

These well-known guests immersed themselves in the traditional rituals of The Greenbrier, including riding up to the original log-constructed Kate's Mountain Lodge for its famous southern fried chicken or a seasonal treat,

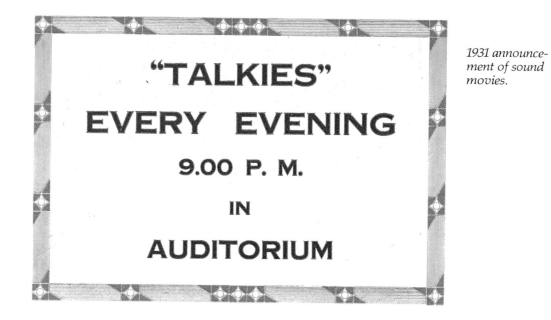

"TALKIES"
EVERY EVENING
9.00 P. M.
IN
AUDITORIUM

*1931 announce-
ment of sound
movies.*

The Dining Room of The Greenbrier in the 1930s.

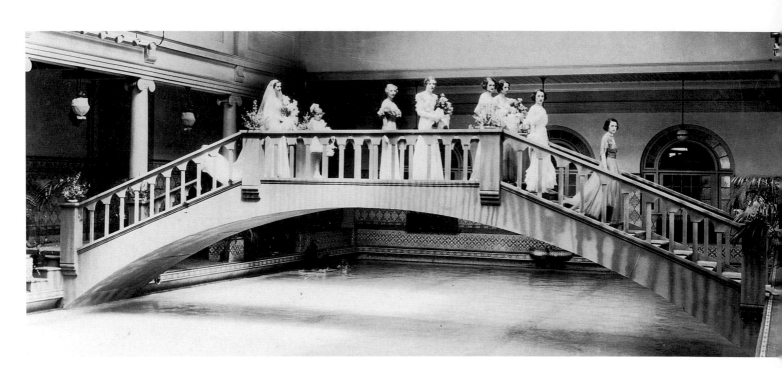

Fashion shows at the indoor pool were popular in the 1930s. This "Parade of Wedding Fashions" was staged in April 1933.

Mr. and Mrs. Gould Shaw of Boston and Palm Beach, two fashionable guests who frequented The Greenbrier in the thirties.

after the hunting parties, of roasted raccoon ("considered a delicacy" one writer reported.) Although golf reigned as the king of sports, horseback riding was a close second, and it was common for the most accomplished riders to bring their horses to explore the two hundred fifty miles of trails through the surrounding mountains. Mah Jong was the most popular indoor sport, except, of course, dancing. By the late twenties, the Charleston—now considered passe—was replaced by the Black Bottom, and by the mid-thirties the Rumba was reportedly the favorite over the Tango. In an era when one hundred million Americans were attending movie theatres weekly, the cinema at The Greenbrier was sure to be popular. There was one distinct difference, however, that was noted in the *Wall Street Journal*: "Statistics will show, we believe, that the percentage of people who attend movies in evening dress is greater at White Sulphur than any place in this or any other country." There was another difference as well. Since General Manager Loren Johnston was an amateur photography buff, guests were encouraged to take home movies, which would later be shown for general entertainment. Polo was another sport the guests could not do without, so for this reason a playing field was created near the airport. There numerous university, military and private club teams competed every Sunday afternoon. In the world of tennis, the Mason and Dixon Championship, held at The Greenbrier each April, was the highlight of the season, because a player's performance in these matches had a direct bearing on the annual selection of the Davis Cup team.

Much of the excitement on the sports scene after 1936 centered around the amazing long-ball hitting of The Greenbrier's new golf pro, Sam Snead. That winter Freddie Martin, for many years the golf manager at The Greenbrier, had witnessed an astounding display of powerful driving by the twenty-three-year-old Snead at a nearby tournament. Martin returned saying he had seen a young man who could hit the ball farther than either Bobby Jones or Walter Hagen, so Snead was hired at $45 per month, plus room and board. But Sam Snead was nearly fired during the first week of his new job. Out on the fifth tee of the Old White Course, he let loose one of his legendary drives that flew the complete 335 yards to the green. Unfortunately, the ball arrived at precisely the moment Alva Bradley (the owner of the Cleveland Indians and, more importantly, a member of the C&O Board of Directors) bent over to pick up his own ball. Snead's ball caught Bradley right on the rump. "It was like something out of a Laurel and Hardy movie the way that man jolted up," Snead recalled years later. Bradley, known to be a man who took his golf seriously, was not amused, and let Snead know it in no uncertain terms. The golf staff and the General Manager were called together and Bradley angrily demanded that the ill-mannered young fairway sniper be properly punished. When it was explained that the offending shot was not Snead's second, but his tee shot, Bradley snorted "Impossible!" So a demonstration was arranged, and much to the C&O director's amazement Snead repeated his feat. "Jumping Judas," yelled Bradley, "Wait'll I tell Babe Ruth about this, he'll be down here to take lessons from you." Bradley then hired Snead as his private instructor, and so the young kid from the Back Creek Mountains of Virginia, not too many miles as the crow flies from White Sulphur Springs, began one of the most fabulous careers in the history of golf.

In his first year at The Greenbrier, Sam Snead gained some notice when he teamed up with Johnny Goodman to defeat Lawson Little and Billy Burke. This didn't exactly make him a household name, as many newspapers headlined their account: "Goodman and Partner Beat Little and Burke." For some time journalists misspelled the name "Sneed," but they learned to report it correctly when Sam burst into the national spotlight in January of 1937 after shooting 69-65-67-69 (at a time when any score in the sixties was considered remarkable) in the Oakland Open. For almost four decades, Sam Snead's photograph and name, spelled correctly, appeared in countless newspaper and magazine articles, and during that extraordinary career he remained The Greenbrier's pro. To legions of golfers the names Slammin' Sammy Snead and The Greenbrier were linked as examples of the best the game of golf had to offer.

As the fall season of 1941 faded, thirty-one years had passed since the Chesapeake and Ohio Railway had purchased White Sulphur Springs, bringing a new splendor to the resort. One journalist of the day captured the sense of delight that struck a visitor after those decades of growth: "Entering the stone gateway, we come upon a scene surprising in its magnificence. For hundreds of yards the trim lawns stretch away to what looks like an Aladdin's palace gleaming ivory-white in the sunshine. This building is so grandiose in its scale, so elegant and stately in its classical lines, that it seems only a magic wand could have created it here among the mountains so far from the haunts of man." This reverie of splendid isolation was shattered, as was much of the rest of the world, by the attack on Pearl Harbor on December 7, 1941. On that fateful Sunday morning, the few guests in the hotel gathered about a small radio in the main lobby unaware that events would soon cause The Greenbrier to be closed to the public for well over six years.

Sam Snead in 1937, The Greenbrier's young golf pro.

The Duke and Duchess of Windsor were the center of attention at the party celebrating the reopening of The Greenbrier after its use as an Army hospital in World War II.

Diplomats and Doctors, Draper and the Duke

hortly after lunch on December 17, 1941, The Greenbrier's General Manager received a cryptic telephone call from the U.S. State Department. Would the resort be prepared, the caller inquired, to accommodate certain diplomats and citizens from the Washington, D.C., embassies of newly-hostile nations? The manager hurriedly called together the hotel staff to consider the unusual proposal, when a second call arrived from the State Department. A decision was urgent, the representative said, because President Roosevelt had ordered the removal of all enemy diplomats from the capital within forty-eight hours. The staff immediately agreed to notify the government that the entire resort was at its disposal for the duration of this delicate emergency situation. By the end of the specified forty-eight hours, The Greenbrier was transformed from a private luxury resort into the focal point of international wartime diplomacy.

The State Department was searching for a suitable location to temporarily house diplomats from the Axis powers until exchanges for American diplomats, also trapped in overseas capitals at the outbreak of war, could be officially negotiated. The Greenbrier fulfilled the government's basic requirements: first, it was relatively isolated and therefore easily guarded, and second, the famous resort offered the kind of first-class accommodations desired, since the State Department hoped to ensure equally fine treatment for interned American diplomats. There was another positive reason for selecting The Greenbrier—two of the key decision-makers in this action, Secretary of State Cordell Hull and Attorney General Francis Biddle, were personally familiar with the resort's quality, facilities and service, as both had frequently vacationed there before the war.

At 5:30 p.m. on December 19th, the first contingent of 159 German and Hungarian diplomats arrived in White Sulphur Springs on a secretly scheduled, eleven-car Pullman train from Washington, D.C. One Washington newspaper described the departing dignitaries gathered outside the German embassy on Massachusetts Avenue as a "well-dressed throng, abounding in fur coats and smart hair-dos, with dozens and dozens of bags, boxes and bundles, piled picnic-style into their special buses." At the same time, a team of eighteen FBI agents was assigned to White Sulphur Springs to enforce the government's strict security regulations controlling all forms of communication into and out of the hotel. Fifty members of the U.S. Border Patrol were transferred to The Greenbrier from their posts along the Canadian and Mexican borders to guard the new guests. The resort was closed to all regular guests, though complying with State Department instructions, The Greenbrier's staff size and quality of service remained unchanged. According to international law set down at the Geneva Convention of 1929, the United States was bound to protect the diplomats and their families, and, as one historian noted, America embraced those accords "with an almost religious fervor." Of course underlying that fervor was the con-

rk **Times.**

LATE CITY EDITION
Partly cloudy and mild today followed by cloudy and colder in late afternoon or night.
Temperatures Yesterday—Max., 52; Min., 39

k Times Company.

CEMBER 20, 1941.

THREE CENTS NEW YORK CITY and Vicinity

IDANAO, BATTLE RAGES;
HONG KONG, HOLD HILLS;
DRAFT MEN FROM 20 TO 44

ONY IS CUT OFF

Kong's Garrison sists at Strong oints on Island

FIGHT TO LAST

Claims Capture of ctoria—Dock Area Reported Ablaze

By The United Press.

NDON, Dec. 19—The fate ong Kong, farthest Imperial st of Britain's far-flung em- was apparently sealed tonight he hard-pressed garrison a gallant but seemingly ss fight against Japanese landed on the main island e Crown Colony.

Colonial Office announced 0 o'clock tonight that a report Japanese sources that Hong was in Japanese hands could confirmed or denied, since ssage had been received from olony since early this morn-

ommunications of Hong Kong Chungking also ceased. yo radio reports heard in ila said Hong Kong had in Japanese hands since 11 ., yesterday, Tokyo time. A ei dispatch reported from n by the Andi Agency of tina to The Associated said the Japanese flag was over the harbor, and the British resistance was rap- being broken. Another i report said the Japanese ed their landing on Hong Island in small boats after ve-hour artillery barrage ir bombing had prepared y. Fortifications opposite n were reported destroyed e large Taikoo dock area flames. The landings apparently made in this with the Japanese quick- pying Jardine's Lookout, enter

Nazi Diplomats Are Sent To West Virginia Resort

Dr. Hans Thomsen, chargé d'affaires, and his wife before leaving yesterday for White Sulphur Springs.
Associated Press Wirephoto

Special to The New York Times.

WASHINGTON, Dec. 19—The German Embassy staff and German newspaper correspondents, numbering about 150, were sent to White Sulphur Springs, W. Va., today pending their departure from the United States when arrangements have been completed. The staff traveled in buses except for Dr. Hans Thomsen, the chargé d'affaires, and his wife, who rode in a limousine. The Swiss Lega-

tion took over custody of the German Embassy.

The Hungarian Legation staff of about twelve is also being concentrated at the West Virginia resort, while Japanese consular staffs from all over the United States are being sent to Hot Springs, Va. The Japanese Embassy staff is remaining here in the embassy for the present. No announcement

Continued on Page Ten

has been made concerning the removal of the Italian Embassy staff.

American diplomats and newspaper correspondents in Germany have been concentrated at Bad Nauheim, a resort in Southern Germany. The staff of the American Embassy in Tokyo is housed in embassy buildings. The State Department, however, was not ready to confirm today a report that the American and Japanese diplomats would be exchanged through the use of an Argentine steamship. Arrangements looking to their repatriation on a reciprocal basis were being made, it was said, but had not been completed.

Contrary to the impression of some enemy aliens that recent Presidential proclamations would not allow them to travel anywhere, Attorney General Biddle announced today that certain latitude would be permitted in this regard.

Pending the issuance of detailed regulations, Mr. Biddle announced that the Presidential proclamations of Dec. 7 and Dec. 8 did not forbid the following:

"Travel within the boundaries or limits of the municipality, town, village, locality or community in which he resides, from place to place and in such manner as will permit him to engage in the activities usual in his community;

"Coming from his home to his place of business, or

"Travel between his home and his place of religious worship, school, college or institution of learning at which he is in regular attendance, or any Federal, State or local government agency with which he is required to transact business."

Whenever an alien enemy wishes to change his address he must first notify the United States Attorney in his district.

Diplomats Installed in Hotel

By The Associated Press.

WHITE SULPHUR SPRINGS, W. Va., Dec. 19—Staffs of the German Embassy and the Hungarian Legation and members of their families arrived here late today and were installed at a hotel.

On official of the State Department who declined to be quoted said that other Germans, some from embassies and consulates in South American countries, were expected to join the party here.

Members of the party will have full range of the hotel grounds, golf course and recreation facilities while here for an indefinite stay, pending departure from the United States.

ARTIST GOES TO BELLEVUE

British Bring Foe to a Halt
In Malaya, but Yield Pena

The New York Times gave front page coverage to the arrival of German diplomats at The Greenbrier in December, 1941. Subsequently, however, there were very few press reports about the stay of the foreign diplomats.

cern for the safety of Americans held oversees. That the Americans were not treated as well in Germany is reflected in the comment of the noted diplomat, George Kennan, who was in charge of one hundred thirty Americans at Bad Nauheim near Frankfurt: "most of us were emaciated when we emerged from the experience."

There was, understandably, much apprehension among The Greenbrier's employees as they adjusted to their new role in government service. The FBI thoroughly investigated each employee, especially those who were foreign-born, and all were issued passes and fingerprinted. Everyone was cautioned that the new residents of The Greenbrier were most likely agents of their respective governments and very possibly directing intelligence-gathering operations in this country. The mayor of White Sulphur Springs, Greenbrier employee William Perry, declared to the press, "Our whole tradition here in White Sulphur Springs is one of patriotism and support of our government . . . We, and I speak for every person in our town, are happy to have this privilege of doing our part during the war crisis."

It was initially understood that the length of The Greenbrier's government service would extend a maximum of three months, with the total number of diplomats and their families amounting to between four and five hundred. But international complications lengthened that time, first from day to day and later from week to week, and swelled the numbers.

By the end of March, 1942, the number of diplomatic guests had grown to over eight hundred; by far the largest component were German citizens, but they were joined by 170 Italians, 53 Hungarians, and 11 Bulgarians. The group included all levels of the diplomatic staffs at each embassy as well as businessmen, bankers, newspaper correspondents, military attaches, engineers, servants, and families. Most of these internees were prominent individuals from the highest stratas of society in their homelands.

For the most part, the sensitive operation proceeded smoothly. Cable traffic between American officials and adversary nations was carried through neutral representatives of Switzerland, Sweden, and Spain. These cables reported daily menus and living conditions at the various internment locations in order that accommodations for all diplomats were kept precisely parallel. For example, when the Germans complained about the food at The Greenbrier, cables from overseas brought typical menus so that they were served the same fare as that in Bad Nauheim. The activities of the diplomatic guests were restricted by the FBI—the golf courses and riding trails were declared off limits for obvious security purposes—but the tennis courts and indoor pool were in constant use. (For years afterwards many who were

children of diplomats at the time returned to The Greenbrier with tales of delightful hours spent frolicking in the pool.) Cottages in Georgia Row were converted into classrooms for the schoolchildren; three weddings were celebrated in the Virginia Room; and six babies, including a set of twins, were born in a nearby hospital in Clifton Forge, Virginia. One of the very few troublesome incidents occurred when the German legation staged a boisterous beer party in the Main Dining Rooms on Hitler's birthday—cleverly described by one waiter as "a hell of a hail of heils"—but the celebration was quietly quelled by a discreet word from the general manager to the German executive officer. The guests passed much of their time playing chess, backgammon, and ping pong or reading the only available newspaper, *The New York Times*.

On April 1st the Italians, Hungarians, and Bulgarians were transferred to the Grove Park Inn, in Asheville, North Carolina, making room for nearly four hundred Japanese diplomats who had been living at The Homestead, in Hot Springs, Virginia, since December. The game of musical chairs continued the next month, when four hundred Germans were repatriated to their homeland and over five hundred Germans traveled north to The Greenbrier from Central and South American nations. By mid-May of 1942, the number of diplomats reached its peak of one thousand. From April through June, the hotel was occupied only by Germans and Japanese and an uneasy truce was maintained by the two nationalities. Gwen Terasaki, an American woman married to a Japanese diplomat and interned with him, reported a continual round of wining and dining and cocktail parties among the high ranking members of both embassies. There was some petty squabbling to be sure—each group was careful to sit at opposite ends of the dining room—and the Japanese group endured some pointed heckling from the Germans when news arrived of Jimmy Doolittle's raid over Tokyo. In spite of the good spirits, however, at times there was an undercurrent of tension alternating with boredom among the internees as they coped with the uncertainty of their futures. A few were quite anxious about the wisdom of their government's wartime policies, and Gwen Terasaki noted that there were five American wives of German diplomats, some of whom were very apprehensive about returning to Nazi Germany.

The Japanese diplomats had had their assets frozen by the U.S. government and were therefore pressed for personal funds. Mrs. Terasaki, who had employed several servants while living in Washington, did her own laundry. "I am sure the elegant Greenbrier Hotel has never before or since had washing and ironing going on in so many of its luxurious rooms," she remarked. The Ger-

Classrooms were set up for the German schoolchildren in Georgia Row.

The Japanese diplomats posed for a group photograph at the north entrance in May, 1942.

mans, on the other hand, still controlled most of their personal accounts. Because they were not permitted to carry American dollars home with them, they converged on The Greenbrier's shopping arcade spending their soon-to-be worthless dollars on fine art prints and expensive antique silver. All of the shops were rapidly depleted of their entire inventory until one bright entrepreneur produced a stack of department store catalogs and the buying spree began anew. When the Germans departed, two extra railroad baggage cars were required to transport all their newly acquired merchandise.

Arrangements for the international exchange of diplomats were completed in increments through May and June, and The Greenbrier's unusual guests began moving out of the hotel, headed for their homes. The resort had hosted a total of 1,697 persons representing five different nations; the staff had handled 8,519 pieces

of baggage. The Japanese diplomats traveled by train to New York, where they boarded the Swedish ocean-liner Gripsholm for the long voyage to Lourenco Marques, the port city now known as Maputo, in the African nation of Mozambique. There they met ships bearing American diplomats from Shanghai and Yokohama for the official exchange directed by the International Red Cross. The German diplomats sailed on the Drottningholm to Lisbon, Portugal, where they were exchanged for Americans who had traveled by train from Berlin. On July 8, 1942, a final group of 151 German aviators left The Greenbrier and the resort's extraordinary 201 days of emergency government service came to an end. There was one interesting footnote: the German, Japanese, and Italian diplomats paid a total of $65,000 in gratuities to The Greenbrier's bellmen, maids, waiters, and porters for excellent services rendered.

Diplomats playing ping-pong in a lobby off the Cameo Ballroom.

*A Japanese diplomat and his family ready for the journey back to Japan,
June 10, 1942.*

The Greenbrier reopened to its regular guests—supplemented by many curious visitors who wanted to see what had been termed "the world's swankest internment center"—in mid-July, but the 1942 season lasted a mere six weeks. Even before the last foreign diplomats were exchanged, management was contacted by representatives of the U.S. Navy and the U.S. Army in search of wartime facilities. The Navy wanted to lease about half of The Greenbrier's rooms, and use the resort as a rest and recuperation center for its officers and enlisted men. The Army wanted the entire hotel for a hospital. In August, a special board convened in Washington, D.C., to decide the fate of The Greenbrier, and the Army was granted approval to proceed with its plans. Following formal procedures, The Greenbrier was condemned under the War Powers Act. However, the government did pay the Chesapeake and Ohio Railway $3.3 million, for The Greenbrier Hotel, all the resort's facilities and seven thousand acres of land—real estate with an estimated value of $5.4 million in August of 1942.

On August 30th, a farewell mint julep party was held before The Greenbrier was drafted into wartime duty. "Tears flowed freely and unashamedly," wrote one newspaper correspondent, "as guests of many seasons here said their last goodbyes to the famous old hotel and the lights blinked out in the upper stories." The next day The Greenbrier officially became the property of the U.S. Army, and the executive officers of the new and unnamed hospital began arriving that very evening.

The conversion of The Greenbrier into a two-thousand bed military hospital progressed rapidly, spurred by the expectation of heavy casualties during Operation Torch, the allied invasion of North Africa. Within a few weeks, an Army inventory team began appraising The Greenbrier's equipment and furnishings to determine which items would be maintained for use in the hospital. The policy was to retain only the most utilitarian kitchen equipment, linens, beds, chairs, and rugs. The hotel staff hastily removed the collection of historical books, photographs and valuable paintings from The Greenbrier and the Presidents' Cottage Museum and loaned them indefinitely to nearby museums and universities. Other items were donated to orphanages, schools and hospitals; some office equipment was transferred to C&O Railway buildings. In the frantic rush to move out, there was neither time nor space to store the most expensive ornamental china, silver, lamps, furniture, prints, and mirrors; in addition, once the White Sulphur Springs Company was liquidated by the C&O, the railroad was

Advertisement placed in The New York Times *on September 4, 1942, three days after the sale of the resort to the U.S. Army. Apparently no one needed six hundred rooms of furniture at the time (note that the offer was for a one-transaction sale) because there were no takers.*

completely out of the resort business. Therefore, the bulk of The Greenbrier's elaborate interior furnishings were quickly auctioned off at an unadvertised sale held at the White Sulphur Springs railroad station. The sale offered a rare opportunity to purchase valuable hotel antiques at unbelievably low prices because in that fall of 1942 the railroad's sole objective was a speedy disposal of unneeded goods.

The new Army facility was eventually named Ashford General Hospital to honor Bailey K. Ashford, M.D., an early twentieth century Army physician whose research dramatically reduced the frightening death toll in Puerto Rico from epidemic diseases. After an investment of nearly $2 million towards the transformation of The Greenbrier into a military unit, Ashford General Hospital was formally dedicated on October 16, 1943. The ceremony was attended by the Surgeon General of the Army, General Norman T. Kirk, Senator Kilgore of West Virginia, and the Duke and Duchess of Windsor. The Duke and Duchess toured the hospital's facilities, signed autographs for the patients and greeted the five thousand visitors who had come to see The Greenbrier in its new incarnation. More than a few members of the public were struck by the incongruity of seeing maroon-clad soldiers strolling the grounds and corridors where grey flannel-clad millionaires had walked only months earlier.

The cover of an information booklet issued to each patient.

The elevator shaft (to the right of the main entrance) constructed to move men and materials to the top two floors of the hospital.

The Duchess of Windsor touring the kitchen of Ashford General Hospital.

The Mess Hall at Ashford General Hospital.
The chandeliers still hang in The Greenbrier's Main
Dining Room.

"Maintaining morale" at Ashford General Hospital.

Colonel (later General) Clyde Beck was the commander of the resort-turned-hospital for four years.

The upper lobby of The Greenbrier became office space for Ashford General Hospital. This view is from what is now the Trellis Lobby into the Victorian Writing Room.

Prisoners of war who worked at Ashford General Hospital.

The press nicknamed Ashford General Hospital "The Shangri-La For Wounded Soldiers" because all the facilities of the former resort were available to the GIs. Much of the hotel's main lobby retained the elegant decor of the pre-war days, although the spaces were put to different uses. The North Parlor became a chapel, the famous ballroom a recreational center filled with ping-pong tables, and what is now the Victorian Writing Room (off the main lobby) the office of the hospital commander, Colonel Clyde Beck. The Virginia Room and the Golf Clubhouse were used as off-duty officers' lounges, the Presidents' Cottage Museum was occupied by the Red Cross, and the old, log-constructed Kate's Mountain Lodge became an officers' club described as "the most beautiful Non-Commissioned Officers' Club in the Army." All of the historic cottages were restored and used as residences by physicians, staff and nurses. And the rooms that now make up the Presidential Suite were utilized as a maternity ward. The lower lobby shops were removed and replaced with laboratories, a dental clinic, and a Post Exchange, complete with a soda fountain. The Mineral Bath Department became a center for hydrotherapy, and occupational and physical therapy. In addition, the golf courses, tennis courts, and indoor swimming pool were always available to the recuperating soldiers.

Ashford General Hospital was designated a Vascular Surgery Center and a Neurosurgical Center. The Chief of Surgery was Daniel C. Elkin, M.D., formerly of Emory University in Atlanta, and under his direction significant advances were made at Ashford General in the fields of blood vessel and nerve surgery. On the fifth and sixth floors of the former hotel, Dr. Elkin established a special six-hundred bed surgical unit with sophisticated temperature and humidity controls, precision instruments, and unique lighting that simulated daylight. In order to transport patients and equipment to these operating rooms, a huge elevator shaft was added to the front facade of the building, beginning below the ballroom and rising to the top floors.

The labor pool to operate and maintain Ashford General Hospital included Army personnel, civilians, and many former employees of The Greenbrier. (A number of the hotel's management team were commissioned officers because of their knowledge of the buildings and grounds.) However, after much discussion, it was decided not to offer a position to The Greenbrier's chef because it appeared unlikely that he could adapt to the demands of Army cuisine. In addition to these employees, the hospital utilized another highly unusual source—a prisoner of war camp located at the airport near the golf courses. The POW camp of seventy-three temporary buildings housed one thousand captured enemy soldiers, first Italian and later German, brought from overseas battlefields. Hundreds of these prisoners worked in the hospital's kitchens, on the grounds crew, in the Post Exchange, at the laundry, and in supply positions. The hospital commander, Colonel Beck, reported to his superiors that this unique program enabled Ashford General Hospital to avoid serious personnel problems. Besides working at the hospital, many of these prisoners were hired by local farmers to harvest crops since many local men were off in the military.

During its four years of operation, Ashford General Hospital admitted 24,148 patients, and 11,346 operations were performed. The vast majority of patients were officers and enlisted men wounded in North Africa, the Aleutian Islands, the Philippines, Italy, and the Pacific Islands. There were a number of American generals as well, among them Omar Bradley, Anthony McAuliffe, Mark Clark, Matthew Ridgeway, and Jonathan Wainwright who, following three years of imprisonment in a Japanese camp, wrote his memoirs there with sportswriter Bob Considine. General Wainwright stayed in the cottage General George Marshall regularly occupied, Top Notch. In addition, General Dwight D. Eisenhower was twice a patient at the hospital, once in January, 1944, before the massive invasion of Normandy, and again in December, 1945. On a third occasion, in the summer of 1945, General and Mrs. Eisenhower stayed at Ashford General following the end of the war; indeed the couple celebrated their 29th wedding anniversary in Top Notch cottage. During this visit General Eisenhower sat on the porch of the cottage for sculptor Archimedes Giacomontonio, who created the first bust ever made of the General; a bronze casting is still on display in The Greenbrier's North Parlor. Mrs. Eisenhower later wrote to the sculptor, "We have often spoken about those pleasant

Visiting Day—Easter 1943.

days you spent at our home in White Sulphur Springs when you were carving a bust of the General. That likeness was one of the finest I have ever seen!"

Two of the very few non-military patients at Ashford General Hospital were retired Secretary of State Cordell Hull and President Roosevelt's close advisor, Harry Hopkins. Civilians supported the war effort by volunteering as gray ladies and many a young local girl made her way to the dances held on holidays in the ballroom. The USO arranged numerous entertainment events, including appearances by comedian Ed Wynn, actor Walter Pidgeon, and golf exhibitions by Sam Snead, Byron Nelson, Jimmy Demaret, and Gene Sarazen. The Red Cross sponsored classes in Spanish, picnics, dancing and bridge parties. The hospital boasted its own band, the Ashford Dance Orchestra, and its own newspaper, *The Ashford News.* Former tennis professional George Lott was in charge of Ashford's tennis program.

With the end of World War II, it became necessary for the Army to decide whether to maintain Ashford General Hospital or declare it surplus property. A meeting of the officers of the hospital was called to discuss what recommendation to make to their superiors. The commander, by then General Beck, voted to retain the prop-

General Dwight D. Eisenhower with the bust sculpted by Archimedes Giacomontonio (left) in July, 1945. A bronze casting of this bust is in The Greenbrier's North Parlor.

Celebrating the end of the war with Japan, August 16, 1945.

erty. General Beck was a Southerner, a native of Memphis, Tennessee, and he had worked hard to maintain the historic resort. In fact, when military leaders had wanted to demolish the old cottages, which form the heart of the nineteenth century resort, he had successfully fought for their preservation. Now faced with a decision, most of the younger officers argued that the loss of POW labor made the estate far too expensive for the Army. The military command in Washington agreed with this position, and on June 30, 1946, Ashford General Hospital was officially closed.

The final flag-lowering ceremony at Ashford General Hospital.

For a few months after the Army's departure, the huge white bulk of The Greenbrier sat empty in the summertime green of the West Virginia mountains. No one knew what would become of the famous resort property, though rumors were rampant. According to one, a Florida gambling syndicate was preparing to convert the hotel into a casino. But because strict Army regulations dictated who was eligible to bid for the surplus hospital, priority was given to government agencies, local governments and non-profit institutions, in that order. At one point the town of White Sulphur Springs resolved to purchase the property and turn it over to the Chesapeake and Ohio Railway. However, the railroad's executives disagreed about whether the resort could ever be an asset again. After almost six anxious months, President Truman signed a bill allowing former owners first priority in purchasing surplus military property. In December of 1946, mostly through the efforts of Robert R. Young, Chairman of the Board of the C&O, the railroad bought back The Greenbrier, paying the government slightly less than the 1942 selling price of $3.3 million, because the tract of transferred land did not include the airport, which was deeded to the town of White Sulphur Springs.

Robert R. Young believed in The Greenbrier and in its continuing role as an attraction drawing passengers to the C&O's main line. His determination brought about a spectacular renewal of the war-worn resort. Young was a familiar figure to many Americans because he fervently promoted efficient, comfortable railroad travel after the war. His famous slogan advocating transcontinental passenger service, "A Hog Can Cross the Country Without Changing Trains, But You Can't," was known to all who used the railroads. However, his interest in The Greenbrier went even further. As a prominent member of American society, with a summer home in Newport, Rhode Island, and a winter home in Palm Beach, Florida, Young was no stranger to the standards of luxury The Greenbrier had always stood for, nor the clientele the hotel had always catered to. Soon after the railroad's purchase of the abandoned resort, Young hired the noted New York interior decorator, Dorothy Draper, to redecorate the C&O's executive offices and suites in Cleveland's Terminal Tower. Quite pleased with the results, he then asked her to begin refurbishing The Greenbrier.

Dorothy Draper was born a Tuckerman of Tuxedo Park, New York. Her family roots went back to colonial Connecticut, and from 1912 to 1930 she was married to George Draper, Franklin Delano Roosevelt's personal physician. Her career began in the late 1920s when she decorated the Hampshire House, in New York City, the largest decorating job awarded to a woman at the time. Her reputation grew as she created interiors for The Quitandinha, in Petropolis, Brazil; Arrowhead Springs Hotel, in California; The Fairmont, in San Francisco; The Plaza and The Carlyle, in New York; The Mayflower, in Washington, D.C.; and The Gideon Putnum, in Saratoga Springs, New York. As her successor, Carleton Varney, wrote of her: "After so many years of widespread imitation of her style, it is hard to reconstruct the impact Dorothy Draper had on interior design. Suffice it to say that having Dorothy Draper as your decorator was like having Yosuf Karsh take your picture or having Luciano Pavarotti sing at your wedding. She was IT, society's most prestigious imprimatur. Whether she designed a single room or a whole hotel, Dorothy Draper's name was the one you wanted to drop." And in the context of her long career, her work at White Sulphur Springs held a special place in her mind. "Of all Dorothy's treasures," Carleton Varney continued, "those far-flung oases of sparkling white enamel and sunny chintz, The Greenbrier was quintessential Draper, the most highly prized jewel in her crown."

Dorothy Draper's first visit to White Sulphur Springs was an eerie experience according to the notes of one who accompanied her on that soggy, gray day in December, 1946. As a limousine brought them from the train station to The Greenbrier, the hotel appeared "almost ghostlike in the whispy veils of ground fog which shrouded its approaches." Under the columns of the North Portico, Dorothy Draper and her assistants were met by a single employee who, with the aid of a flashlight (the electrical power was shut off), led them "into the somber darkness of the entryway and up to a vast unfur-

Dorothy Draper

nished lobby floor, where in silent emptiness a forest of naked columns stood at attention." The decorating team immediately began inspecting the hotel, starting on the top floor, and working their way down. Within hours, having opened the heavy doors of every room and closet to see what might remain for her use, Mrs. Draper had chosen a comprehensive theme for her redecoration of The Greenbrier—"Romance and Rhododendrons"—a theme that combined her vision of White Sulphur's romantic past and her attraction to the rhododendron, West Virginia's state flower.

The scope of the task before her was staggering; at the time it was the largest redecoration attempted in the history of the American hotel industry. But Mrs. Draper was given carte blanche by Robert Young, which helped. She was free to let her colorful imagination create an entirely new interior decor for The Greenbrier. For the next sixteen months she supervised the massive job of undoing the Army's conversion, virtually rebuilding the inside of the hotel. She broke up the cavernous space that was once the upper lobby and designed the series of elegant rooms that now occupy that floor. She moved the hotel's registration desk to the downstairs lobby so that the noise and bustle of guests checking in and out would not disturb the more formal lobby upstairs, and she chose color schemes and furnishings in the guest rooms so that no two were exactly alike. A few statistics give some idea of the magnitude of Dorothy Draper's redecoration: she ordered thirty miles of carpeting, 45,000 yards of fabric, 15,000 rolls of wallpaper—including the custom-designed rhododendron pattern along the guest room corridors—and some 34,567 individual decorative and furniture items, each of which was numbered and tagged for a specific room. Forty thousand gallons of paint were necessary to carry out her colorful plans. This meant that most of the paint either had to be specially manufactured or blended to achieve her color specifications, a total of over one thousand variations in all.

Dorothy Draper overlooked nothing, redesigning six hundred individual guest rooms in the hotel and cottages, all the public lobbies, sports facilities, offices—even the employees' uniforms. "A great hotel," she said, "is like a woman's costume—an overall effect is only attained by attention to detail." Her trademark was not only bright colors but the coordination of all her colors, and that coordination included thousands of pieces of china, table linens, towels, blankets, writing paper, menus, laundry bags, golf score cards, cocktail napkins, hotel brochures, golf course flags, display cases, prints and paintings on the walls, and matchbook covers. As a writer for *Holiday* magazine described the result, "The Draper touch, and The Greenbrier manner are both of a thoroughness that leaves no stone unturned, and down to the last light switch and wastebasket, down to the Do Not Disturb card you leave on your door knob, everything has been designed and placed to be part of The Greenbrier community."

Of course there were problems. Because of lingering war shortages, Draper had difficulty locating precisely the kind and quality of furnishings she demanded. She decided the only solution was to hire a stable of craftsmen to build the hundreds of tables, desks, lamps, sofas, mantles and chests—both modern and antique repro-

what's happening at White Sulphur Springs?

We've embarked upon an
extraordinary project of transformation,
designed to surpass
even The Greenbrier of old.

Opening date can't be promised just yet,
but we do promise a splendidly intimate
new note of charm, executed
under the guiding hand of Dorothy Draper.

The Greenbrier
AT WHITE SULPHUR SPRINGS, WEST VIRGINIA

Accommodations at The Greenbrier and Cottages by Reservation Only

NEW YORK, 11 West 42nd Street   CHICAGO, 77 West Washington Street   WASHINGTON, Investment Building   BOSTON, 73 Tremont Street

Magazine advertisement that appeared in late 1947.

Applying the final touches in April, 1948—landscaping in front of the hotel. Behind the workmen is the restored facade, where the Army had added the elevator shaft. (See page 137.)

ductions—she had envisioned in her comprehensive scheme for the new interior. Next a more dramatic problem arose. When workmen climbed ladders to inspect the cracks in the delicate plaster-sculpted ceiling of the ballroom, they were horrified to discover that the lathwork under the plaster had corroded. Then to everyone's astonishment, a large section of the ceiling crashed to the dance floor. Mrs. Draper was not to be deterred, however. She liked the original ceiling and so immediately ordered an entirely new one constructed, an exact duplicate of the original intricate cameo design. As the final crowning touch, she added a nine-foot Czechoslovakian crystal chandelier to the restored ballroom, a piece she had designed after an old Russian print. The new chandelier blended so well, legend has it, that Dorothy Draper had the pleasure of laughing each time she heard a guest nostalgically, but mistakenly, recall dancing beneath it before the war.

Dorothy Draper had a natural feel for balancing the old and the new. New, bold, black and white marble flooring was added to accent the main lobby, while five English crystal chandeliers from the pre-war hotel still graced the Colonnades Dining Room. The few mirrors, breakfronts, tables, and chairs that had remained in the hotel during its use as a hospital were placed strategically within her new environment and then supplemented with scores of antiques. The upper lobby and many of the suites were transformed into showplaces of English, Italian, French, and American antique vases, clocks, busts, jars, prints, and mantles. All of the handsome oil portraits hanging in the dining rooms of The Greenbrier were purchased by Dorothy Draper in 1947, including works by such well-known American artists as Gilbert Stuart, John Singleton Copley, Rembrandt Peale, and painter-turned-inventor, Samuel F.B. Morse. In the North Parlor, described by one viewer as "the apex of Dorothy Draper's most sublime work," she placed an impressive seventeenth century oriental Coromandel screen against one wall, covered the floor with a one-hundred-fifty-year-old French Aubusson rug (which was replaced with a reproduction fifteen years later, upon the advent of stiletto heels on ladies' shoes, which caused irreparable damage) and retained the English Sheffield chandelier that had hung in the room since 1930. One of the most startling instances of Mrs. Draper's ingenuity was her decision to create the pair of paintings flanking the fireplace in the North Parlor by audaciously cutting in two the single painting "Action at Ticonderoga."

"The public is hungry for a fresh point of view presented an an unexpected and attractive form," Dorothy Draper maintained, an attitude especially appropriate following years of enforced olive-drab during wartime. At The Greenbrier she concentrated on the three basic ingredients she thought essential to any decorating job: "masses of beautiful color, a sense of balance and scale, and an awareness and love of smart accessories." In short, Dorothy Draper believed that "good showmanship" was a crucial element in the success of a hotel's interior decor. When newspaper and magazine writers

The main lobby of The Greenbrier as it looked before and during World War II (above) and as it has appeared since Dorothy Draper's redecoration (below).

finally beheld the completed Greenbrier project, they were enthusiastic in their praise of that showmanship. "The new, improved Greenbrier is alive with gay wallpapers, it sings with pinks, greens and blues," wrote one. "A technicolor surprise," and "Dorothy at her flaming best," others remarked. "The decor is refreshing, like having Aqua Velvet splashed on your face," was one writer's reaction. So new and different was her highly individual style of decorating that a new verb crept into the vocabulary of interior design—"Draperized."

The renovation of The Greenbrier spread beyond guest areas of the hotel: the kitchen was completely modernized, plumbing and wiring were rerouted from military to civilian functions, and on Dorothy Draper's recommendation, the landscape architect Richard K. Webel, of Long Island, was retained to oversee major improvements to the grounds. Perhaps his most striking landscaping creation was the patio and garden outside the newly-added Old White Club where boxwoods, fruit trees, and bright flowers were enclosed by a graceful serpentine brick wall reminiscent of those Thomas Jefferson designed at the University of Virginia. To find bricks of just the right quality, Mr. Webel had to go as far afield as old Charleston, South Carolina, where a crew of his discovered thirty-six thousand handmade bricks while working on an old plantation. The two-hundred-year-old bricks were then transformed into the curving four-hundred-twenty-four-foot-long wall still standing today.

While all this physical renovation was in progress, an entirely new program was under discussion by top level C&O executives. Edward R. Stettinius, Jr., former Secretary of State under President Roosevelt and a member of the railroad's board of directors, had proposed the establishment of a diagnostic health clinic at the resort. With his broad experience in industry—first as assistant to the President of General Motors, and then as Chairman of the Board of United States Steel—Stettinius recognized that many of the nation's top corporate leaders aged prematurely largely because they neglected to maintain their health through periodic and consistent physical examinations. He argued that while business executives routinely practiced preventative maintenance on their equipment, they avoided taking similar care of their own physical well being. To remedy this shortsighted practice, he suggested that if physical examinations were offered in an attractive resort setting, instead of in hospitals designed to care for the sick, more executives would attend to their health.

And so The Greenbrier Clinic was created on July 1, 1947, when James P. Baker, M.D., was appointed Medical Director. The third floor of the Bath Wing was converted into offices, laboratories, and examination rooms and the Clinic opened its doors exactly one year later

with two physicians and a staff of four. "We didn't know if this idea of preventive medicine would catch on," Dr. Baker said. "Our clinic is unique," he continued, "in that it is designed exclusively for diagnosis. Here we do no treatment. We examine thoroughly and advise the individual or his personal physician what we have found. Individuals have the opportunity to identify and correct conditions that, if left unattended, could adversely affect their work and well-being in later years."

Dorothy Draper's Victorian Writing Room has remained unchanged over the years.

Dorothy Draper's new chandelier was hung under wraps in February, 1948 ...

...and unveiled a few days before the reopening party began on April 15, 1948.

As the gigantic rebirth of The Greenbrier neared completion in early 1948, C&O officials and the management of the hotel began detailed planning for a very special party to celebrate its reopening. With the exception of a few brief weeks in the summer of 1942, The Greenbrier had been closed to the public for over six years, and Robert R. Young wanted the party to be a memorable event. Having invested $12,413,871 repurchasing and renovating the property, Mr. Young allocated another $65,000 to throw what *Life* magazine called "the most lavish on-the-house house party of the century."

The grand reopening party of April 15 through 18, 1948, was surely one of the most unforgettable moments in the long and brilliant history of White Sulphur Springs. The guest list was a stunning inventory of the most prominent names in American industry, government, entertainment and society circles. As *Time* magazine put it, Robert R. Young invited "three hundred of the biggest wigs he could find." In fourteen private railroad cars, by limousine and private plane arrived such personalities as the Duke and Duchess of Windsor, Bing Crosby, William Randolph Hearst, Jr., John Jacob Astor, Clark Clifford, and Cyrus Eaton, not to mention Mrs. Joseph P. Kennedy, who returned to the site of her 1914 honeymoon with her daughters Patricia, Eunice, and Kathleen as well as son John, then a young Congressman. (This was to be the last time Kathleen "Kick" Kennedy visited with her family—she died less than a month later in an airplane crash in the south of France.) And there were other notables too: magazine publishers Malcolm Forbes and Henry Luce; Chairman of the Chase National Bank, Winthrop Aldrich; social hostesses Elsa Maxwell and Perle Mesta; U.S. Attorney General Tom Clark; the governors of West Virginia, Virginia, and New Jersey; as well as numerous members of European royalty. America's number one glamour girl, Brenda Frazier, and her husband, football star Johnny "Shipwreck" Kelly, mingled with British cinema tycoon, J. Arthur Rank, and society polo player, Winston Guest. Indeed, sprinkled throughout the gathering were some of the best-known family names in America: Armour, DuPont, Biddle, Pulitzer, Vanderbilt. During the long weekend, quipped *Life* magazine, "the hotel register read like a sampling of the Social Register, Dun & Bradstreet's and the Congressional Directory."

Most of the guests participated in a pro-amateur golf tournament that attracted such famous professionals as Sam Snead, Ben Hogan, Johnny Bulla, Henry Cotton, and George Fazio. The professional competition was won by three-time British Open champion, Henry Cotton, who captured his first American victory at this

British golfer Henry Cotton, accepting the first place prize money for the professional half of the Pro-Am tournament during the 1948 reopening party. From left to right: Cotton, Merrill Meigs, tournament organizer Christopher Dunphy, Governor Clarence Meadows of West Virginia, Mrs. John Kelly (Brenda Frazier), Johnny Bulla and Johnny "Shipwreck" Kelly.

event; Patricia Kennedy won the Ladies' Amateur match. Though the Duke and Duchess of Windsor (and their clothing) were usually at the center of attention, everyone agreed that Bing Crosby was a close second, causing a traffic jam whenever he stopped, as guests flocked to get his autograph. At The Greenbrier, Crosby claimed, "I had to wash and iron my shirt before sending it to the laundry," and he went on to insist that the maid cleaned his room with a mink mop and used a lorgnette to inspect under his bed. Crosby's latest movie, "The Emperor Waltz," was premiered during the party, alternating with another new movie (which seemed appropriate to the occasion), "Mr. Blanding Builds a Dream House."

The climax of the merry weekend was the Diamond Ball on Saturday night. In the Cameo Ballroom the specially invited guests dined on beluga caviar, Green Turtle Soup Greenbrier, English Pheasant Smitane with wild rice, broiled fresh mushrooms over Virginia ham, accompanied by pink champagne. Afterwards, a gold cigarette case trimmed with diamonds was raffled off for charity and the guests danced until three in the morning to the music of the Meyer Davis Orchestra.

Band leader Davis recalled that when he had played at The Greenbrier during the Duke of Windsor's 1919 visit, the then Prince of Wales had joined the band on the drums, and so after hearty applause, the Duke agreed to do so one more time, keeping the beat to "How are Things in Glocca Morra?" Behind the scenes there was consternation among some American government officials who believed that a photograph of the former King of England playing the drums might not be exactly dignified. But when such a picture appeared in hundreds of newspapers across the country, American and British citizens seemed to take it all in stride. Even Bing Crosby was drawn into the evening's festivities, abandoning his usual iron-clad rule against entertaining at parties. It was reported that his renditions of "The Whiffenpoof Song" and "Now is the Time," brought the noisy crowd to silence.

There was about the party the aura of an extraordinary event, something beyond the normal assembly of society. Columnist Cholly Knickerbocker proclaimed, "We doubt that even the Sultan of Turkey, the Emperor of China, or the Czar of Russia, when those fabulous courts were at their peak, ever attempted anything on a

The widely published photograph of the Duke of Windsor at the drums during the Diamond Ball. To the right is bandleader Meyer Davis.

Mr. and Mrs. Robert R. Young, the hosts for The Greenbrier's reopening party.

more colossal scale." Others were perhaps not as extravagant in their praise, but based their comments on personal experience: one dowager reported that "there's been nothing like it since the Bradley Martin Ball of 1896"; another visitor noted that "the likes of this party has not been seen in this country in many years—not since the golden days of Newport in its heyday." Still another guest, focusing on the collection of business leaders at the party, commented that "Joe Stalin would have gladly given up eating borscht if he could have captured Robert Young's entire houseparty at The Greenbrier. For in one stroke Stalin would have had in his hands the creme de la creme of American capitalism." At one point, during the Diamond Ball, a gloomy party-goer is said to have approached Meyer Davis and sighed, "This is the last of the great social events of a changing age, civilization may be dancing at the brink of a precipice." The normally unflappable Davis was taken aback for a moment, but promptly retorted, "Whenever civil-

zation dances at the brink of a precipice, it's always to the music of Meyer Davis."

The press loved it. The reopening party was covered by *Town and Country, Harper's Bazaar, Holiday* and *Time* magazines as well as scores of newspapers. *Life* devoted four pages, entitled "Life Goes to the Big Weekend at White Sulphur," to the affair; *Mademoiselle* presented a selection of spring honeymoon apparel with the redecorated Greenbrier as the setting; and *Vogue* featured a photographic essay, "What They Wore at The Greenbrier's Opening." *New York Mirror* magazine called Robert R. Young "A New Champion Party-Thrower!" And, of course, reporters uncovered numerous anecdotal details: the Duke and Duchess of Windsor arrived with one hundred twenty pieces of luggage, fourteen of which were for their three-day stay; the Duke's valet laid out three complete outfits, from shoes to neckties, side-by-side for his selection before a luncheon; one wealthy woman appeared at the Diamond Ball wearing a diamond necklace "worth a cool million"; Mrs. Kennedy was seen waltzing at the Ball with her son, John; Bing Crosby crooned "Auld Lang Syne" at the train station for departing guests; however, he got off the train one stop down the line and doubled back for another day of golf. Many of the stories concerned Dorothy Draper, who beamed throughout the weekend as congratulations poured in from all quarters on her accomplishments at The Greenbrier. It was said that Mrs. Draper and her crew literally fled out the back door of the newly completed Presidential Suite as the Duke and Duchess arrived at the front door, that she spent thousands of dollars on house plants arranged about the hotel for the opening and was outraged to see a gardener using a black hose to water the grass when she had specifically ordered red hoses. According to *Time* magazine, Dorothy Draper demanded that no coal locomotives be allowed to stoke up within five miles of White Sulphur Springs lest their smoke mar her spotless white hotel, but the C&O was compelled to put its foot down on that request.

When all the fanfare had died down, it was left to Cleveland Amory, one of America's most popular chroniclers of high society history, to put the reopening party in its proper perspective. In *The Last Resorts*, his definitive account of resort life in the United States, Amory declared flatly: "The affair was the outstanding resort Society function in modern social history."

The Duchess of Windsor with Mrs. Robert R. Young (right). Anita Young was the sister of noted artist Georgia O'Keefe.

Above: Bing Crosby charmed all the guests at the reopening party. Right: This photograph appeared in Life *magazine's coverage of the reopening party showing three of the Kennedy sisters (l to r): Patricia, Kathleen, and Eunice. The men are John Kelly (left) and John Pierrepont. (Photograph by Liza Larsen, courtesy* Life *magazine.)*

Opulent Americana in a Splendid Setting

When The Greenbrier reopened its doors to the public on April 19, 1948, visitors found the hotel in mint condition. Not only did the old clientele return, but thousands of new guests arrived, eager to see Dorothy Draper's state-of-the-art decor and to borrow her colorful ideas for their own homes. Sam Snead rejoined the staff and again captivated golfers hoping to improve their games by playing with the man who had won the 1946 British Open. The reopening party generated a tremendous amount of publicity, and it had certainly done the hotel no harm to be widely known as one of the favorite haunts of the Duke and Duchess of Windsor. Among fashionable Society, with the institution of The Greenbrier's annual Spring Festival (a party staged to continue the tradition of the famous reopening party), the hotel once again became a social hub.

The Spring Festival was a special event not to be missed under any circumstances. In fact, in the 1950s and 1960s, the festivals were a must on the American social calendar. Scheduled each year for the second week in May, just after the Kentucky Derby, the Spring Festival combined a lavish house party with outstanding golf competition in The Greenbrier Open. For those who attended the festivals in the 1950s, the presence of the Duke and Duchess of Windsor added still more glamour to an event that was already the most sensational of the season. Not only were the Duke's golf game and the Duchess's designer gowns the subject of many a newspaper column, they were a source of constant comment

among their fellow guests, many of whom were luminaries themselves. "Here is opulent Americana at its richest," quipped a writer for *Holiday* magazine after one particularly brilliant festival.

The peak of each Spring Festival's week-long rush of activities was the gala Saturday night dinner dance in the Cameo Ballroom to the music of the Meyer Davis Orchestra. "The atmosphere is gay and as sparkling as the wine," journalist Al Hine wrote of the 1952 event, "and you feel that some old Greenbrier ghost, looking in through the tall windows, would nod approvingly and happily at this continuation of the elegant rout they knew and loved well. They might wrinkle their brows momentarily at a rumba or a mambo," he continued, "but the smiles would clear as Meyer Davis' men swung into a waltz and the Duke of Windsor with his Wallis—a Baltimore belle herself—moved gracefully across the floor." At one Spring Festival, a guest was overheard remarking about the Duke and Duchess, "How darling and democratic of them to dance in the same ballroom with us." Her husband surveyed the dazzling crowd under the chandelier and muttered in retort, "I wouldn't say the Windsors are exactly slumming."

Indeed there were those who defined the rather elusive concept of "Society" in post-war America by the class of people who gathered at the Spring Festivals. When social historian Cleveland Amory attempted to differentiate the precise boundaries of the slippery phrase "American Society," he turned to a European observer, the Austrian

The Greenbrier in the early 1970s.

Archrivals Sam Snead and Ben Hogan share a light moment before one of their frequent Greenbrier matchups.

Baron Hubert Panz. "What is Society in America?" Amory asked the Baron (who had won the 1952 Festival's annual waltz contest), and his immediate response was: "Is it not to go to your Greenbrier Hotel in your Spring Festival and to bet on the Duke of Windsor's team and to sit only a couple of tables from the Henry Fords? Is that not Society, no?"

Complementing, and in some cases outshining, the glittering social assembly at the Festivals was the high caliber of golf played by both amateurs and professionals. Sam Snead annually hosted an impressive field of contenders at The Greenbrier Open and frequently swept the matches against some of the best golfers in the world. In fact, The Greenbrier Golf Pro's name was so closely associated with the event, in 1957 the tournament was officially renamed The Sam Snead Festival. And when athletes and guests relaxed in the Old White Club after the competition, they were often pleasantly surprised to hear an unexpected figure playing jazz trumpet, none other than Samuel Jackson Snead himself. Sports pages in newspapers across the country were filled each May with accounts of the exploits of such famous golfers as Arnold Palmer, Jimmy Demaret, Gary Player, Cary Middlecoff (the 1949 winner), Dow Finsterwald, Mike Souchak, Dutch Harrison (the 1957 winner), Billy Casper, Henry Cotton, Henry Picard, Ed Oliver (the 1956

winner), Jimmy Revolta, Peter Thompson, Vic Ghezzi, George Fazio, and Julius Boros. However, throughout the 1950s, the match-ups between Sam Snead and Ben Hogan generated the most intense interest. It was a time when both were at the peak of their form and dominated golf in America.

Although superb golf always characterized the tournaments during the Spring Festivals, the competition in 1950 and 1959 stood out as exceptional. When the roster of golfers for the 1950 Open was released, golf aficionados were both amazed and delighted to see that Ben Hogan was on the list. Only fifteen months earlier, on February 2, 1949, the reigning U.S. Open champion had barely survived a terrifying automobile accident in western Texas. Many had doubted he would ever walk again, much less play competitive golf. Hogan's recovery after the crash captured sports page headlines, not to mention the hearts of his many fans. His entry in The Greenbrier Open, one of the first tournaments he entered after the near-fatal crash, therefore created an inordinate aura of excitement.

As it turned out, the game was all that was expected and more. The four rounds evolved into a classic Hogan-Snead encounter, heightened by the fact that Snead had beaten Hogan only a few months earlier in the playoffs of the Los Angeles Open. But Hogan's play more than matched his previous style. "Playing with the tenacity of a bulldog," as one newspaper put it, Bantam Ben Hogan shot rounds of 64-64-65-66 for a twenty-one under par total two hundred fifty-nine, equaling the record score for seventy-two holes on a par seventy course. "I was satisfied," the modest Hogan commented later, "but see nothing extra in my performance." Golf writers thought otherwise, however, proclaiming "the great Hogan is back." Golf historian Herbert Warren Wind took the proclamation one step further: "Hogan was not only back, he was back on top."

Nine years later, Sam Snead again entered The Greenbrier Open. He had already won four times, most recently the year before when he had beat Gary Player. After two respectable rounds of sixty-eight and sixty-nine, Snead was in second place behind Dutch Harrison. May 16, 1959, was a very windy day on The Greenbrier course, but Snead, playing just eleven days shy of his forty-seventh birthday, hit one perfect drive after another. "It was on the twelfth that I began to realize something wonderful," Snead later wrote. "I could feel in my gut that the yips had, for once, decided to leave me be. It was a high feeling, a confident feeling. I knew that if I could just drive as good as I knew, the putts would take care of themselves." Indeed he shot the last seven holes in twenty-one strokes, seven under par. When the final putt caught the lower corner of the cup and fell in, Slammin' Sammy Snead had fired an

The Final Putt for 59. Sam Snead lines up and sinks his last stroke for a career-best 59 in May, 1959. At right he is congratulated by his amateur partner Bruce Forbes.

Ben Hogan gladly accepts his check as winner of the 1950 Greenbrier Open from the Duke of Windsor as the Duchess looks on.

Gary Player at the 1959 Greenbrier Open.

Bob Hope at the 1953 Spring Festival.

An historic moment: Arnold Palmer (far right) won his first professional money at The Greenbrier's Spring Festival in May, 1955. Palmer and his partner Spencer Olin (next to him) split the pro-am winner's check of $1,700 when they tied Ed "Porky" Oliver (far left) and his amateur partner Carling Dinkler (second from left). The man in the hat is Christopher Dunphy who organized the Spring Festival tournaments and next to him is Dutch Harrison, the winner of the professional competition.

incredible fifty-nine. A huge cheer went up from the crowd and echoed for days a sportswriters grasped to find appropriate adjectives to describe the event: "Fantastic," "Sensational," "Astounding," "Spectacular," "Wondrous," "Phenomenal," "Sizzling." *Sports Illustrated* magazine called the round "magnificent" and raved, "Sam shot the greatest competitive round of golf in the history of the game."

"This is the highlight," Snead jubilantly declared as he walked off the eighteenth hole that day. "I've always wanted to break sixty in tournament play. I was hoping I'd be able to break sixty before I hung up my sticks. Now that I've done it, I'm not going to hang up those sticks." The next day Snead followed his fifty-nine with a fourth round sixty-three to win his one hundred third tournament and equal Ben Hogan's record two hundred fifty-nine.

NOTE: YARDAGE MEASURED FROM BLUE MARKERS

SNEAD — SUMMERS — LOW BALL

Yds.	Par	Hcp.	Hole	Snead	Summers	Low Ball +/-0	W. Par
389	4	7	1	3		3	4
120	3	17	2	3		3	3
412	4	3	3	3		3	5
372	4	9	4	3		3	4
367	4	11	5	4	4	4	4
293	4	15	6	3		3	4
409	4	1	7	4	5	4	5
391	4	5	8	4	4	3	4
286	4	13	9	4	4	4	4
3039	35		OUT	31		30	37

The "GREENBRIER" Course

Yds.	Par	Hcp.	Hole	Snead	Summers	Low Ball	W. Par
236	3	14	10	3		3	3
425	4	4	11	4		4	5
400	4	10	12	3		3	4
395	4	12	13	3	3	3	4
174	3	18	14	2		2	3
483	5	6	15	3		3	5
526	5	2	16	4	4	3	5
200	3	16	17	3		3	3
439	4	8	18	3		3	5
3278	35		IN	28		27	38
6317	70		TOT.	59		57	75

HANDICAP		DATE	PUBLISHED BY GOLF-MAP CROWNSVILLE, MD.
NET SCORE		5/16/59	

PLAYER — ATTESTED

Sam Snead's scorecard for the best round of his career.

While the Spring Festivals marked the peak of each year's social season, there were numerous special meetings and conferences that also kept The Greenbrier in the news. July of 1949, for instance, was an especially busy month. Early that month John L. Lewis, one of the most powerful labor leaders in modern American history, led a delegation of United Mine Workers of America representatives in negotiations with coal operators who controlled two-thirds of the nation's coal output. The selection of The Greenbrier as the site for these talks was quite symbolic. For years coal operators had informally gathered at White Sulphur Springs, and therefore Lewis was meeting them, so to speak, in their own backyard.

Shortly after these negotiations ended, Secretary of Defense Louis Johnson hosted a meeting of the Secretaries of the Army, Navy, and Air Force with the Joint Chiefs of Staff for a top-secret discussion of post-war military strategy. This was the first time such a meeting of high-ranking officials of the armed services had been held outside Washington, D.C. The officials occupied the Presidential Suite (the Duke and Duchess of Windsor's accommodations during the Spring Festival), and in the afternoon more informal discussions continued on the golf courses where, incidentally, Army Chief of Staff, General Omar Bradley, took the honors as the best golfer of the group by shooting a seventy-five. While defense officials mapped their plans, one hundred twenty-five fashion editors traveled by a special C&O train to White Sulphur Springs to view the new Fall dress and jewelry fashions. Between fashion shows, the editors excitedly passed the news that General Eisenhower was expected to join the military conference. However, poor weather forced cancellation of his plans. Other editors reported meeting bandleader Bob Crosby on the golf courses who, as Bing's brother, introduced himself as "the one without Hope." Dorothy Draper spoke to the fashion editors emphasizing her basic message, that decorators "have got to be bold. They've got to be daring. They've got to have lots of color. Color is magic." But what really caught the editors' eyes were Dorothy Draper's famous Greenbrier washcloths, which were a brilliant red (to provide splashes of color in otherwise white bathrooms) and measured fourteen-by-fourteen inches. "The fashion festivities hadn't been underway for more than an hour," one journalist noted, "before washcloths were showing up as neckpieces, miniature turbans, halters, belts and dangle accessories. The Greenbrier people were a little surprised, but not alarmed, and they even smiled resignedly as the washcloths disappeared a few days later."

Two examples of French designer Pierre Balmain's creations shown in 1950 in the Cameo Ballroom.

Secretary of Defense Johnson, pleased with the success of the July military meeting, returned to The Greenbrier three months later to entertain the Prime Minister of India, Jawaharal Nehru. Accompanied by his daughter, Indira Gandhi, the Prime Minister rested for a few days during a nearly month-long tour of the United States. The Nehru party took the Presidential Suite and their visit was climaxed by an elaborate state dinner served in their honor. Over one hundred fifty prominent individuals from the worlds of politics, banking, journalism, and industry attended, among them U.S. Supreme Court Justice, Stanley Reed; former World Bank Chairman, Eugene Meyer; Chief of the Air Force, Hoyt S. Vandenburg; B.F. Fairless, President of U.S. Steel; I.B.M. President, Thomas Watson; Chesapeake and Ohio Railway Chairman, Robert R. Young; and Harvey Firestone, Jr., of Firestone Tire and Rubber.

Forty-five state governors convened in White Sulphur Springs for the forty-second Annual Governor's Conference in June of 1950; this was the second time this group met

at The Greenbrier, the first having been in 1923. The important conference was covered in great detail in *Time*, *Newsweek*, and *Life* magazines. "For four days at White Sulphur Springs, W.Va., last week there was a rare and heartening gathering of politicians," reported *Life*. "What was rare and heartening about it was that, instead of partisanship, politicking and partying, the conference was characterized by a genuine spirit of cooperation." This cooperation hardly excluded fun, however. Most of the governors arrived at The Greenbrier with their families, Ford Motor Company provided brand-new Fords equipped with license plates bearing each governor's name, and Howard's Creek was stocked with one thousand trout. It is said that much of the informal talk among the governors that year centered around New York Governor Thomas Dewey's announcement that he would not seek re-election because of illness.

This 1950 Governor's Conference was a continuation of the long and venerable tradition of political meetings—especially of state governors—that had been held at White Sulphur Springs since the late nineteenth century. It was subsequently followed by two Southern Governors' Conferences (the latter, in 1963, being of interest in that a group of Civil Rights protesters gathered outside the front gate, a singular occurrence in the history of The Greenbrier), a special interim meeting of the National Governors' Conference, and in May of 1972 a meeting of the Republican Governors. At these and other political gatherings, some of the most prominent names in American politics enjoyed the hospitality of The Greenbrier, among them Everett Dirksen, Robert F. Kennedy, Nelson Rockefeller, Robert Byrd, Sam Ervin, Earl Warren, George Wallace, Eugene McCarthy, and Jacob Javits. At governors' conferences, later Presidents Jimmy Carter and Ronald Reagan occupied the same suite just two weeks apart from one another.

Indian Prime Minister Nehru in October, 1949.

Secretary of State Dean Acheson addressing the 1950 Governor's Conference.

President Eisenhower, accompanied by his brother Milton, arriving by train for the North American Summit Conference on March 26, 1956.

Sam Snead took a break from the PGA Tour to return home to The Greenbrier for a round of golf with President Eisenhower before the opening of the Conference.

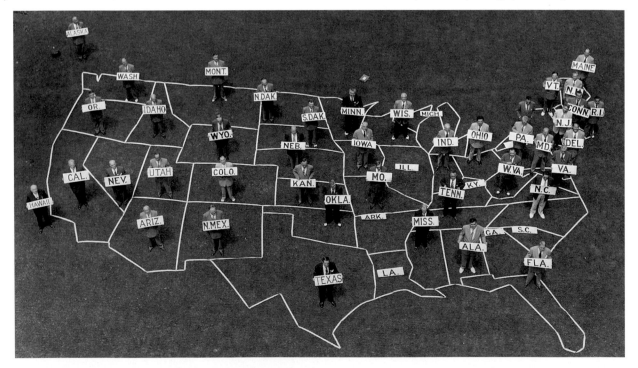

This remarkable photograph of the 45 governors attending the June 1950 Governors Conference appeared in Life magazine. The giant map (36 by 60 feet) was made of tape by Greenbrier engineers. (Photograph by Hank Walker, courtesy Life magazine.)

The most important post-war government meeting at The Greenbrier, however, was the North American Summit Conference, hosted in March, 1956, by President Dwight D. Eisenhower. For this much-publicized event, the president of Mexico, Adolfo Cortines, and the prime minister of Canada, Louis St. Laurent, traveled to White Sulphur Springs to engage in a series of informal discussions covering a wide range of international issues. The most unique feature of the summit was the lack of any rigidly scheduled agenda. Instead, the heads of state met in easy chairs in the drawing room of the Presidential Suite to practice what journalists called "armchair diplomacy." As the president described the meeting, he was "asking two neighbors to drop in for dinner." For most of the sessions only the leaders of the three nations were present, plus the respective foreign ministers, in-cluding Canadian Secretary of State for External Affairs, Lester Pearson, and U.S. Secretary of State John Foster Dulles.

President Eisenhower arrived by train at The Greenbrier earlier than the other guests so he could get in a round of golf before the conference began. Braving chilly March weather with temperatures barely reaching into the thirties, the president shot a ninety-three on the Old White Course. It was one of his first times out on the links since his heart attack six months before. The President complained to Sam Snead that his golf game was suffering from his restricted backswing; that it was even causing him to lose sleep. Snead's advice, it seems, went directly to the point: "Stick your butt out more, Mr. President," he said. Though some of the Secret Service agents standing by were shocked, the President just blinked and said, "I thought it *was* out." But not far enough, in Snead's opinion, for good balance.

The official party at the 1956 Summit Conference. To the right of President Eisenhower is Louis St. Laurent, the prime minister of Canada, next is Lester Pearson, secretary of state for external affairs of Canada. To the left of Eisenhower is Adolfo Cortines, the president of Mexico and next to him, John Foster Dulles, the U.S. secretary of state.

Throughout the three-day affair the national leaders were treated to culinary specialities from all parts of the United States: Philadelphia brie cheese, Kentucky Bibb lettuce, Virginia ham, Key West green turtle soup, Carolina rice, Maine lobster, Maryland crabmeat, California pears, and brandied Georgia peaches. On the final evening of the conference, the State Dinner began with beluga caviar followed by Gulf Stream Poppano Rellano, Roast Pheasant en Voliere, and genuine Virginia ham with hearts of palm. Dessert courses were served with ornate flower baskets made of pulled sugar. And at a luncheon in the Golf Clubhouse, the centerpiece was a figure of President Eisenhower, sculpted from styrofoam, demonstrating a powerful golf swing. Secretary of State Dulles told The Greenbrier's Executive Food Director that although he had traveled the world over, he had never witnessed anything to surpass such fine culinary service. "It was a houseparty in a delightful mountain resort," reported the *Christian Science Monitor*, "the principal purpose being to develop bonds of friendship between the leaders of these three countries. Mr. Eisenhower seems to have found just the environment he wants." The *Monitor* proposed that The Greenbrier serve as the location of a new White House annex; indeed, during the conference some may have believed this was the case, because hotel telephone operators answered all incoming calls "Good Morning, Greenbrier White House."

All of the U.S. Presidents from Eisenhower through Bill Clinton have visited The Greenbrier, but each before he began his White House term of office. In June of 1958, ten years after he and his family had attended the gala reopening party, John F. Kennedy returned, this time to deliver an address on international trade. In October of 1963, President Kennedy's press secretary, Pierre

Salinger, took the train from Washington's Union Station to White Sulphur Springs, ostensibly to relax and play some golf with Sam Snead. However, before the vacation ended, a serious plan evolved for The Greenbrier to serve as the site for a February, 1964, meeting between President Kennedy and French President Charles De Gaulle. Salinger returned to Washington with a proposal that President De Gaulle and his party occupy the State Suite, President Kennedy and American officials the Presidential Suite, and that official talks be held in the Crystal Room, midway between the suites. Of course, due to President Kennedy's assassination a few weeks after Salinger's visit, the French-American meeting was never to happen.

Richard Nixon was a frequent guest at The Greenbrier during his two terms as vice-president. He and his family spent Memorial Day weekends at the resort five times between 1953 and 1958, usually staying in Top Notch cottage. The vice-president, often accompanied by the then Deputy Attorney General and later Secretary of State William P. Rogers, always included a few rounds of golf with Sam Snead during his visits. On one occasion Mr. Nixon shot a respectable eighty-eight, while Snead fired an even more respectable sixty-one.

Lyndon Johnson was a guest at The Greenbrier, too. Senator and Mrs. Johnson arrived on June 30, 1950, and while being escorted to their cottage in South Carolina Row, Mr. Johnson remarked that visiting The Greenbrier was "just like coming home to Texas." Vice-President Johnson attended a meeting in White Sulphur Springs in May of 1961 and later came within an hour of a presidential visit in 1966, but his trip was canceled at the last moment. Years earlier, in October of 1940, Representative Lyndon Johnson had spent a week at The Greenbrier, and during that visit he met with an influential Aus-

A magazine advertisement for the 1956 Cadillac set in front of The Greenbrier's main entrance.

During one of his frequent trips to The Greenbrier, Vice-President Hubert Humphrey teamed up with West Virginia Governor Hulett C. Smith for a round of golf.

tin, Texas, businessman, who made him a lucrative offer, a partnership in an oil drilling firm. That encounter between the thirty-two-year-old Congressman and his potential partner is the opening vignette in Robert A. Caro's biography of Johnson, *The Path to Power.* As Caro tells the story, the two men discussed the proposal while sitting on the lawn in front of their cottage, while a friend of Johnson's observed. The friend was puzzled when Johnson politely yet firmly declined the partnership, explaining that if the public knew he had oil interests it would kill him politically. But the friend knew quite well that being an oilman had never hurt a politician in Texas. He wondered what office Johnson had in mind. Only then did George Brown, Johnson's friend and close associate, realize that Johnson's ambitions went further than becoming the U.S. Senator from Texas. To Brown, ruminating later on their conversation that day, it was suddenly clear that the young politician with just over three years of experience in the House of Representatives, the man so poor that he had just bought his first properly fitting suit, was already calculating his path to the presidency of the United States.

Although Lyndon Johnson never visited The Greenbrier while president, during his administration a part of The Greenbrier traveled to the White House. The wedding cake for the December 9, 1967, marriage of Presi-

dent Johnson's daughter, Lynda Bird, to Captain Charles S. Robb was created at The Greenbrier by the resort's renowned pastry chef, Clement Maggia. The two-hundred-dred-fifty-pound, five-tier, six-foot cake was made from an old-fashioned recipe and then decorated by Maggia with icing scrolls, pulled sugar roses, love birds, and lace work. It was carefully transported to the White House, the two larger lower tiers in a private truck and the three smaller tiers in a station wagon. Mr. Maggia, however, never saw the delighted faces of the wedding guests because he died a few days before the wedding, and The Greenbrier's young pastry expert, Eric Crane, assembled Maggia's masterpiece in Washington for the ceremony.

Gerald Ford attended a conference of bankers at The Greenbrier while Vice-President; he had visited many times as a member of the House of Representatives. Jimmy Carter participated in several meetings while Governor of Georgia and Ronald Reagan traveled from California for the 1972 Republican Governors' Conference at The Greenbrier. In 1983, George Bush discussed economic policy with the American Bankers Association. Bill Clinton was a Greenbrier guest in 1985 and 1989, both times speaking to groups as the Governor of Arkansas.

Presidential hopefuls also visited The Greenbrier. During his 1962 stay, Senator Barry Goldwater wrote in the VIP Register: "This small touch of heaven gets us through the rest of the year." Of all the prominent postwar political figures to visit The Greenbrier, perhaps the most frequent guest was Hubert Humphrey. Between 1957 and 1973, Humphrey registered no less than fifteen times. Many of these visits were personal vacations, though some, like the trip he made in November of 1965 to meet with the prime minister of Sweden, Tage Erlander, were for informal talks. During one such visit, Vice-President Humphrey is said to have decided he wanted to go turkey hunting, which was not exactly a routine request. But since this was the vice-president of the United States and a particularly valued guest, a guide was hired to take Humphrey off into the woods in search of game. As the day wore on, it seemed that the distinguished hunter was repeatedly missing his mark; it looked as if the foray would yield no results. Then, in a last ditch effort, some members of The Greenbrier's staff managed to enlist a rather old and slow turkey from a nearby farm and quietly let it loose in front of the vice-president. He missed. The turkey was rounded up and discreetly unleashed again. Another miss. Finally, on the third try, Humphrey hit his mark and tramped back to the State Suite thrilled with the day's outing.

Of course the list of well-known visitors to The Greenbrier in the 1950s and 1960s went beyond the names of

Debbie Reynolds and Eddie Fisher during their 1955 honeymoon.

national political figures. Other names tucked away in the hotel files included Johnny Carson, Joan Crawford, Steve Allen, Phil Silvers, Claudette Colbert, Dr. Norman Vincent Peale, Rudi Vallee, Art Buchwald, Lou Groza, Dr. Jonas Salk, and Ray Bolger. Bob Hope is said to have shot his best round of golf at The Greenbrier. Debbie Reynolds and Eddie Fisher spent part of their 1955 honeymoon at the resort. Radio commentator Paul Harvey occasionally broadcast his programs from the parlor of Top Notch cottage and once joined the Reverend Billy Graham for a round of golf. General and Mrs. Mark Clark visited in 1954, and in an interview Clark revealed that he had also come to White Sulphur Springs in 1943 for secret meetings at Ashford General Hospital. Colonel Harland Sanders, of Kentucky of course, told a newspaper writer that he had come to The Greenbrier "to show upstarts from neighboring states how a mint julep is really made." Princess Grace and Prince Rainier of Monaco arrived in the spring of 1963 with their children for a private family vacation. Since it was not an official state visit, there were no formal functions, press coverage, or security agents, and the Prince and Princess were therefore able to spend a few quiet days to themselves.

But one of the more unusual meetings to have taken place at The Greenbrier was that between Cleveland businessman, Cyrus Eaton, and the Soviet ambassador to the United States, Mikhail Menshikov. Eaton had taken over as chairman of the board of the Chesapeake and Ohio Railway in 1954 when Robert R. Young left to head the New York Central Railroad. At a rather posh dinner in the Presidential Suite in 1959, the American businessman and the Russian ambassador exchanged toasts to their differing national economic systems, first to capitalism, and then to communism. However, Mrs. Eaton surprised the group by proposing one additional toast—to all the people in the world who believe in neither. After a moment's hesitation, everyone at the dinner table cheerfully joined in. Later, Cyrus Eaton wryly explained why he chose White Sulphur Springs as an appropriate place to meet a Soviet ambassador: "The Greenbrier makes a favorable impression on Communists," he said, "because it is probably the most capitalistic spot in America."

Certainly the C&O Chairman spoke with authority on the subject. As one of the most important business figures in twentieth century America, he knew all there was to know about the inner workings of American capitalism. Eaton also knew the time-honored role of The Greenbrier in hosting the best and brightest of

Princess Grace and Prince Rainier with their children, Albert and Caroline in April, 1963.

C&O Chairman of the Board Cyrus Eaton (right) welcoming Soviet Ambassador Mikhail Menshikov in May, 1959.

The Rev. Billy Graham (second from right) and broadcaster Paul Harvey (far left) made up a foursome with Greenbrier President Truman Wright (left) and Resident Manager Wes Keenan in September 1967.

America's corporate life, an unbroken tradition that had begun in the nineteenth century. In the 1950s and 1960s, The Greenbrier advertised itself as "America's Informal Business Capitol," and in the 1980s one writer described the resort as an "alternate Camp David for America's permanent government."

Given the reality of hotel economics in the post World War II era, it had become clear that establishments of over a few hundred rooms could no longer continue to exist without larger business meetings. When Truman Wright assumed the position of Managing Director of The Greenbrier in 1952 he was well aware of the economic forces shaping the destiny of resorts. There was, however, little space within the hotel designed specifically to accommodate the needs of expanded business conferences, a common situation throughout the industry in the 1950s. Even Dorothy Draper's major redecoration after the closing of Ashford General Hospital had not significantly changed the amount of meeting space at The Greenbrier. Therefore, in May of 1953 work began on a new conference wing after several crucial decisions were made to preserve the grand and historic ambience of The Greenbrier. First, it was agreed that the conference area—consisting of the Chesapeake Room with a theatre below and smaller meeting rooms above—would be a self-contained unit so that the bustle of conferences would not disturb the quiet elegance of the lobbies, dining rooms, and shops. Second, the Cleveland architectural firm of Small, Smith and Reeb was commissioned to design the addition; the same firm that had successfully blended the North and Virginia Wings into the original hotel's Georgian style in 1930. And third, Dorothy Draper was invited to continue her famous Greenbrier style throughout the new conference rooms, banquet hall and movie theatre.

Construction of the West Wing went on for over a year. Due to delays in the arrival of equipment, the wing was not completed on time, and the management was faced with the difficult problem of denying clients who were prepared to use the facilities. It was becoming the kind of situation that caused the hotel managers long sleepless nights. Fortunately, however, The Greenbrier's chief engineer came up with an ingenious solution. In a brilliant move, he converted the indoor swimming pool into a temporary meeting room. The pool was drained, a floor was built to cover the yawning gap where the water had been, and then a carpet was added as were chairs from other areas of the hotel. As a result, an entirely new meeting space was available when hundreds of General Motors executives arrived several days later.

Over the years, the number and size of conferences has increased, but more importantly, meetings have become much more complex, demanding a level of pro-

Hermann Rusch (above) had an incalculable impact on food service at The Greenbrier. As Executive Food Director from 1955 to 1978 he not only supervised the daily operation of the kitchen staff but established The Greenbrier's Culinary Apprenticeship Program. For decades he was associated with the U.S. Olympic Committee, as the U.S. team's supervising chef and later as Chairman of Food and Housing. He often ended his presentations to culinarians with a phrase synonymous with his style and example: "Cooking is an art, a noble science. Cooks are ladies and gentlemen." Bottom photo: In 1956 Hermann Rusch made the original selections for The Greenbrier's famous Gold Service Dinner. Charleston Gazette food writer Delmar Robinson described the Gold Service at The Greenbrier as "a great resort at its golden best."

fessionalism on the part of the hotel staff and meeting planners that barely existed in the 1950s. Much of The Greenbrier's success has been due to the fact that the stately resort has accommodated the business community without losing the storied qualities of the past. Since the mid-1950s, approximately seventy percent of The Greenbrier's guests each year attend meetings, in groups as small as half a dozen and as large as one thousand. Today it is not unusual to see associations return annually, as they have done for forty, fifty, sixty years or more. For many American industries and firms, the annual meeting at The Greenbrier is an established tradition thoroughly entwined with the history of their enterprise.

Still, White Sulphur Springs has continued to be known as a social and recreational resort. Improvements in these areas have kept pace with the expansion of conference facilities. Indeed, the soil excavated from the site of the West Wing was used for the foundation of a new Gun Club overlooking the resort on Kate's Mountain. Further up the mountain a new Kate's Mountain Lodge was built—replacing the log-constructed lodge that dated from 1918—a popular spot for private, informal dinners because of its commanding view of the countryside. In 1956 The Greenbrier's engineers installed an outdoor swimming pool, a task that proved extremely delicate because the pool was designed to sit directly over a number of underground tributaries feeding the ancient spring of sulphur water. The artist's colony of the prewar years was revived in the mid-1950s when Alabama Row was restored for The Greenbrier's Arts and Crafts colony. The tiny Dollhouse, which has graced the grounds since 1919, reopened to delight children and adults alike. The Presidents' Cottage Museum was also restored and then furnished with antiques from the prewar Greenbrier, as well as additional antiques purchased in New York and London. The historical documents, photographs and memorabilia exhibited in the Museum had, until then, been well cared for in a museum in nearby Lewisburg. Appropriately enough, the Presidents' Cottage Museum opened again in 1958, the centennial of the Old White Hotel's opening.

Complementing all of the attention to new construction and historic buildings was a decision that bore more directly upon a guest's stay at the resort. When Hermann Rusch was appointed Executive Food Director in 1955, The Greenbrier could boast that its food service was managed by one of the finest chefs in the world. Rusch, a native of Switzerland, guided the preparation of meals at the resort for twenty-two years and won countless awards, both for himself and The Greenbrier. In 1957, he inaugurated a unique Culinary Training Program to give American chefs the expertise that had previously only been taught to Europeans. Rusch's demanding course, combining practical on-the-job training with classroom instruction, became the model for subsequent programs across the nation. "One of the greatest advantages of training at The Greenbrier," wrote *Washington Post* food critic William Rice, "is that the young cooks are working at the craft day in and day out, not merely learning in an academic setting . . . Meals are done in the grand style and there is an enormous amount of banquet activity, thus making tasks such as canape and buffet platter decoration or tallow and ice carving part of the normal training." The Culinary Training Program, which continues today, involves a minimum of two years of apprenticeship, depending upon the experience of each student.

Carleton Varney, president of the Dorothy Draper Company.

On another front, in the mid-1960s Dorothy Draper retired after a remarkable career and a twenty-year association with The Greenbrier. A few years earlier, Carleton Varney, a native of Boston, had joined her firm and immersed himself in her style. (He would eventually purchase her company after her death in 1969.) Understandably, Varney approached both his new position and Dorothy Draper herself with awe. Indeed, he soon found that she hadn't been called "Her Serene Highness, the Queen of Interior Design" for lack of either ideas or

The first room Carleton Varney decorated at The Greenbrier was the Crystal Dining Room, shown here in during a 1962 Christmas Gold Service dinner party hosted by C&O Railway President Walter Tuohy. (Of the three gentlemen in the front row, Mr. Tuohy is on the right.)

personality. It was therefore with great anticipation that he and Dorothy Draper rode the train down from New York in1960 to visit her most famous creation. "My first look at The Greenbrier staggered me," he recalled, "I had never seen a building quite that enormous, quite that grand. It was everyone's fantasy Georgian antebellum mansion, the one everyone dreams of occupying, from which women emerge as Scarlett O'Hara and men stride through the library as Rhett Butler. This was the realization of that dream of the Old South, and Mrs. Draper had, with her usual sweeping statement, added a few more layers of glamour. The place had room after room of the most beautiful spaces I have ever seen."

Carleton Varney's work at The Greenbrier began just as the West Virginia Wing neared completion. He decided to continue Dorothy Draper's famous Greenbrier motifs in the new wing, specifically the rhododendron wallpaper and apple-green doors in the corridors, and then he individually decorated the eighty-eight new guest rooms. The highlight of the wing is the State Suite with its four large bedrooms and a princely parlor that together create an effect rivaling the imposing Presidential Suite. The first party to stay in the State Suite was Senator Barry Goldwater and his family in May 1962.

The three million dollar West Virginia Wing was the last addition to The Greenbrier designed by the Cleveland architectural firm of Small, Smith and Reeb. They produced a facade for the new structure which echoed their classic lines on the Virginia Wing (which in turn had evoked the front porch of George Washington's home, Mount Vernon). One floor would be devoted to

the facilities of The Greenbrier Clinic which had succeeded far beyond expectations. In its first year, less than fifty examinations were completed in the Clinic, but by the early 1960s that number approached 2,500 annually creating a desperate need for more space in the old location above the indoor pool. In the new quarters equipped with the latest technology Dr. James P. Baker and his associates continued to practice their philosophy of preventive medicine as they had since he founded the Clinic. "We encourage the patient to discuss his or her symptoms, if any, and to talk about their health habits and worries," Dr. Baker said. "This usually gives the key to what examinations are necessary." This style of personal attention from each physician has been one of the defining characteristics of The Greenbrier Clinic ever since.

The new wing included an Exhibit Hall plus two new meeting rooms, called Governor's Hall and the Mountaineer Room, and The Greenbrier promoted this Exhibit Center as part of its increasing commitment to conference business. Thirty years later The Washington *Post* revealed that there was considerably more to the story. This Exhibit Center was in fact part of a huge underground bunker built by the federal government for the wartime relocation of the United States Congress. The publicly acknowledged conference facilities constituted 22,000 square feet of space, but behind the walls were another 90,000 square feet of Congressional bunker, every square inch of which was part of a classified project not seen by the public until 1995. Even the unclassified areas had a purpose behind ostensible Greenbrier conference uses—in case of war, the Senate and the House

Dr. James P. Baker was the Medical Director of The Greenbrier Clinic from its opening in 1948 until his retirement in 1973. A unique diagnostic and preventive health facility, The Greenbrier Clinic's approach to health care is characterized by the professionalism of its staff as well as a high level of individual attention from each physician.

of Representatives would gather in the Exhibit Center for emergency legislative sessions. The complete story of this secret emergency relocation center will be covered in the next chapter.

The April 1963 issue of *Town and Country* magazine described The Greenbrier as "the pearl of American resorts." The magazine compared it to the great French estates of the Loire Valley: "No private residence exists anywhere in the United States where a man can entertain hundreds of guests, as did the kings and nobles of France. However, the industrial aristocracy of the United States entertains at 20th century Greenbrier. So extensive are the grounds that 1,200 guests seem no more than a good-sized gay country house party."

In contrast to that kind of huge house party, a small meeting of railroad executives at The Greenbrier in the summer of 1961 produced substantial changes in that industry. Mergers between Eastern railroads were being heatedly discussed at that time because the railroads' century-old monopoly on long distance transportation in the United States had been permanently undercut by the advent of interstate highways and transcontinental airlines. In addition, the late 1950s recession hit

the railroad industry particularly hard, leading to the Greenbrier conference. In one merger, The Greenbrier's owner, the Chesapeake and Ohio (C&O), combined with the Baltimore and Ohio (B&O) to establish a new company that eventually took a new name, the Chessie System. ("Chessie" was the famous sleeping cat used for forty years as the C&O Railway's advertising symbol and pictured on thousands of calenders promoting the notion that passengers might "Sleep Like a Kitten on the C&O.")

The Greenbrier became a subsidiary of the Chessie System even though railroad ridership plunged dramatically in the 1960s with each new mile of interstate highway and each new airport. This decline in passenger service challenged one of the fundamental assumptions underpinning the railroad's ownership of the resort, namely, that The Greenbrier meshed perfectly with passenger traffic marketing. Despite this, the resort adapted to changing transportation patterns. Beginning in January 1965, the construction of Interstate 64 directly by White Sulphur Springs encouraged much more automobile traffic. In addition, The Greenbrier worked closely with local and Federal Aviation Administration officials to develop the Greenbrier Valley Airport about ten miles away near Lewisburg, which opened in June 1968. This 6,000 foot runway (later expanded to 7,000 feet) tied the resort into the nation's rapidly growing air

One of the most successful corporate symbols in American history, Chessie the sleeping cat was associated with the C&O Railway for decades. This memorable image is from a 1956 calender. When the C&O affiliated with the nation's oldest railroad, the Baltimore and Ohio, the combined roads took the cat's name for their new holding company, the Chessie System.

Greenbrier Valley Airport, ten miles west of The Greenbrier near Lewisburg, WV, opened in June 1968 and brought the resort into the Jet Age. It is pictured here on a busy June day with commercial aircraft and corporate jets. © Grubb Photo

transportation network, critically important for commercial service as well as corporate jets and charter flights. It is no coincidence that the new airport also improved plans for the wartime evacuation and relocation of Congress to the bunker under the West Virginia Wing.

By the early 1970s the Chairman of the Chessie System, Hays T. Watkins, felt it was time to take a close look at The Greenbrier's future because the railroad's passenger service had been turned over to Amtrak and the resort's revenues were not commensurate with Chessie's investment. That investment grew in 1973 with the construction of Colonial Hall, the hotel's largest banquet and meeting space, and the addition of the Hilltop tennis complex, consisting of ten new outdoor courts and a Tennis Club. With investment rising and revenues flat, Mr. Watkins brought in the consulting firm of Booz, Allen and Hamilton to study The Greenbrier's operations and submit recommendations for improvements. The consultants were instructed to consider all options, including leasing to a management company, retaining the property with a new operating strategy or selling it. (Selling the resort would have been complicated by the bunker. Any sale

would have had to be conducted in consultation with the federal government.) Looking back, Mr. Watkins' reassessment of The Greenbrier turned out to be a pivotal moment in the resort's history, as significant as the C&O purchase of the resort in 1910, the expansion of 1930 or the postwar Dorothy Draper redecoration.

In the end, Mr. Watkins decided to continue Chessie System ownership and bring in new management under the leadership of John S. Lanahan. Mr. Lanahan replaced E. Truman Wright, who had guided the fortunes of the White Sulphur Springs resort longer than anyone since the days of the Calwell family over a century earlier. For twenty-three years Truman Wright had personally embodied the traditions and standards of The Greenbrier. The task for John Lanahan was to preserve the resort's legendary tranquil charm yet remain versatile enough to attract new guests, especially a younger generation of guests.

Tennis was a booming preoccupation with younger guests in the mid-1970s. To serve them, The Greenbrier's new Hilltop facility increased the total number of available courts, but all of them were outdoors. One part of the new strategy, however, was to focus on building up the traditional off-season months (November through March) with year-round facilities. Therefore, crews excavated a site adjacent to the Golf Clubhouse for an immense new Indoor Tennis Center. This building is deceptively large because it contains not only five Dynaturf courts but two lower levels to store two hundred golf carts. The Tennis Center could easily have disrupted the sense of scale in the area—overshadowing the historic Springhouse and the Golf Clubhouse—had not designer Joseph Jakubowsky positioned it over a natural gully permitting it to set discreetly alongside its companions. The Center opened with a gala party on October 15, 1975 and for the next four years it was the site of annual Seniors tournaments, televised on PBS, featuring the top players in the game. As a result of these improvements, *Tennis Magazine* designated The Greenbrier one of the "Top 50 Greatest Tennis Resorts

in the United States," and in 1996 upgraded the resort to a Top 10 national ranking.

Mr. Lanahan then turned his attention to the historic cottages because they were the logical location for guest room expansion. In the late 1970s a concerted effort began to upgrade the larger units into guest houses after years of use as staff residences. This project continued over fifteen years and eventually transformed the cottages into some of the finest accommodations at The Greenbrier. As a result, these multi-bedroom units feature a large parlor or dining room, a private bath adjoins every bedroom and Carleton Varney's distinctive Greenbrier decor enlivens all the guest houses. They have become popular locations for family holiday reunions, small social group gatherings and business entertaining. Top Notch cottage was extensively rebuilt and enlarged making it as desirable as a premier suite in the hotel. In addition to these renovations, a new guest

The largest meeting room and banquet hall at The Greenbrier is Colonial Hall. It is the site of the New Year's Eve Gala as well as banquets like this one throughout the year.

In this photograph from the late 1970s, the Indoor Tennis Center (left) clusters with the older courts in front of the Golf Club. Between the tennis building and the clubhouse is the first tee of the Old White Course.

house with an extraordinary view was built alongside the first fairway of The Greenbrier Course. Completed in 1976, the four bedroom Valley View Estate House sits on the hill occupied by Wolf Row (the lair of the bachelors!) a century and a half earlier. It is a favorite for small groups seeking seclusion and quick access to golf.

A more substantial challenge was the renovation of Paradise Row, the oldest on the grounds, because it consisted of interconnected single rooms, each much too small by today's standards. The solution was to retain the brick walls dating from the 1830s and within that space create parlors with a bathroom, wet bar and fireplace. In 1981 new large bedrooms and full baths were added directly behind each parlor. Anticipating the popularity of small suites in hotels, these fifteen one bedroom suites offer particularly spacious accommodations for couples in what were once honeymoon quarters.

Since the opening of the Old White Course in 1913, golf has been the number one sporting activity at The Greenbrier. One of the most dramatic improvements to Greenbrier golf began in the summer of 1976 when Jack Nicklaus arrived to rebuild The Greenbrier Course. Over the next twenty-two months every hole on the course, which opened in 1924, was remodeled: all eighteen greens were rebuilt, a new two and a half acre lake added another dimension to the 2nd, 16th and 17th holes, traps around the greens were widened and deepened while new fairway bunkers brought the number of bunkers to forty-four. Par increased from 70 to 72 and the overall length of the course stretched to 6,721 yards from the championship tees. Upon completion, John Lanahan

remarked, "We asked Jack to do the impossible. We wanted him to create a championship course from the blue tees and a weekend course from the whites. We think he's done just that."

Jack Nicklaus returned to The Greenbrier over the 1978 Memorial Day weekend to dedicate the new course. Asked to describe his course, he responded, "We feel that golf should be a visible game. A player should be able to recognize the challenge from the tee or landing area. The visibility also provides memorable views and high aesthetic value and that's what we believe we have accomplished here." Playing the dedication round in fine form (after all, this was the year he won his third British Open), Nicklaus shot one under par. About one thousand local golf fans formed an enthusiastic gallery to watch him team up with baseball Hall of Famer Joe DiMaggio who shot "somewhere in the low to mid-80s" and was quick to note that he out drove Nicklaus on three holes.

The Greenbrier commissioned Jack Nicklaus with a specific goal in mind: to provide challenging championship conditions for the 1979 International Ryder Cup Matches. Since 1927 British and American professional teams had competed for national pride and the Ryder Cup trophy on a biennial basis, but at The Greenbrier ranking European players for the first time joined the British team. The change was made to improve the competition between the two teams because the United States had dominated the series—winning all but three of the previous twenty-two matches, with one tie.

Top Notch Estate House. This "cottage" was built in 1912 as the summer home of George Stevens, the President of the C&O Railway, but was substantially enlarged in the mid-1970s. The top photograph shows the living room as it looks today.

Looking down on the new lake created by Jack Nicklaus during the rebuilding of The Greenbrier Course.

Seve Ballesteros of Spain added excitement to the 1979 British/European team. He was then a twenty-two year old phenomenon who had won his first major tournament, the British Open, a few months earlier. His teammates included Nick Faldo, Sandy Lyle, Mark James, Peter Oosterhuis, Bernard Gallacher, Tony Jacklin and captain John Jacobs. They were, however, no match for a powerhouse American team featuring Lee Trevino, Fuzzy Zoeller, Lee Elder, Hubert Green, Lanny Wadkins, Gil Morgan, Hale Irwin, Tom Kite and captained by Ryder Cup veteran Billy Casper. (Tom Watson withdrew from the team during practice rounds to join his wife when she delivered their first child.) Although the American team won, it was, in the words of one British newspaper, "No Easy Ryder." At the end of the second of three days, the U.S. team held a slender one point lead and early in the final day's play the two teams were even. The last day featured the kind of fascinating singles match-ups that highlight international competition: Nick Faldo versus Lee Elder, Sandy Lyle versus Lee Trevino, Tom Kite versus Tony Jacklin. On a sunny September afternoon millions of golf fans watched the last round on ABC television as the American team pulled ahead to another victory.

Senior PGA Tour officials took note of the new Greenbrier Course and in 1985 a series of three Senior competitions began on the Nicklaus course. The first American Express-sponsored tournament belonged to Don January, who dominated the Senior Tour in the mid-1980s. He beat Lee Elder by two, scoring 70-64-66. Pro Jimmy Powell grabbed the headlines, setting the Greenbrier Course record by firing a first round 62. Don January came back the next July to win again, this time beating Jim Ferree in a playoff while Miller Barber and Lee Elder

Jack Nicklaus completely redesigned The Greenbrier Course for championship play. Here he is teeing off on Number 6 during the dedication round in May 1978.

The 1979 International Ryder Cup Matches

The victorious American team, with captain Billy Casper in foreground holding the Ryder Cup trophy. From left to right: Mark Hayes, Larry Nelson, Lee Trevino, Fuzzy Zoeller, Lee Elder, Hubert Green, John Mahaffey, Lanny Wadkins, Gil Morgan, Hale Irwin, Tom Kite, Andy Bean.

The British/European team, from left to right: Tony Jacklin, Sandy Lyle, Mark James, Ken Brown, Peter Oosterhuis, Nick Faldo, John Jacobs (captain), Mike King, Brian Barnes, Seve Ballesteros, Antonio Garrido, Bernard Gallacher, Des Smith.

Above: Don January won consecutive PGA Senior Tour tournaments on The Greenbrier Course in 1985 and 1986. Below: Arnold Palmer keeping an eye on the path of his shot on The Greenbrier Course in July 1986

At the 1979 Ryder Cup. Lee Trevino (top) was his usual highly entertaining self; Tom Kite (middle) and Seve Ballesteros (bottom) were playing in their first Ryder Cup Matches—they would face each other as Ryder Cup captains eighteen years later.

Former hostages arriving at The Greenbrier in April 1981, three months after their release following 444 days of captivity in Iran. At left, with a beard, is Richard Queen, in the yellow jacket carrying a briefcase is Bruce Laingen, the former Charge d'affaires at the U.S. Embassy in Tehran.

If Ryder Cup and Senior Tour competition kept golf fans' attention directed toward The Greenbrier, almost all Americans' attention turned to White Sulphur Springs in 1981 when diplomats and embassy personnel held hostage for over a year by extremists in Iran gathered at the resort for a State Department-sponsored reunion. Concerned about potential difficulties adjusting to everyday routines after the ordeal, the State Department brought the same medical team that met the hostages upon their release to The Greenbrier to conduct further individual and small group consultations. The former hostages appeared in great spirits and after formal sessions they took full advantage of the resort's facilities, fanning out with their families on bicycles, in carriages and on foot to the tennis courts, hiking trails, gun club and golf courses. As Time magazine quipped, "Tehran was never like this." One former hostage who could not attend chose to extend greetings to his friends by buzzing the Golf Clubhouse in a screaming F-14 jet fighter. In truth, by the time the former hostages arrived at The Greenbrier they seemed more wearied by the demands of being national celebrities than the after effects of months in captivity. Most expressed a strong desire to

tied for third. The galleries at that 1986 tournament delighted in the play of the popular Chi-Chi Rodriguez and the legendary Arnold Palmer. Australian Bruce Crampton jumped to a commanding lead in 1987 with ten birdies for an impressive first round 63 and didn't look back. He coasted to the championship with a 54-hole total of 200. That year Gary Player returned to The Greenbrier for the first time in many years and shot a very respectable final round 65, including a hole-in-one at the 17th. In general, these Senior competitions gave some participants a sense of returning to their youth because many had competed in the Sam Snead Festivals of the 1950s and 1960s. This was the case not only for Palmer, Player and Crampton, but also for Dow Finsterwald, Peter Thomson, Billy Casper, Julius Boros, Mike Souchak and Dave Marr.

The Greenbrier is owned by the CSX Corporation, a railroad-based transportation company headquartered in Richmond, Virginia formed in 1980 by the merger of the Chessie System and the Seaboard Coast Lines.

In the late 1980s and early 1990s virtually all of the guest rooms in the hotel were rebuilt and upgraded. In some cases two rooms were combined creating a junior suite like the one shown above.

return to normal life and the medical team found them physically and emotionally ready to do so. Aware that this was their last organized gathering, the group appreciated quiet moments in a secluded setting with friends before going their separate ways.

The former hostages and their families were guests of the CSX Corporation, the current owner of The Greenbrier. CSX was formed on November 1, 1980 when the Chessie System merged with the Seaboard Coast Lines, a Florida-based railroad, and The Greenbrier became a wholly-owned unit of the new company. The name was derived by joining the "C" for Chessie to the "S" for Seaboard and adding "X" as the multiplier symbol because the new company would become more than the sum of its parts. This long-term ownership (at that point it had been seventy years since the initial C&O Railway purchase) has created an almost palpable aura of stability at The Greenbrier.

Shortly after the merger, Greenbrier president John Lanahan moved up to a position in the parent company with the satisfaction that his leadership had created a

financial foundation for the resort that was more sound than at any other period in its long history. In six years revenues had tripled. Just as important, generating more profit returned more investment to The Greenbrier. Lacking a debt load to service, long range strategy could focus upon sustained maintenance and expansion.

This was the objective of William C. Pitt, III, who rose from director of operations to president and managing director. As he took the helm, Mr. Pitt faced something new at The Greenbrier and that was competition on an unprecedented scale. The international resort industry expanded at a dizzying rate in the 1980s and much of that growth was concentrated in the luxury market. The competitive increase was especially intense in group business because companies and trade associations could now choose from more properties in more diverse locations.

In the face of this situation The Greenbrier could not afford to rest on its considerable laurels. The enemy of a property as extensive and historic as The Greenbrier is deferred maintenance, therefore a systematic and comprehensive upgrading began in 1984 with a two-phase refurbishment of the conference facilities. First, the meeting rooms already in place—named after presidents of the United States who have visited White Sulphur Springs—were rebuilt and totally redecorated by Carleton Varney. Then a two-story extension to the conference center added the McKinley, Hayes and Taft Rooms which are linked to the kitchen so they serve both as meeting rooms and as private dining rooms. Because the new wing is clearly visible through the windows of the Main Dining Rooms it was blended with particular care into the existing architecture.

As soon as the new wing opened, attention switched to upgrading the hotel's plumbing and wiring, in some ways a more troublesome and complex problem. This project demanded detailed coordination over three consecutive winter seasons because large sections of the building were closed off and workmen then crawled behind hundreds of walls and ceilings installing miles

The tranquility of a fresh snowfall at The Greenbrier.

Christmas at The Greenbrier means weaving seasonal decor into the established ambience of the stately lobbies.

of pipes and electrical equipment. The staggering maintenance costs at The Greenbrier are illustrated by this project: Dorothy Draper had totally redecorated the hotel's interior and refurnished its rooms in the late 1940s for nine million dollars—forty years later, in contrast, it took eight million dollars just to replace basic utilities. To keep this in perspective, this work was only half of a larger project to upgrade guest rooms. The second half was carried out between 1990 and 1994 when most hotel bathrooms were rebuilt with marble floors and walls and then fitted with new fixtures. Whenever renovation is undertaken at The Greenbrier consistency of quality is a critical consideration to ensure that the new work matches existing materials and styles. In this case that meant spending upwards of $17,000 per bathroom for hundreds of guest rooms. Once both projects were completed, it was but a slight overstatement to claim that all guest rooms were totally rebuilt over a ten year period.

Top photo: Governor and Mrs. Bill Clinton at a Greenbrier meeting of the Southern Regional Education Board in June 1985. At right is Kentucky Governor Martha Collins. Bottom: Chrysler Corporation Chairman Lee Iacocca at a press conference during a March 1985 meeting of Democratic members of the House of Representatives.

Perhaps the most significant change in visiting patterns in recent years has been the increasing number of people traveling to The Greenbrier in the winter months. For decades it was axiomatic that the resort was slow from November through March, but in the mid-1970s extensive holiday and weekend programs began attracting thousands of guests. Thanksgiving is sold-out frequently. In fact, Thanksgiving now competes with the Fourth of July for "busiest day of the year at The Greenbrier," with New Year's a close contender. Many families have established a tradition of annual gatherings at The Greenbrier for the Twelve Days of Christmas. Each December the hotel's lobbies and dining rooms undergo a miraculous transformation as the Director of Social Activities creates a spectacular Christmas environment and designs a series of holiday activities for all family members.

For five years in the 1980s the highlight of winter seasons was the Gillis Long Issues Conference, a meeting of Democratic members of the House of Representatives who traveled by special Amtrak train for weekend retreats. Each year the nineteen railroad cars of representatives and their families, legislative staffers, press members and sponsors arrived at the station and were greeted by a band as the days of tennis, children's activities, theme parties, and lots of political talk began. On each Saturday afternoon the keynote address featured such luminaries as entertainer Bill Cosby, Chrysler Chairman Lee Iacocca and New York governor Mario Cuomo. Bill Clinton and Hillary Rodham Clinton—in her role as President of the Children's Defense Fund—participated in panels during the 1988 meeting. (Republicans were not ignored: in 1989 The Greenbrier delivered ten thousand handmade chocolate truffles to George Bush's Presidential Inaugural Dinner.)

The Greenbrier's Cooking School is an off-season program that blossomed well beyond expectations. When classes began in January of 1978, it was the first resort cooking school in the United States. Julie Dannenbaum was the first director—she had founded Creative Cooking, Inc. in Philadelphia and then branched out to summer sessions at the Gritti Palace in Venice, Italy and winter sessions at The Greenbrier. When Julie Dannenbaum retired in 1991, Anne Willan introduced La Varenne at The Greenbrier based upon her cooking school in France. From the outset the Cooking School included home-grown talent, that is, the chefs who create The Greenbrier's renowned cuisine also teach classes, share recipes and demonstrate techniques perfected in the resort's kitchen. Both Anne Willan and the culinary staff draw from their international networks to bring in

Anne Willan (right), Director of La Varenne at The Greenbrier, posed with her friend Julia Child during a March 1997 cooking school session.

guest chefs, with Julia Child the perennial favorite. Walter Scheib, who moved from The Greenbrier to the White House in 1994, is also a visiting Cooking School chef.

After visiting The Greenbrier during a chilly March 1991 weekend Washington *Post* book critic Jonathan Yardley reported on his stay in *States of Mind: A Personal Journey Through the Mid-Atlantic.* He described enjoying the Indoor Pool, the Spa and the Main Dining Room

where, he noted, he and his wife were served by "a waiter who, like everyone else we'd encountered . . . had mastered the art of friendliness unencumbered by either servility or pomposity." Yardley saw the resort in the off-season and in bad weather, leading to an interesting observation: "A case can be made that precisely such conditions are the toughest and fairest test of a resort; if it can keep the customers happy when business is slow and the climate is inhospitable, it is doing its job. By such a test The Greenbrier proved itself admirably worthy."

In the spring of 1987 Ted Kleisner, a third-generation inn-keeper who had served as The Greenbrier's director of operations for four years in the early 1980s, returned to take the position of vice-president and managing director. He arrived just in time to oversee the construction of the six million dollar Mineral Bath and Spa Building adjacent to the Indoor Pool. (In classic Greenbrier fashion, each section of wall was immediately painted white as it went up so that the red brick would not distract from the main building.) The result is a new and luxurious facility for the oldest and most fundamental ritual at White Sulphur Springs, bathing in the mineral waters. It is a long way from "taking the waters" two hundred years ago to the opulence inside this building, but it is the same soothing water flowing from the same spring. To be sure new treatments and massages are continually added, however, the range of services includes two traditional and unique Greenbrier Spa treatments, the Scotch Spray and the Swiss Shower. Continuing these high-pressure water therapies, which prepare the skin for massage, required custom-designed equipment duplicating that which had been used in the old facility for seventy-five years.

Top: Spring Row wends its way across historic ground. Before the Civil War this was the site of Georgia Row, Young Bucks Row, the dining room and the original Spring Row, a series of log cabins built in 1810. The Hilltop Tennis Courts sit above Spring Row. Bottom: A Spring Row parlor.

The new Mineral Bath and Spa brings to mind the adage that "the more things change the more they remain the same." At The Greenbrier that translates into selecting changes and improvements that fit comfortably into the resort's established personality. Another example of this impulse is the construction of Spring Row, the first new guest house row built on the property since the Civil War. When completed in 1989, the units of Spring Row reflected the old Virginia vernacular architectural style of Paradise Row. (Mr. Kleisner, a veteran of Savannah, Georgia's restoration, made sure that historical continuity was not disrupted.) The name comes from its location on land occupied by a much earlier Spring Row, once the cottages closest to the sulphur spring. The new Spring Row consists of thirty-three one bedroom suites

The imposing facade of The Colonnade Estate House has remained virtually unchanged since 1838, making it the finest example of antebellum architecture at The Greenbrier. The interior of the building, however, was completely updated in 1989 and includes a dining room (below) grand enough to accommodate a 22-guest dinner party. Because President Martin Van Buren was a guest in this house, the china in The Colonnade is a reproduction of the pattern he used in the White House.

with either fine views of the central lawn or sweeping views of the golf courses. A croquet court blends into Spring Row, bringing back a sport that was a fixture of resort social life a century ago.

As the Spring Row project neared completion, restoration began on The Colonnade, the summer home of South Carolina planters Richard Singleton and Wade Hampton who had figured so prominently in the resort's early history. Because The Colonnade is the best preserved example of antebellum architecture on the property, special care was taken in its adaptive restoration into a three-bedroom guest house featuring two parlors and a private dining room seating twenty-four. The exterior of the structure, however, remains virtually the same as in 1838 when President Martin Van Buren visited the cottage to mingle with influential members of southern society.

For years the question was debated: if golf is the number one activity at The Greenbrier what is second? The answer, it seemed, had to be either tennis or riding. By the mid-1980s it was clear that the answer was neither of these, it was shopping. The first signs came with the rebirth of the Alabama Row Art Colony through an infusion of new craftspeople who created a series of attractive shops in the historic cottages. In conjunction with upgrading the adjacent Presidents' Cottage Museum, a neglected area of the resort once again became an engaging destination.

Up to that point, most shops in the hotel were owned and operated by individual concessionaires. That changed in 1986 when the barber shop space became available and it seemed reasonable to create a shop owned by The Greenbrier where all resort logo items could be sold in one location. To everyone's astonishment, The Greenbrier Shoppe generated $700,000 in sales in the first year and with that The Greenbrier jumped feet first into retail. But to do so meant expanding into an entirely new kind of business usually considered beyond the scope of a hotelier's concern. More specifically it meant establishing a new department within the resort's internal organization and acquiring a new range of sales skills.

As a result, by the mid-1990s the lower lobby corridor became a cozy village of alluring shops. Over a ten year period each shop was rebuilt, redecorated, restocked and developed its own individual personality. Some shops are tied to resort activities: The Greenbrier Gourmet, Kate's Mountain Outfitter's-Orvis, The Sam Snead Shop, the Swim Shop. The Carleton Varney Gift Shop is uniquely connected to The Greenbrier, bringing Carleton Varney's internationally-recognized style to guests who identify the resort with his flair. The Candy Maker is an example of moving out of the kitchen to a prime retail location and integrating candy manufacturing into a sales operation—you can watch them make the candy before you buy it.

Everyone seems to agree that moving the candy making operation from the kitchen to the shop corridor was a sensational idea.

Draper's Cafe is not only a versatile restaurant for breakfast, lunch and private dinners, it is a classic example of creating a unique Greenbrier venue by focusing upon a unique Greenbrier personality.

Draper's Cafe developed in the context of this lower lobby transformation. Prompted by the pressing need for a larger breakfast and lunch venue, this new restaurant evolved into an admiring tribute from Carleton Varney to his mentor, Dorothy Draper. Reproduced throughout are the colors, tones and stylish decorative adornments that Dorothy Draper introduced into interior decorating vocabulary. As a final touch before opening in 1990 the walls were covered in an aubergine because it is precisely the color she used in her New York City apartment.

Around the corner from Draper's is a shop dedicated to another personality who has loomed large in the twentieth century story of The Greenbrier, Sam Snead. In the Spring of 1993 The Greenbrier hired Sam Snead for the third time (the other times were in 1936 and 1948) and he returned as Golf Pro Emeritus to the resort where it all began for him. After an eighteen-year hiatus, the winningest player in the sport's history was back roaming his old home courses hitting in the seventies while he was in his eighties and regaling guests with tales from his remarkable career. During his forty years representing The Greenbrier, Snead won seven major titles, 81 official PGA tournaments and most of

Top: Two all-time greats in golf history, Tom Watson and Sam Snead, teamed up for a round on a beautiful day in May 1994. Bottom: Karsten Solheim and his wife, Louise, announced a 20 year agreement in 1990 to underwrite competition between the U.S. LPGA Tour and Europe's Women Professional Golfers' European Tour (WPGET). Here they pose with JoAnne Carner (left), U.S. captain and Mickey Walker (right) European captain.

The 1994 American Solheim Cup team celebrating their triumph. Top (L to R): Brandie Burton, Kelly Robbins, Captain JoAnne Carner, Michelle McGann (alternate), Donna Andrews, Beth Daniel, Meg Mallon, Patty Sheehan. Lower (L to R) Dottie Mochrie, Tammie Green, Sherri Steinhauer, Betsy King.

his 135 total victories. As Greenbrier President Ted Kleisner put it, "Sam Snead's name is synonymous with The Greenbrier, so it makes our reunion an especially satisfying occasion." For Sam it was like coming home. "It feels like I've never left," he told reporters. His keen eye for a profitable wager remained intact: "I always loved to get a pigeon who had a strong grip, a fast back swing, and a pocket full of money."

As soon as Sam reported back for duty it was time to revive the classic Sam Snead Festival of the 1950s and he was the center of attention at the first tournament in May 1994. But he moved to the sidelines that October, slipping into the gallery to follow the much-anticipated third Solheim Cup tournament. Solheim Cup competition began in 1990 when Karsten Solheim, founder and CEO of Karsten Manufacturing Company (the maker

of Ping golf equipment), agreed to underwrite a Ryder Cup-style tournament between teams of women professional golfers from the United States and Europe. After the first match, an overwhelming American victory, there was significant doubt that the Europeans could effectively compete in this format. That dramatically changed after the second tournament when the European team astounded the golf world with one of the great upsets of modern sports history. Sportswriters struggled for words strong enough to convey the magnitude of the American defeat: "startling!" "amazing!" "monumental!" At that moment tension began building for the Greenbrier rematch.

Mickey Walker returned in 1994 as the European captain with her star Laura Davies of England, considered the number one player in the world. The European

General Colin Powell paused for the photographer at the North Portico during his June 1994 visit to The Greenbrier.

team featured a number of contributors to the spectacular victory two years earlier: Helen Alfredsson, Catrin Nilsmark, Trish Johnson, Alison Nicholas, Pam Wright and Liselotte Neumann. The American captain, JoAnne Carner, voiced her team's determination to rebound when she told reporters, "I'm not going to guarantee a victory, but I will guarantee we aren't going to lose." Carner led a team strengthened by Solheim veterans Patty Sheehan, Beth Daniel, Betsy King and Dottie Mochrie.

In brilliant autumn weather the competition held tight on The Greenbrier Course during the first two days of alternate-shot and best-ball foursome play. At the end of day one Europe led 3–2, and at the end of day two the matches were even. But in the singles competition on the last day the American team displayed clear superiority, winning eight of ten matches. Dottie Mochrie and Brandie Burton were the stars for the U.S. team, the only ones to win all three of their matches. In their singles matches Mochrie beat Catrin Nilsmark and Burton overcame the formidable Laura Davies, 2 up. The final score, 13–7, made the American victory appear more lopsided than it was, but with it securely in place the

Waterford crystal Solheim Cup trophy returned to the United States. Because the matches were covered live on television both in the United States and in Europe for the first time, Beth Daniel's comment went right to the point: "Women's golf is the real winner this week."

As The Greenbrier moves into the twenty-first century, the interplay between past and present, between change and continuity, is as apparent as ever. The 1990s began with the National Park Service designating The Greenbrier a National Historic Landmark, meaning it possesses "exceptional value to the nation as a whole." While there are sixty thousand properties listed on the National Register of Historic Places, only two thousand of them are also identified as National Historic Landmarks—the distinction is the quality of national historical significance.

At the same time, activities at the resort expanded to cater to new guests and to families. These additional

The Hunt Club is a log cabin built in the early 1930s as The Greenbrier's first skeet and trapshooting site. It sits on a quiet spot along Howard's Creek about a mile downstream from the Golf Club. After a 1996 restoration, fishing and hunting outings now start at the cabin and its rustic interior is a prime location for private parties and dinners.

activities include white water rafting, cooking classes, the Falconry Academy, mountain biking, all of which appeal to those seeking to supplement golf and tennis. The decommissioning of the underground bunker in 1995 led to a popular program of guided tours through a remarkable facility that illustrates the Cold War's pervasiveness when as unlikely an institution as a luxury resort became part of emergency defense planning. The Greenbrier Wingshooting Preserve opened in 1996 affording sportsmen an opportunity to hunt pheasant, quail and chukar in a secluded natural environment. Creating the preserve entailed restoring a charming log structure along Howard's Creek, now known as the Hunt Club, offering a site for private parties and dinners. Shopping might be considered a nineties activity and opportunities expanded off property in 1996 when a Greenbrier Shoppe opened fifty miles west at Tamarack, the West Virginia arts center, and the Christmas Shop at the Depot transformed the 1930 train station. A distinctive recent trend has been the sharp increase in families vacationing at The Greenbrier, thus an expanded children's program, running at its peak in the summer and at holidays, makes it possible for parents to partake in the lengthening list of activities.

Of course none of this diminishes the importance of golf. Sam Snead's return to The Greenbrier provided the concept behind an extensive rebuilding of the Golf Clubhouse. The continuity of his Greenbrier career inspired a new interior. Over two winter seasons the building's inside was cleared out while the exterior was preserved; new locker rooms stretched through the downstairs and a new restaurant—Sam Snead's at The Golf Club—took shape upstairs. That restaurant segues into Slammin' Sammy's (a longtime moniker for Snead) which became

The official opening of Sam Snead's at the Golf Club occurred at a party celebrating Sam's 85th birthday. When asked who was the greatest golfer of all time, Sam calculated that he was; "Jack Nicklaus was second and Ben Hogan and Arnold Palmer fought for third." Inset: The exhibits on the Golf Clubhouse walls illustrate the impressive accomplishments of Sam Snead's career in fascinating detail. Among the scores of photographs, magazine covers, letters and newspaper clippings the one that captures the most attention is the collection of golf balls from Sam's 35 holes-in-one.

Congressional Luncheon
in honor of
George W. Bush
President of the United States

Colonial Hall
The Greenbrier
Friday, February 1, 2002

Congressional Dinner
Honored Guests
Vice President Dick Cheney
and Mrs. Lynne Cheney

Colonial Hall
The Greenbrier
Wednesday, January 30, 2002

Almost two hundred Republican Members of Congress gathered for a winter retreat at The Greenbrier from January 30 to February 1, 2002. President George W. Bush addressed the group's final luncheon. In the upper left photograph The Greenbrier's President Ted J. Kleisner (center) and General Manager Jack Damioli greet the President upon his arrival. Vice President Richard B. Cheney spoke at the dinner for members of the House of Representatives. The photograph of the Vice President at the top right was taken during an earlier Greenbrier visit in June 1994. In the center, Bono, the lead singer of the popular Irish band U2 and a participant in the retreat, strikes his rock star pose with The Greenbrier's Executive Chef, Peter Timmins, a fellow Dubliner.

the gathering place for food, beverages and late-night dancing. The entire Clubhouse is a showcase for an awesome collection of memorabilia documenting not only Sam Snead's career but the history of golf in America. In typical Greenbrier fashion, a new facility is given a distinctive personality by dipping into the resort's storied past and adapting it to today's uses. The refurbished Clubhouse opened on May 27, 1997, Sam Snead's 85th birthday. The event was celebrated with heartfelt toasts in the evening after Sam celebrated in the afternoon on the Old White Course by shooting a 78.

The Clubhouse project illustrates a larger issue for The Greenbrier at this point in its history: the ongoing effort to balance an imperative to change and grow on the one hand with a desire to conserve the resort's unique character on the other. Seen in the light of all that has gone before over the last two centuries, to dine at Sam Snead's at the Golf Club or gaze out from the Colonnade Estate House porch or surrender to the waters of the Mineral Bath and Spa is to sense that at The Greenbrier even what is new and clearly up-to-date is imbued with historical antecedents. That sense of heritage is an important component whenever the resort's managers and owners weigh decisions about the future. In turn this reflects the wishes of longtime guests as well as the deep spirit of tradition among The Greenbrier's eighteen hundred employees.

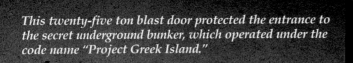

This twenty-five ton blast door protected the entrance to the secret underground bunker, which operated under the code name "Project Greek Island."

Project Greek Island

O n Friday, May 29, 1992 Greenbrier President Ted Kleisner called an unusual mix of staff members to his office for a meeting that none of those present will ever forget. "Today we are going to acknowledge," he announced, "a secret thirty-five year partnership with the United States government. This partnership is about to be disclosed in an upcoming article in the Washington *Post* which reveals the existence of an emergency relocation center, a bunker, on our property and describes the facility in such detail that we can no longer deny it." As staffers stared in stunned silence, Mr. Kleisner inserted a video tape into a VCR saying, "This message to the Board of Directors of CSX Corporation [the owner of The Greenbrier] will give you some background on this sensitive matter."

In the quiet room every eye was riveted on the screen where a man stood at a podium with a large official-looking emblem attached to the front. He spoke calmly and deliberately: "Welcome. Since the early 1950s the CSX Corporation and its predecessor organizations have been engaged in an extraordinary partnership with the Federal government—to assist in the preservation of our constitutional framework. This association has been one of this nation's most closely guarded secrets. Your possession of this video tape means that an event has occurred which has resulted in the public disclosure of this confidential relationship."

The event referred to was the impending *Post* article which was followed by an explosion of media coverage about the supersecret underground bunker. Certainly a dramatic story, headline-writers made the most of it: "Secret Underground Capitol Confirmed," "Wartime Hideaway Revealed," "The Secret Is Out! Bunker Was Ready In Case of Nuclear Attack." A Mississippi headline packed the most punch: "For Congress, Apocalypse Wow!" Another one invented a new name for The Greenbrier: "Hotel Armageddon."

The news was indeed mind-boggling. Underneath the stately five-star resort sat a huge concrete and steel bunker designed to house Congress in the event of a national crisis. Just as startling, the facility's existence had remained secret for a generation. But that ended with the *Washington Post Magazine's* lengthy article entitled "Last Resort: The Ultimate Congressional Hideaway." Writer Ted Gup had, over a period of years, pieced together the elements of a story that put thirty-five years of Greenbrier history into an entirely new light.

As the government official giving the CSX Board briefing explained, the story begins in the early 1950s when the ideological and military rivalry between the United States and the USSR intensified into what journalist Walter Lippmann named the "Cold War." The threat of war was substantially complicated by nuclear weapons—in 1953 both sides possessed atomic and

For three days in May 1992 newspapers and television networks reported the astonishing news that a secret wartime bunker for Congress was at The Greenbrier. The article breaking the story appeared in the Washington Post Magazine.

hydrogen bombs. In this context President Dwight D. Eisenhower and his advisors began planning what they called the "continuity of government" program. It appeared likely that Washington, D.C. would be a target and the destruction of the capital city would cripple both the nation's ability to defend itself and the ability of the three branches of government to carry out their obligations to the American people. The President's advisors believed some planning was needed to ensure that government might continue functioning in these dire circumstances. Those plans involved moving the various segments of government away from Washington and housing them in emergency relocation shelters.

The Office of Defense Mobilization, a unit of the Executive Office of the President, proposed the construction of a number of shelters within the "federal reloca-

tion arc," described by one official as "a series of facilities that runs in an arc from the District of Columbia to Pennsylvania, out to Virginia and West Virginia and south to North Carolina." While the President could plan for the executive branch, he could not impose such directions on the legislative branch. Therefore, in August 1955 President Eisenhower called the Congressional leadership to the White House and appealed directly to Speaker of the House Sam Rayburn, House Minority leader Joseph W. Martin, Jr., Senate Majority leader Lyndon B. Johnson and Senate Minority leader William Knowland. The President argued that the legislative branch had an obligation to create a survival plan because the constitutional system of checks and balances might otherwise collapse in a time of national crisis. The leaders agreed and signed on with the project, beginning the process that led to a bunker at The Greenbrier.

At that time, the Congressional leaders made a decision that affected The Greenbrier for decades to come. Because they anticipated little likelihood of success in the normal legislative process, the leaders unilaterally and covertly authorized the Office of Defense Mobilization to survey and select a number of suitable sites for the construction of a fallout shelter. In other words, the project was initiated in secrecy and remained a highly classified operation throughout its almost forty year duration.

There was another reason for secrecy. Shelters built during this period were essentially of two designs: one type was built deep underground and relied upon the physical protection of massive rock formations. These shelters tended to be openly built, obvious in their purpose, and very expensive. The second type of facility offered more modest protection and its utility depended upon assurances that a potential enemy did not know of its existence. The legislative branch shelter was to be of the latter type.

Site selection for this type of shelter was critically important. The U.S. Army Corps of Engineers identified about a half dozen suitable locations for a Congressional fallout shelter and The Greenbrier was selected for a number of reasons. For one, the resort was within the federal relocation arc. It was far enough away from potential targets so as not to suffer collateral damage in case of attack and yet still accessible by rail, air and ground transportation. For another, it is situated in a small valley surrounded by mountains that would protect the site. In addition, The Greenbrier offered an extensive physical plant so the shelter could utilize an existing support infrastructure, that is, shelter maintenance activities could be discreetly blended into the resort's routine maintenance. There was also an intangible reason

The bunker at The Greenbrier was designed for the relocation of Congress and Lyndon Johnson, while Senate Majority Leader, was one of four leaders who authorized the project. Greenbrier President Truman Wright is shown welcoming Vice President Johnson in May 1961.

In the 1950s, the railroad was the most efficient way to move a large number of individuals. One reason for selecting The Greenbrier was the railroad line running directly to Washington, D.C. This 1963 photograph shows the relationship of the hotel to the train station in the foreground. The bunker is underneath the West Virginia Wing which sits behind the main hotel.

for selecting The Greenbrier: the earlier World War II relationship. The government had worked with The Greenbrier and its owner, the C&O Railway, to house foreign diplomats in 1942 and to create Ashford General Hospital. In matters requiring an extraordinary level of cooperation and discretion on the part of a private company, prudence suggested working with an organization whose reliability was a matter of record.

No record seems to exist of the precise moment when government officials first contacted the C&O Railway about plans for the resort, but it seems likely that sometime during his March 1956 conference at The Green-

brier President Eisenhower discussed the proposition with Walter J. Tuohy, the President of the Railway. It also seems likely that as a result of their discussion Mr. Tuohy made a commitment to discuss a cooperative venture because on March 28, 1956— the day the President departed The Greenbrier— an intriguing letter was written to Mr. Tuohy.

The message arrived under the letterhead of the Architect of the Capitol. This official directs the construction and maintenance of all Congressional buildings and facilities. The letter consisted of only two sentences, introducing J. George Stewart, the Architect of the Capitol, and asking for Mr. Tuohy's assistance "on matters of vital importance to the Congress of the United States." The wording was deliberately vague— this was to be the only piece of paper linking Congress to the Greenbrier

Above: The Greenbrier's location in a small valley virtually encircled by mountains was another factor in site selection. Mountain walls rising 1,500 feet above the valley floor offered protection from fallout and made the site a difficult target. This view is from Greenbrier Mountain across to Kate's Mountain. At left: President Eisenhower talking with C&O Railway President Walter Tuohy on March 26, 1956 when the President arrived at The Greenbrier (see page 161). The President authorized the "continuity of government" program creating emergency federal government shelters. Mr. Tuohy was responsible for negotiating an agreement to build one on C&O property.

ARCHITECT OF THE CAPITOL
WASHINGTON, D. C.

SECRET

March 28, 1956

Mr. Walter J. Tuohy, President
Chesapeake and Ohio Railway Company
Terminal Tower
Cleveland 1, Ohio

Dear Mr. Tuohy:

This is to introduce Mr. J. George Stewart, Architect of
the Capitol, who is calling upon you on matters of vital importance
to the Congress of the United States.

We, the undersigned, representing the leadership of the
United States Congress, will appreciate any cooperation you may
give us.

Sincerely yours,

[signature]
Speaker of the House of
Representatives

[signature]
Majority Leader of the Senate

[signature]
Minority Leader of the House
of Representatives

[signature]
Minority Leader of the Senate

A copy of the letter from Congressional leadership to C&O Railway President Walter Tuohy that is the only document specifically (however vaguely) linking Congress to the bunker at The Greenbrier. It is under the letterhead of the Architect of the Capitol because that official worked directly with the project.

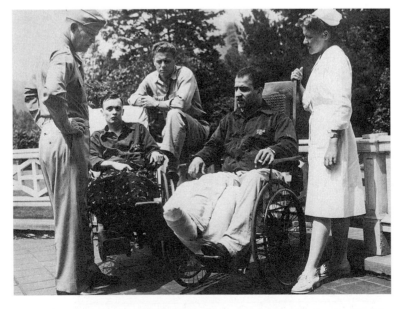

General Eisenhower was at The Greenbrier three times during its World War II use as an Army hospital. Ten years later, during the Cold War, the government was again engaged in emergency planning and turned to its earlier partner.

bunker. It was signed by the four leaders who had met with President Eisenhower seven months earlier: Sam Rayburn, Lyndon Johnson, Joseph Martin and William Knowland.

Shortly after Mr. Tuohy received the letter, a small group of C&O executives heard the details about these "matters of vital importance" during informal meetings with government officials at The Greenbrier, the Mayflower Hotel in Washington, D.C. and aboard railroad business cars. They quickly agreed on first steps. First, the shelter would be located directly behind the hotel building, in an area known as Copeland's Hill. Second, drill rigs immediately started test bores in the hill and simultaneously a memo to Greenbrier personnel explained that the drilling was "to determine subterranean conditions as part of a study of the desirability of constructing an exhibit hall." Third, a New York architectural firm was authorized to design an underground structure that included an exhibit hall which was part of a much larger operation.

Thus began a project for which there was no precedent. For that reason, the government and the C&O Railway started working on a legal agreement. Representatives of the C&O, the Army Corps of Engineers, The Greenbrier and the Architect of the Capitol (serving as the Congressional leadership liaison) spent months negotiating a contract spelling out details in this uncharted area of cooperation between the government and a private company.

Before any discussions began, the FBI fingerprinted and checked the backgrounds of everyone involved for security clearances. This acute security consciousness characterized the project from the beginning until termination almost forty years later— no one participated without a thorough background check culminating in the signing of a security agreement. Few persons cleared after this point knew the Congressional connection, only those at the highest levels. Conversations about the ultimate user of the facility referred vaguely to "the client."

When the Board of Directors empowered C&O executives to proceed with detailed negotiations they deliberated cautiously because there were far-reaching consequences. At the center of the agreement was a dormant and unrecorded lease. Should that lease ever be activated, the government immediately took over the entire Greenbrier property. C&O officials wanted assurances this would happen only in case of a bonafide national emergency. The dormant lease could be activated by one of three individuals: the President of the United States, the Secretary of Defense or the Secretary of the Army. To protect the C&O from an open-ended lease, the railway could require the government

This announcement appeared in The Greenbrier's employee newsletter in February 1957 to explain the new work.

to buy The Greenbrier for $27.5 million, a price subject to revision over time.

Another consequence of any agreement was that The Greenbrier and the C&O Railway would work within the security restrictions dictated by the government's needs. For example, the government could not own the bunker outright because legal ownership would create a paper trail and compromise security. The obvious solution was Greenbrier ownership of the bunker with the government paying rent. That is essentially what happened, but another problem arose. At the time, Congress could pay no more than $25,000 per year in rent without the approval of two committees. The leadership wanted to avoid that process because it too would compromise security. So slowly the idea of adding a wing to The Greenbrier as a form of compensation came under discussion. There was another advantage to building an addition to the hotel— putting it directly above the shelter solved the problem of disguising the underground facility's construction.

This was important because as plans developed the underground bunker was going to be more than 100,000 square feet, which meant difficult-to-conceal construction.

Correspondence regarding negotiations between the government and the C&O Railway concerning "Project X" was transmitted under cover sheets like this one.

The solution was quite clever: build in plain sight, making parts of the classified facility (the Exhibit Hall and two meeting rooms) open to Greenbrier guests as part of the above ground wing. One further factor was considered at this point. For security reasons, the government could not overtly direct the construction project, so the agreement called for the C&O Railway to act as an "undisclosed agent" in building the bunker. Naturally, railway officials anticipated questions from shareholders and resort guests about the nature of the project and without the addition of a new wing they felt unable to satisfactorily explain their role.

Contract talks moved into a more intensive phase in the spring of 1958. Congressional leaders were anxious to finalize an agreement and a variety of issues were rapidly negotiated and resolved. These included the following items: the government would subsidize improvements to The Greenbrier's water, sewerage and steam generating plants because the new bunker facilities would strain the existing equipment. The Greenbrier was responsible for "maintaining the premises as a habitable facility," meaning that routine maintenance

was to be done by Greenbrier employees. The government agreed to pay all costs for the underground bunker and the above ground wing in one lump sum upon signing the agreement. If the C&O ever wanted to sell The Greenbrier, the government held the right of first refusal. There could be only one government activation of the facility. The Greenbrier could build new facilities or remove old facilities as long as it did not destroy the utility of the underground bunker. The government agreed not to attempt to acquire the property by condemnation; it agreed not to store explosives or radioactive materials on the premises. Knotty tax and insurance issues were eventually worked out.

In the midst of these negotiations the project received an official code name. For a year planners had filed records in "Project X" folders but after June 1958 planning for the work on the hill behind The Greenbrier was identified as "Project Casper." For security purposes, the code name changed periodically and by the early 1980s it was "Project Greek Island."

The C&O Railway and the U.S. government signed a twenty-year lease agreement on November 26, 1958.

M. I. Dunn was the C&O's Vice-President for Operations who oversaw construction of the bunker and the West Virginia Wing from the Railway's headquarters in Cleveland. He designated L.T. Nuckols, the retired C&O Chief Engineer, as the on site construction manager.

The construction of the West Virginia Wing explained the large project on the hill behind the hotel. Throughout construction this architect's drawing was displayed near the Dining Room to illustrate what was being built. In 1973 the addition of Colonial Hall (see page 211) filled the gap between Chesapeake Hall and the new wing.

That same day the railway deposited a check for $12 million to cover the projected cost of Project Casper. Three days later a local sawmill owner began clearing trees from Copeland's Hill and two weeks later a contractor won the excavation bid. On December 12, 1958, a brief article in two state newspapers reported: "The Chesapeake and Ohio Railway announced plans today for the construction of an Exhibit Hall adjacent to the auditorium of The Greenbrier Hotel. The cost of the addition was not disclosed." And with that the Cold War arrived in White Sulphur Springs, West Virginia.

Bunker construction continued for more than two years. The excavation work completed in Spring 1959 created what local people for years referred to as "the big hole." With that finished, workers built an eight-foot fence and subsequent work went on out of public sight behind white-painted boards. There were indications of a large-scale construction project despite the fence. For one thing, there was a seemingly endless amount of concrete poured into the excavated hole. A local supplier who provided equipment estimated that his company hauled 4,000 loads to the site, delivering 50,000 tons of concrete. Another indication was the

EXHIBIT CENTER The air-conditioned Exhibit Center offers 16,400 square feet of exhibit facilities in the main hall and 6,300 additional square feet on the balcony with decor and lighting especially designed to display new products and line extensions to the best effect either in booth areas or open shows. Architectural planning has provided a traffic flow which makes each area the "best spot" in the hall.

MOUNTAINEER ROOM Perfect comfort for a meeting of 125 is offered by the Mountaineer Room with permanent, theatre-type seating. Fully air-conditioned and sound equipped. Dais is 19 by 4 feet.

GOVERNOR'S HALL Featuring continental style, permanent seating for 475, the Governor's Hall offers a versatile spot for meetings. Fully air-conditioned and sound equipped. The stage is 8½ feet by 37 feet.

Part of the bunker was "hidden in plain sight." This page from a 1962 Greenbrier brochure shows the portions that were used as part of the resort's conference facilities. It was important that the new facilities appear to be an integral part of normal resort operations.

Taken in 1959, this is the only known photograph of bunker construction. The excavated area in the foreground became the storage area for huge tanks of diesel fuel and water. Workers were hired by the C&O Railway, not by the government. Did they know what they were building? As one put it: "You were told not to ask questions."

amount of dirt hauled out. St. Charles Catholic Church across the street from the site got a new parking lot atop a hollow that was filled in with bunker dirt. The Greenbrier's nine hole golf course, the Lakeside Course, expanded into an eighteen-hole course as a result of the tremendous availability of fill dirt.

Rumors about a hidden purpose for the project started circulating almost as soon as the first shovel full of dirt moved. In February 1959 an article appeared in the Charleston *Gazette* headlined "Greenbrier Rumor Denied: No Presidential Hideout Planned" The rumor was denied by C&O Railway officials who insisted that excavation for the Exhibit Hall accounted for the stories. Months later *Gazette* editors wrote in a letter to Greenbrier Vice-President Truman Wright: "We hear

you are building a bomb shelter for the President of the United States." Mr. Wright's answer was repeated in various forms for years: "Your letter is indeed interesting. I have no idea with whom you spoke, but your informant was typical of some of the wild rumors we have heard around The Greenbrier. I know nothing of a bomb shelter for the President. We are constructing an Exhibit Hall, new meeting rooms, adequate housing to take care of the expansion of The Greenbrier Clinic and approximately one hundred air-conditioned guest rooms."

Over the years almost everyone claiming to know there was a bomb shelter under The Greenbrier was convinced it was built for the President of the United States. For those cleared on the identity of "the client" it was a bit easier to deny the story knowing that the

Workers at the Mosler Safe Company in Ohio pose next to one of the blast doors that protect vehicular entrances to the bunker. Doors this size were usually built with two panels, or "leafs," but these were "single leaf," which maximized strength by eliminating the vulnerable seam. The doors were transported to The Greenbrier by train on a special flatbed car low enough to clear bridges and tunnels.

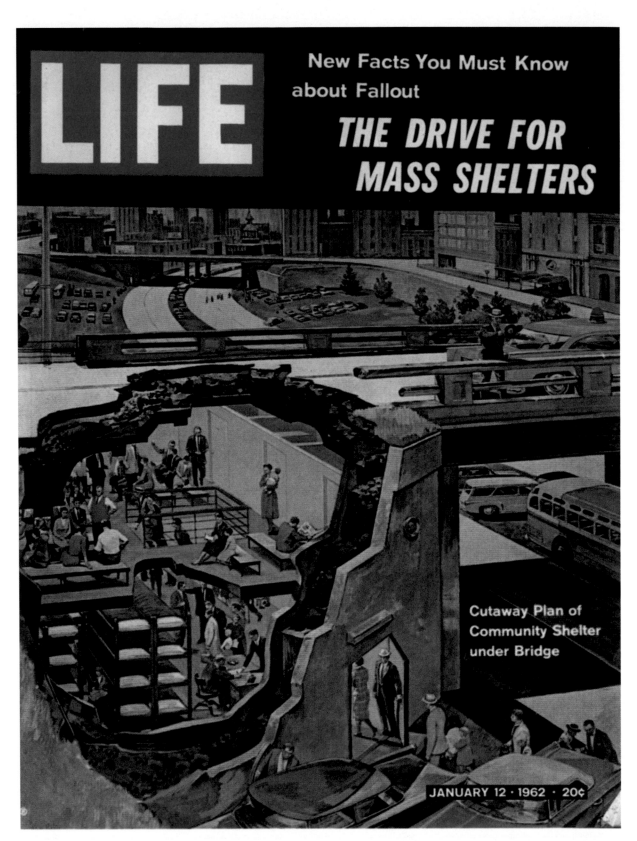

This Life magazine cover from January 1962 illustrates the widespread concern about fallout shelters during the period the bunker was built at The Greenbrier. Speaking of mass fallout shelters, the magazine editorialized: "Shelters are simply an admission that a nuclear war, however unlikely, is not an impossibility. Justification of shelters is simple: under certain ghastly circumstances, they might save millions of lives." (Illustration by Ron Kiley, used by permission of Life magazine.)

facility was designed for Congress—it was not an underground White House, it was an underground Capitol.

There was another reason for the speculation about a bomb shelter at The Greenbrier. This large-scale construction project involving significant excavation went on during the peak years of fallout shelter agitation. As the Cold War intensified, civil defense officials studied proposals for extremely expensive national fallout shelter systems. (President Eisenhower rejected a 1958 commission's proposal for a $22.5 billion system, an amount equaling a third of the federal budget at the time.) With a spiraling arms race in the late 1950s and early 1960s and heightened tensions over Suez, Hungary, Berlin and Cuba, anxiety steadily increased. Widely circulated magazines of the day carried stories of family and community fallout shelters. The launching of Sputnik, the Soviet satellite, in October 1957 drove an intense clamor for a major defense build

The Exhibit Hall is a huge space that was frequently used for conference exhibitions and social functions (see page 210), but it would have been converted into workstations for Congressional officials in case of activation. Because it is underground, it helped explain the excavation work during construction of the West Virginia Wing.

up, including the construction of fallout shelters. The building of The Greenbrier bunker was undertaken in the context of these events as well as at the time of routine "duck and cover" exercises in the nation's schools.

The emergency relocation center at The Greenbrier was far more than simply a shelter where members of Congress might survive war and fallout. Rather, the underground structure—and the entire resort in accord with the lease agreement—would become the new location of the federal government's legislative branch. For this reason the underground facility (which came to be called "the substructure" during construction) included not only dormitories, a dining room and a power plant for survival purposes but also large areas designed for the reassembly of Congress as a legislative body. The Exhibit Hall had a mission beyond its hotel use: it was the designated work space for various members of the institution of Congress—the Sergeant at

Arms, the Chaplain, the Speaker of the House, etc. Adjacent to that huge space, Governor's Hall was to be the postwar site of the House of Representative just as the Mountaineer Room was for the Senate. Congressional records would also have been transported to the site in case of activation.

More than that, the substructure contained a sophisticated communications center. Since those gathered inside this particular center would be America's elected representatives, facilities were available for them to communicate with their constituents and with state government officials at a time of great national crisis. State of the art equipment was installed to ensure that they could communicate with other emergency government centers. For these communications reasons, two eighty-foot radio towers encased in concrete silos sat underground outside the bunker ready to be raised upon activation of the facility. Cables running under the golf courses connected the relocation center to the tops of the surrounding mountains. On the peak of Greenbrier Mountain to the north was a television tower and atop Kate's Mountains across the valley were micro-

Part of an extensive communications center, these radio studios offered members of Congress a means of communicating with their constituents.

Just beyond the west end of the West Virginia Wing (top), hidden by brush, is one of two radio antenna housing units. Removal of the tarp reveals a concrete box—actually the top of a twenty foot underground concrete silo—from which an antenna emerges (bottom) that extends 75 feet upwards.

wave telephone towers. The bunker's communications capabilities included a complex telephone system designed and installed by AT&T and connected to the Kate's Mountain tower.

These cables were like tentacles reaching out from the substructure connecting it the outside world. Other life-supporting tentacles reached out so that the bunker might function. A six-inch pipe ran half a mile to a spot near Howard's Creek (close to the third green of the Old White Course) where an infiltration gallery— a well— provided water. This water source constantly replenished three huge 25,000 gallon storage tanks within the bunker. A shorter tunnel enclosed the air intake system which began near the Hilltop tennis courts where a small and obscure building hid the vital source of fresh air. An exhaust system carried smoke from generators and an incinerator to a smokestack deep in a wooded area just outside the facility.

Another project that kept the facility connected to the outside world was the extension of the White Sulphur Springs airport adjacent to The Greenbrier's golf courses. This landing strip could handle the aircraft of the 1950s and early 1960s flying "the client" to the relocation center. The fact that the resort sat on a major railroad line running directly to Washington, D.C. was also important—until the late 1970s, plans for special trains to transport members of Congress to The Greenbrier were in place as a back up to airlift evacuation. The opening of Greenbrier Valley Airport ten miles away near Lewisburg in 1968 superseded these plans.

The bunker was structurally complete in the summer of 1961 and maintenance of the facility turned over to The Greenbrier on July 1. The location of the bunker on the grounds of a resort with an extensive physical plant now came into play. Since time would be critical in any crisis situation requiring activation of the facility, it was imperative for the facility to be ready on very short notice. An essential part of the relocation plan was the bunker's state of constant operational readiness.

This nondescript building near the Hilltop Tennis Courts is the bunker's fresh air source. Air passes down a tunnel to the substructure where special filters would remove radio-active contaminants.

eral Accounting Office tallied the total cost of building both the emergency relocation center and the West Virginia Wing at $14,069,398. The completion of the project had an eerie timeliness: the books closed only days before the nerve-wracking climax of the Cuban missile crisis, the one time when the bunker hovered at the edge of activation. The facility was rapidly prepared for use as tensions mounted that month following the discovery of Soviet offensive missiles on Cuban soil and President Kennedy's subsequent confrontation with Soviet premier Khrushchev. Had that brush with nuclear war escalated further, the facility would definitely have been activated. For a few long days in October 1962 it appeared the time was at hand to put the bunker to its intended use.

Because of this operational readiness plan, the complex system of machinery, equipment, plumbing and electrical wiring required a detailed preventive maintenance program. For this important element of the plan the government relied on The Greenbrier's staff, particularly the Engineering Department. Dozens of Engineering personnel were cleared on the project and worked the bunker in addition to their normal resort duties. The Greenbrier paid the wages of those who worked inside the bunker and the government reimbursed The Greenbrier. This procedure was also followed in paying materials and utilities expenses.

Attention turned to building the West Virginia Wing above ground and the first room was available in April 1962. The new wing connected to the main hotel via an underground tunnel that led to the movie theatre; this provided access to the eighty-eight rooms in the wing and also to The Greenbrier Clinic. But like so many other things about Project Greek Island more was involved than met the eye. Encased in thick concrete walls, the tunnel was actually one more arm reaching out from the bunker, this time to a reserve area. The movie theatre (and the employees' cafeteria located directly behind the movie screen) also had a backup mission as an additional work and meeting space supplementing areas inside the bunker.

The C&O's Chief Engineer officially closed out the construction project on October 16, 1962 and the Gen-

For three decades the underground facility remained ready for use on a few hours notice, one phone call away from activation. For this reason a cover company called Forsythe Associates was created so that communications specialists were on site at all times. It was critically important to the plan's success that communication systems be fully operational at the time of evacuation and activation. To disguise their true assignments, Forsythe members overtly worked as audiovisual consultants with The Greenbrier's cable, television and telephone systems. However, individuals on the Forsythe staff were civilian federal employees, most with military communications backgrounds, and they devoted the majority of their time to their covert mission inside the bunker.

Together with cleared Greenbrier employees, Forsythe Associates kept the bunker in a state of fine-tuned readiness. A maintenance manual existed for every piece of equipment in the bunker and each step was followed rigorously, a process that included regular testing. For example, the diesel generators in the power plant were fired up on a weekly schedule, the retractable radio antennae opened and extended out several times a year, the cryptographic systems were used frequently and the telephones daily. Because

This landing strip adjacent to The Greenbrier's golf courses was part of the early evacuation planning. The view is looking west, with U.S. Route 60 to the right. The airport was closed in 1986 and a portion of the runway in the foreground was removed in 1998 during construction of The Meadows golf course.

keeping up with technology was so important, the Forsythe staff and cleared Greenbrier employees spent a great deal of time in schools at classes and seminars. As one worker put it, "Once a piece of equipment was purchased and installed you couldn't call the repairman to make a house call at a secret bunker."

Refinements and adjustments to the operation continued throughout the 1960s and 1970s. In 1965 The Greenbrier organized a system for stockpiling and rotating food supplies. Frozen food came in through the resort's normal food purchasing channels, but a portion was diverted to freezers inside the bunker. These food stocks were routinely circulated and resupplied by cleared members of The Greenbrier staff. In another case, a system was installed to extract and replace the fuel oil in three 14,000 gallon storage tanks to prevent deterioration. A much larger project was the two-level

Luther Way was The Greenbrier's Chief Engineer from 1952 to 1980 and managed the personnel who maintained equipment inside the bunker. As many as fifty Greenbrier mechanics, electricians, plumbers, masons, painters, carpenters, and tinsmiths as well as air conditioning and refrigeration specialists worked as needed in the bunker. In addition, selected members of the Security Department, kitchen staff and management were cleared on the project. All were sworn to absolute secrecy.

The Greenbrier's Public Relations Department released this photograph in 1962 to promote the newly opened West Virginia Wing. Note the parking lot in the right foreground adjacent to St. Charles Catholic Church. It is actually a huge landfill created with excavated bunker dirt.

addition of Colonial Hall and the Eisenhower Parlors below it in 1973. This new meeting and banquet space almost abutted the eastern exterior wall of the bunker. Therefore, the Architect of the Capitol traveled down from Washington, D.C. to personally inspect the site to ensure that it would not disrupt emergency use of the facility. The new construction meant modifying the truck entrance to the Exhibit Hall section of the bunker but in another area, along the corridor leading to the movie theatre, the work created an additional reserve area. This is in the Eisenhower Parlors, below ground, which could be closed off and pressurized creating an area for five hundred more bunk beds.

Inside the bunker itself technological improvements continued, especially in the 1980s when the clinic area was enlarged and re-equipped, a new AT&T telephone

system brought in, chillers were replaced as part of upgrading the air-conditioning system and a halon fire suppressant system added inside the power plant. All these improvements were to ensure that the facility remained viable in a world of rapidly changing technologies.

Throughout this process it was necessary, as always, to maintain the security envelope surrounding Project Greek Island. A few methods were used to keep the operation secret. Following military procedure, only those individuals with a "need to know" were briefed about the existence of the bunker— that meant people who needed to know about the operation in order to perform their jobs. However, individuals cleared on the project were told only as much as they needed to know to complete their immediate

Top photo: The Exhibit Hall during its first public use, for a medical meeting in August 1962. If activated, this area would be split up into 24 sections with work spaces for Congressional officials including House and Senate Majority and Minority Leaders, the Sergeant at Arms, the Architect of the Capitol, and the House and Senate Chaplains. Bottom: Two rare photographs taken during the period the bunker was operational. At left, the 430 foot west tunnel lined with thousands of cases of military C-rations. Later, freeze-dried provisions replaced these rations. Right, one of the eighteen dormitories with the original bunks. For thirty years each bed was assigned to a member of Congress and as membership changed the beds were reassigned.

tasks. For example, an electrician working on a specific job was escorted directly to that site but not allowed access to other areas. In addition, there were levels of clearance; in some cases cleared individuals were told the facility was a classified government communications center and the explanation ended there. The number of personnel involved was limited because the fewer who knew, the less the chance of a security breach. Finally, anyone receiving any clearance signed a nondisclosure agreement spelling out the fines and prison sentences which were part of the security enforcement system.

Members of Forsythe Associates kept a low profile around the resort, yet they were visible in their role as

Top: Building Colonial Hall and the Eisenhower Parlors below it in 1973 in between the West Virginia Wing (at right) and Chesapeake Hall (at left). Bottom: From the air as it looks today.

Share a Ride

On the walls of the bunker were reminders of the need to maintain security. This poster hung in the communications center.

This camera could raise up atop the West Virginia Wing elevator tower giving those inside the bunker a view of the immediate hotel area. It could also be trained on surrounding mountains to inspect communication towers.

For thirty years, Greenbrier guests stepped off the elevator at the level marked "E" for Exhibit Center (above) and followed the sign unaware they were walking by a cover door (below) that folded out allowing a blast door to close off an entrance into the bunker.

consulting audiovisual specialists. For example, their work repairing the resort's television equipment went on in a public room near the Exhibit Hall. They lived nearby, attended church in town and sent their children to local schools, all of which made them accepted members of the community. However, they also routinely slipped through obscure doorways off of the Exhibit Hall and into classified areas of the bunker. For everyone involved, security meant not telling even the closest family members the true nature of their work.

For the duration of the Cold War the existence of Project Greek Island was never revealed. Although

books and magazine articles described some federal government evacuation and shelter planning, none ever hinted at this particular facility. A 1975 article in *Harper's* magazine asked, "Which members of which branches of government are included on the ultra secret lists of those to be evacuated?" Senator Hubert Humphrey responded that he had toured a facility for Congress ("I saw the entrance, how it opened. I saw the kitchen, the beds, the food storage.") but he gave no clue to its whereabouts. A 1984 book, *The Day After World War III: The U.S. Government's Plans for Surviving a Nuclear War*, analyzed a number of emergency scenarios for executive branch agencies, but concerning Congress the author quoted House Speaker Thomas "Tip" O'Neill: "They have a plan . . . It's something that's highly privileged and confidential, and I wouldn't be able to discuss it."

The most important method for keeping The Greenbrier relocation center secret was the tight control maintained for thirty years by the leadership of Congress. The "need to know" principle followed by Forsythe Associates and cleared Greenbrier employees applied to support personnel in Washington, D.C. Anyone involved in funding, technical consultations, military coordination, or any number of complicated activities related to shelter planning and maintenance learned that the source of authority for Project Greek Island went

Because of the "Danger High Voltage" sign, this isolated door in the woods behind the West Virginia Wing seemed to be an entrance to an electrical equipment area. In fact it is a cover door disguising the large blast door shown on page 192.

The May 1992 Washington *Post* story had such a stunning impact because it talked not in vague terms about some kind of bunker under The Greenbrier, rather it gave a detailed description of the facility and clearly identified "the client." As the writer, Ted Gup, explained: "The Greenbrier facility was custom-designed to meet the needs of a Congress-in-hiding . . . Its discovery offers the first conclusive evidence that Congress as a whole was even included in government evacuation scenarios and given a role in postwar America." As soon as the story broke, the joint bipartisan Congressional leadership issued a statement acknowledging the facility adding, "it was always clear that if the secret of the facility's location were to be compromised, so too would be the viability of the Congressional facility."

directly back to the Congressional leadership. On a few occasions it was suggested that a government interest at The Greenbrier might be acknowledged in some indirect way, but each time the idea was floated it was met with a firm and decisive "no" from the leadership.

The leaders had met with *Post* editors in several off-the-record consultations before publication in an attempt to persuade them not to reveal the bunker and its location.

The connection between the bunker and Congress was clearly represented in the TV Conference Room which was dominated by a photomural of the Capitol building in Washington, D.C. Members of Congress might film messages here to be transmitted to the public. The Capitol backdrop would reinforce the idea that this was an emergency location for the government's legislative branch.

After internal discussions the newspaper went ahead because, as the executive editor explained, "In the end, we concluded this was a historically significant and interesting story that posed no grave danger to national security or human life." They reached that conclusion, he said, because "an awful lot has changed since this facility was designed and built. Nuclear weapons were less speedy, less powerful and less numerous than they are today."

After the whirlwind of media coverage that weekend—which, given the decades of tight security, included the almost unimaginable scene of anchorman Tom Brokaw and correspondent Andrea Mitchell discussing the bunker on NBC Nightly News—things died down quickly. On June 1, House Speaker Thomas S. Foley wrote in a letter to Defense Secretary Richard B. Cheney: "In light of recent press exposure of the emergency relocation facility in White Sulphur Springs, West Virginia, it is my intention to recommend ending support for the facility." (What is most remarkable about this sentence is that it was the first time a leader of Congress ever publicly stated the shelter's location.) In other words, with the Speaker's letter Congress relinquished control of Project Greek Island.

Another factor in the Speaker's decision was that members of Congress had recently undergone intense negative publicity about their perquisites (the "perks" of office) and the last thing they needed was hundreds of headlines about a supposed "five-star luxury bomb shelter." As one newspaper put it: "For a Congress frantically downplaying its perks and privileges, the news that it planned to ride out the apocalypse at a five-star resort hotel isn't likely to endear the institution to a cranky electorate." Most of the media coverage focused on the "posh" Greenbrier assuming that the underground facility was of the same order. Three years passed before the public saw that this was not the case.

Also on June 1, 1992, Forsythe Associates ceased to exist. Control of the facility passed to the Defense Department who began a review of the usefulness of the operation. Should it be mothballed? Was there some other agency it might serve? Could it be modified in some way? The facility continued as a classified operation and strict security measures remained in effect so that Greenbrier

Fritz Bugas was the on-site manager of the Congressional relocation center from 1971 until the facility officially closed in July 1995. To people at The Greenbrier, he was the Regional Manager of Forsythe Associates.

visitors knew about the bunker but were not allowed access. Eventually the Defense Department began what can best be described as a "base-closing procedure." Former Forsythe employees worked alongside government auditors inventorying dozens of rooms filled with office, cafeteria and kitchen equipment, communications gear, bunk beds, spare parts, weapons, medical supplies, documents and thousands of other items stockpiled inside the bunker for the postwar reassembly of Congress. Decisions were made where to transport this government property, arrangements were made to do so and any number of contractual and legal agreements were modified or

Greenbrier President and Managing Director Ted J. Kleisner explained his role in Project Greek Island to NBC correspondent Stone Phillips during the filming of the Dateline program that provided the first publicly broadcast footage of the bunker on November 3, 1995.

A relaxed former President George Bush posed in Governors Hall after his tour of the bunker in January 1997.

Governors Hall would have been used for meetings of the House of Representatives. Before tours of the bunker began the room was set up to look as it might had that body been in session.

terminated. Finally, moving out began: for twenty-nine consecutive Monday mornings a tractor-trailer pulled up to the west cover door and drove off hours later completely loaded with a portion of the contents.

By the summer of 1995 this process was finished and when the government's lease agreement with the CSX Corporation expired on July 31 so did Project Greek Island. On that date the entire facility reverted to The Greenbrier. But even before the contract lapsed, feelers were sent out to the national media concerning an exclusive story on the bunker's opening. Clearly, the first viewing of a Cold War bunker's inner workings would be of national interest and The Greenbrier sought broad publicity for the event. The NBC program Dateline agreed and crews arrived in September for a week of filming a story they called "Forbidden City." When Dateline broadcast the segment on November 3, 1995 twelve million Americans watched correspondent Stone Phillips explore the bunker's rooms and corridors guided by Fritz Bugas, the official in charge of Project Greek Island for more than

twenty years. In fifteen minutes of television time one of the great secrets of the Cold War passed into history.

Two days after the program the first bunker tours were given for Greenbrier employees. This was a special expression of gratitude to the hundreds of staff members who had, by a kind of unspoken understanding, indirectly participated in the cover operation by not publicly talking about rumors everyone had heard for years. By Christmas, tours for resort guests were wending through the facility. For the few former Forsythe Associates staffers now working for The Greenbrier, it was most unsettling to see groups of awestruck guests in an area that recently had been the most secret place in America. Thus ended perhaps the single most important story in The Greenbrier's long history: for more than thirty years the most powerful nation on earth was prepared to transform the resort into the seat of its legislative branch of government and to do so at a time of utmost national crisis. The Greenbrier, for its part, had been a willing and committed partner.

Congressional Record

United States of America

PROCEEDINGS AND DEBATES OF THE *106th* CONGRESS

WASHINGTON, MONDAY, JULY 10, 2000

THE GREENBRIER

Mr. BYRD. Mr. President, tucked into a sheltered green valley in Southern West Virginia is a magical place, a place where fascinating history, natural majesty, and sumptuous comfort have combined since the first days of our nation's founding to create a spot that is justly world-renowned. That place, Mr. President, is called The Greenbrier, in White Sulphur Springs, West Virginia. It has been a special place for several decades now, overflowing with game for the Shawnee Indians, a spa since colonial days, a place of high society idylls and balls, fought over during the Civil War, a World War II diplomatic internment site and then a rest and recuperation hospital for wounded soldiers, and a secret government relocation site—all cloaked behind the well-bred, white-columned face of a grand southern belle of a resort.

Mr. President, in May, my wife Erma and I celebrated our 63rd anniversary. Erma is my childhood sweetheart, the former Erma Ora James. We have written a lot of history together over the past 63 years, and I could not ask for a better coauthor.

This year, as we have in the last several years, we celebrated at the fabled Greenbrier resort in White Sulphur Springs. I am certainly not original in my inspiration to celebrate moments of marital bliss there—President John Tyler, the first President to be married in office, spent part of his 1844 honeymoon there, and Mr. and Mrs. Joseph P. Kennedy arrived at the Greenbrier on October 11, 1914, for a two-week honeymoon. Many, many, other famous names are inscribed in the Greenbrier's guest register. The history that Erma and I have created together is a blink of the eye compared to that of The Greenbrier, whose healing waters were first enjoyed by hardy colonists in 1778, as they had been by Shawnee Indians for untold years before that.

The Greenbrier has been a resort almost since the day in 1778 that Mrs. Anderson, one of the first homesteaders in the Greenbrier area of the "Endless Mountains," as the region was identified on colonial maps, first tested the wondrous mineral waters on her chronic rheumatism. Word of Mrs. Anderson's recovery spread rapidly, and numerous log cabins were soon erected near the spring. The "summer season" at the spring was born, albeit in a somewhat primitive state.

Still, the fame of the spring along Howard's Creek continued to spread. Thomas Jefferson mentioned "Howard's Creek of Green Briar" in his "Notes on the State of Virginia" in 1784; that same year, George Washington focused the Virginia legislature's attention on the commercial prospects of the "Old State Road" running between the Kanawha River valley,

through The Greenbrier's lands, to the piedmont and tidewater sections of Virginia. Along the route of today's roadway between the hotel and the golf clubhouse stands a monument to this vision. The Buffalo Trail monument commemorates the point at which the pre-colonial Indian Buffalo Trail crossed the Allegheny Mountains on its way from the Atlantic Coast to Ohio. This trail became the James River and Kanawha Turnpike, which for over a century carried commerce and development from the settled East to the future states of West Virginia, Kentucky, Ohio, Indiana, Illinois, and Missouri. By 1809, a tavern with a dining room, a bar, a stable, mills, and numerous cabins constituted a hospitable stopping place along the still-rugged route West. And rheumatism sufferers were joined at this watering hole by others more interested in the creature comforts and social interaction than in relieving joint pain.

By 1815, the first spring house was built over the spring head, and a thriving resort was attracting visitors who typically stayed for several weeks at a time. A hotel and many surrounding cottages, some quite sumptuous, were erected over the years. Commodore Stephen Decatur, hero of the Barbary Wars, brought his wife for a 16-day stay in 1817, and Henry Clay of Kentucky, Speaker of the House of Representatives, spent some time at White Sulphur Springs during several summers over some 30 years. The cool mountain breezes under the shelter of ancient oaks, combined with stylish fans and gentle rocking chairs on a shady porch, made the Greenbrier a comfortable spot in those sweltering summers before air conditioning.

In many ways, the Greenbrier has changed little over the years. The gracious sweep of lawn, the stately trees, the ranks of white cottages and imposing hotel facades hark back to that earlier era. Many of the cottages, most too sumptuous to be called merely "cottages," have their own special histories. One of the cottages was owned by Jerome Napoleon Bonaparte, who was a nephew of the French Emperor. General John J. Pershing, Commander of the Allied Forces in World War I completed his memoirs in the cottage named "Top Notch." Early morning horseback rides are still popular, and Erma and I recently enjoyed the romantic carriage ride through the grounds. Hunting, fishing, and even falconry are still practiced. But more gold courses, tennis courts, and swimming pools encourage a more active lifestyle than in those early days. The Greenbrier is justly famous for its golf and for the Sam Snead Golf School. Though I do not play, I still enjoy the beautifully landscaped courses with their wide sweeps of lawn and water dotted with sandy island obstacles. The partaking of the sulphur water, that elemental component of the original spa experi-

ence, is now complemented by health and beauty facilities and services that pamper every part of you. A visit to the Greenbrier has grown ever more restorative over the years.

Henry Clay, that great man from Kentucky, the State of the Senator who now presides over the Senate with a dignity and degree of charm and skill and poise as rare as a day in June, often visited at the Greenbrier, as I have said.

Henry Clay was an early political fan of the Greenbrier, surely the most gracious and comfortable stopping place on his many trips between Washington and his home in Kentucky. Other well-known figures and luminaries who visited the resort prior to the Civil War were Presidents Martin Van Buren, Andrew Jackson, Millard Fillmore, Franklin Pierce, and James Buchanan. I have already noted that President John Tyler honeymooned at the Greenbrier. Dolly Madison, Daniel Webster, Davy Crockett, Francis Scott Key, and John C. Calhoun, and many other political notables have also contributed to engrossing dinner conversations there in more recent years, including Senate greats such as Everett Dirksen, Sam Ervin, Jacob Javits, and Barry Goldwater. Other politicians preferred the outstanding golf at the resort, including President Eisenhower, President Nixon (as a Vice President), President Woodrow Wilson has also graced the Greenbrier, though I do not know if he was a golfer.

The Greenbrier has always been a favorite spot of other celebrities, as well. The Vanderbilts, Astors, Hearsts, Forbes, Luces, DuPonts, and the Kennedys have sojourned there, as did Prince Ranier and Princess Grace with their children Albert and Caroline. The Duke and Duchess of Windsor danced the night away in the grand ballroom. Bing Crosby has sung there, and Johnny Carson, Steve Allen, Dr. Norman Vincent Peale, Rudi Valle, Art Buchwald, Dr. Jonas Salk, Cyrus Eaton, and the Reverend Billy Graham have all made mealtime conversations there sparkle more than the crystal chandeliers in the dining room. Babe Ruth and Lou Gehrig are just two of the sporting greats who have autographed the guest register. Clare Booth Luce wrote the first draft of her most enduring place, "The Women," during a three-day stay in 1936. Like Tennyson's brook, the fascinating list of notables could go on and on forever. People watching—that is watching people—has always been a spectator sport at Greenbrier functions!

The Greenbrier has experienced trauma as well as galas. During the Civil War, the Greenbrier's location astride a strategic rail line into Richmond, Virginia, put her in the line of fire. Troops were billeted in her guest rooms, but both sides spared a favorite pre-war vacation site and fighting raged along the Greenbrier River. Being in what became Southern West Virginia, during the debate over succession in 1863, the Greenbrier's fate as a West Virginia or a Virginia citizen was uncertain. I am surely glad that West Virginia was the winner!

During Reconstruction, the hotel's healing waters also helped to heal the wounds of war, as grand society from both sides of the conflict continued to meet at the Greenbrier. General Robert E. Lee's was a frequent visitor. In General Robert E. Lee's single post-war political statement, he led a group of prominent Southern leaders vacationing at the Greenbrier in drafting and signing what became known as "The White Sulphure Manifesto" of 1868. This document, widely reprinted in newspapers across the country, declared that, upon the reestablishment of self-governance in the South, the Southern people would "faithfully obey the Constitution and laws of the United States, treat the Negro with kindness and humanity and fulfill every duty incumbent on peaceful citizens, loyal to the Constitution of their country." The war was truly over.

In 1869, one of the most famous photographs ever taken at White Sulphur Springs included Robert E. Lee and a group of former Confederate Generals, among them Henry Wise of Virginia, P.G.T. Beauregard of Louisiana, and Bankhead Magruder of Virginia. Other ex-Confederate officers who visited the resort were Alexander Lawton of Georgia, Joseph Brent of Maryland, James Conner of South Carolina, and Robert Lilley of Virginia. Former Union General William S. Rosecrans visited General Lee while Lee was vacationing one summer at the Greenbrier.

The Greenbrier has served the nation well in two other wars, as well—World War II and the Cold War. At the outbreak of World War II, the hotel served as a rather gilded cage for several thousand foreign diplomats and their families, from Germany, Italy, Hungary, Bulgaria, and, later, Japan. It was then taken over the federal government for the Army's use as a rest and recuperation hospital for wounded soldiers, before returning, like the soldiers it housed, to civilian life.

Much has been made, in recent years, of the Greenbrier's secret life as a covert agent of the U.S. government. In 1992, the existence of an emergency government relocation center built secretly deep beneath the Greenbrier was revealed. The result of an extraordinary partnership between the CSX Corporation and the federal government, the bunker contained facilities to house and operate the entire United States Congress in the even of nuclear attack. It had its origin in plans created by President Eisenhower to ensure the survival of the constitutional system of checks and balances. The President had to convince Congressional leaders, including Senate Majority Leader Lyndon B. Johnson, to go along with the plan, which was carried out in the greatest secrecy for over forty years. The secrecy was necessary, because the bunker at the Greenbrier was not designed to withstand a direct hit, but, rather, to ensure security through a combination of physical design and camouflage. The remote shelter of the West Virginia hills proved a perfect combination of cover, concealment, and denial.

Now, the bunker is open to the public for tours. It is fascinating to see the level of detail that was included in the bunker, but it is also sobering to reflect upon the real fear of Armageddon that existed in this country during those years and which justified this kind of contingency planning. As you finish the tour and return to the sunlit world of golf, lazy country walks, luxurious settings, and fine dining that is the hallmark of the Greenbrier experience, it is difficult to recall those not-so-distant times when school children practiced hiding under their desks in the event of a conventional or nuclear exchange.

I encourage my fellow Senators, and, indeed, anyone listening, to visit the Greenbrier, to tour the bunker, and to relish the history and the service that are so much a part of this precious piece of West Virginia. Avoid the current high gas prices and road congestion, and take the train as so many have before you. Leave steamy, contentious, Washington behind for a time, and step out at the Greenbrier's rail depot wondering at the beauty, the cool breezes that smell of fresh, clean air and wildflowers. Allow yourself to be swept along by the attentive, unobtrusive service of an earlier age and be deposited in a bright, flower-bedecked room before a pre-dinner stroll about the grounds. You will be walking with the celebrities of the past as you write a wonderful new chapter in your own history.

I close with the immortal words and images of the poet William Wordsworth, who lived from 1770 to 1850, when the Greenbrier was yet in its early days. But his lines eloquently capture the sights one can now happen upon when strolling through the magical grounds of this wonderful outpost of gentle civilization amid the mountains, and they capture the happiness such beauty inspires:

> I wandered lonely as a cloud
> That floats on high o'er vales and hills,
> When all at once I saw a crowd,
> A host, of golden daffodils;
> Beside the lake, beneath the trees,
> Fluttering and dancing in the breeze.
>
> Continuous as the stars that shine
> And twinkle on the milky way,
> They stretched in never-ending line
> Along the margins of a bay:
> Ten thousand saw I at a glance,
> Tossing their heads in sprightly dance.
>
> The waves beside them danced; but they
> Out-did the sparkling waves in glee:
> A poet could not but be gay,
> In such a jocund company:
> I gazed—and gazed—but little thought
> What wealth the show to me had brought:
>
> For oft, when on my couch I lie
> In vacant or in a pensive mood,
> They flash upon that inward eye
> Which is the bliss of solitude;
> And then my heart with pleasure fills,
> And dances with the daffodils.

Senator Robert C. Byrd and his wife Erma celebrating their 63rd wedding anniversary at The Greenbrier in May 2000. It was this trip that prompted Senator Byrd to deliver this speech about The Greenbrier on the floor of the United States Senate which was reprinted in the Congressional Record.

Like the Greenbrier, the forests in West Virginia. I yield the floor.

NOTES ON SOURCES

The only previous history of The Greenbrier is William Olcott's *The Greenbrier Heritage*, published by The Greenbrier in 1967. For a general history of White Sulphur Springs and the surrounding resorts in the nineteenth century, the best source remains Perceval Reniers, *The Springs of Virginia: Life, Love, and Death at the Waters* (The University of North Carolina Press, 1941). A more recent analysis of the springs and their place in American culture is Marshall W. Fishwick, *Springlore in Virginia* (Bowling Green State University Popular Press, 1978). An impressive survey of the mineral spring resorts, well-illustrated, is Stan Cohen's, *Historic Springs of the Virginias: A Pictorial History* (Pictorial Histories Publishing Company, 1981). William A. MacCorkle's *The White Sulphur Springs* (The Neale Publishing Company, 1916) gives the best picture of The Greenbrier shortly after the 1910 purchase by the C&O Railway, plus it includes reprints of nineteenth century sources.

In the nineteenth century a kind of personalized travel writing flourished. For a review of this material see Robert S. Conte, "The Celebrated White Sulphur Springs of Greenbrier: Nineteenth Century Travel Accounts," *West Virginia History*, Spring-Summer, 1981. Primary sources include Philip Holbrook Nicklin—who used the pseudonym Peregrine Prolix—*Letters Descriptive of the Virginia Springs* (Philadelphia: H.S. Tanner, 1837; reprinted by AAR/Tantulus, 1978) and Mary M Hagner—who used the pseudonym Mark Pencil—*The White Sulphur Papers, Or Life at the Springs of Western Virginia* (New York: Samuel Colman, 1839). See also *A Trip to the Virginia Springs, Or the Belles and Beaux of 1835, By A Lady* (Lexington, Virginia, 1843) and *Life at The White Sulphur Springs*, Mary J. Windle (Philadelphia, 1857).

These books describing the ante-bellum White Sulphur Springs are supplemented by numerous magazine articles, especially in the *Southern Literary Messenger (SLM)*. See "Visit to the Virginia Springs During the Summer of 1834," *SLM*, vol. 1, no. 9 (May, 1835) reprinted in part in *SLM*, vol. 1, no. 6 June, 1939); "Another Visit to the Virginia Springs, or the Adventures of Harry Humbug, Esq.," *SLM*, vol. 1, No. 13 (September, 1835); "Journal of a Trip to the Mountains, Caves and Springs of Virginia By a New Englander," *SLM*, vol. IV, nos. 4, 5 and 6 (1838). See also, "The White Sulphur Springs," *New England Magazine* (September, 1832), and "A Trip to the Virginia Springs," *Knickerbocker Magazine* July-November, 1852).

Published letters, journals and diaries are also an important source for the years before the Civil War. See John E. Semmes, *John H. B. Latrobe and His Times, 1803-1891* (Baltimore, 1917); Frederick Marryat, *Diary in America, With Remarks on Its Institutions* (Philadelphia, 1839); Harriet Martineau, *Society in America* (London, 1839); G.W. Featherstonhaugh, *Excursion Through the Slave States from Washington On the Potomac to the Frontier of Mexico* (New York, 1844); Count Francesco Arese, *A Trip to the Prairies and in the Interior of North America, 1837–1838* (New York, 1934); James K. Paulding, *Letters from the South Written During an Excursion in the Summer of 1816* (New York, 1817); Mary J. Windle, *Life in Washington* (Philadelphia, 1859); The Earl of Carlisle [Lord Morpeth], *Travels in America* (New York, 1851); J.S. Buckingham, *The Slave States of America* (London, 1854); J. Milton Mackie, *From Cape Cod to Dixie and the Tropics* (New York, 1864); William K. Scarborough, ed., *The Diary of Edmund Ruffin* (Baton Rouge, 1972); William D. Hoyt, Jr., "Journey to the Springs, 1846," *Virginia Magazine of History and Biography*, vol. 54 (1946); Bernard Mayo, "Henry Clay, Patron and Idol of White Sulphur Springs: His Letters to James Calwell," *The Virginia Magazine of History and Biography*, vol. 55, no. 4 (October, 1947); E: Lee Shephard, ed., "'Trip to the Virginia Springs': An Extract from the Diary of Blair Bolling." *The Virginia Magazine of History and Biography*, vol. 96, no. 2 (April, 1988).

On the use of the mineral water, Dr. John I. Moorman's work contains the best analyses of nineteenth century applications. His first publication was *A Directory for the Use of the White Sulphur Springs Waters* (Philadelphia, 1839) followed by *The Virginia Springs With Their Analysis* (Philadelphia, 1847). This volume expanded in 1859 and 1867 editions and evolved into his most comprehensive work, *The Mineral Springs of North America* (Philadelphia, 1873). For information on Dr. Moorman see Guy Hinsdale, M.D., "John Jennings Moorman, M.D.: A Biographical Note," *Annals of Medical History*, vol. II, no. 4 July, 1934). For selections from Dr. Moorman's private writings see Robert S. Conte, "The Memoir of Dr. John J. Moorman, Resident Physician at White Sulphur Springs," *The Journal of the Greenbrier Historical Society*, vol. III, no. 6 (1980).

On the Civil War and Robert E. Lee's visits see *The War of the Rebellion: A Compilation of the Official Records of the Union and Confederate Armies* (Washington, 1880-1901); Douglas Southall Freeman, *R.E. Lee: A Biography* (New York, 1934-35); Cecil D. Eby, Jr., *A Virginia Yankee in the Civil War: The Diaries of David Hunter Strother* (Chapel Hill, 1961); H.A. Dupont, *The Campaign of 1864 in the Valley of Virginia* (New York, 1925); Charles Bracelen Flood, *Lee: The Last Years* (Boston. 1981); Robert E. Lee, Jr., *Recollections and Letter of General Robert E. Lee* (New York, 1904); John S. Wise, *The Lion's Skin: A Historical Novel and a Novel History* (New York, 1905); Christiana Bond, *Memories of General Robert E. Lee* (Baltimore, 1926); Charles A. Pilsbury,

"A Southern Watering Place," *Potter's American Monthly* (October, 1880).

Material on the late nineteenth century resort includes: Edward A. Pollard, *The Virginia Tourist* (Philadelphia, 1870); Mary B. Dodge, "Virginia in Water-Colors," *Lippincott's Magazine* (July, 1872); Edward King, *The Great South* (Hartford, 1875); "The Virginia Springs," *The Nation* (September 20, 1877); John Esten Cooke, "The White Sulphur Springs," *Harper's New Monthly Magazine* (August, 1878); "A Life's Mistake," *Frank Leslie's Popular Monthly* (April, 1879); George W. Bagby, *The Old Virginia Gentleman and Other Sketches* (Richmond, 1938); J.G. Pangborn, *Picturesque B. and O.* (Chicago, 1883): "Virginia Summer Resorts," *Harper's New Monthly Magazine* (October 3. 1885); Charles Dudley Warner, "Their Pilgrimage," *Harper's New Monthly Magazine* (August, 1886); "A Reminiscence of the While Sulphur Springs," *Harper's New Monthly Magazine* (August 4, 1888); Robert S. Conte, "Oakhurst: The First Golf Club in America," *The Journal of the Greenbrier Historical Society*, vol. IV, no. 5 (1985).

For information on the resort in the first decades of the twentieth century see Aubin Audelotte McDowell, *White Sulphur Springs as Known in History and Tradition* (Washington, D.C., 1909); Harrison Rhodes, *In Vacation America* (New York, 1915); John Martin Hammond, *Winter Journeys in the South* (New York, 1916); Louise Closser Hale, *We Discover the Old Dominion* (New York, 1916); William A. MacCorkle, *The Recollections of Fifty Years of West Virginia* (New York, 1928); Agnes Rothery, *Virginia: The New Dominion* (New York, 1940); J.O. Dahl and Crete M. Dahl, "Greenbrier—A Heritage of Hospitality," *Hotel Review Pictorial*, vol. XXVI, no. 4 (April, 1931); Guy Hinsdale, M.D., "Doctors at the White Sulphur Springs," *Bulletin of the History of Medicine*, vol. XIII, no. 5 (May, 1943).

The best single source on the internment of diplomats at The Greenbrier is Arnold Kramer, "In Splendid Isolation: Enemy Diplomats in World War II," *Prologue: Journal of the National Archives*, vol. 17, no. 1 (Spring, 1985); for a first-hand account see Gwen Terasaki, *Bridge to the Sun* (Chapel Hill, 1957); also David Brinkley, *Washington Goes to War* (New York, 1988). An interesting comparison to the experience of the diplomats at The Greenbrier is Charles B. Burdick's account of American diplomats in Germany, *An American Island in Hitler's Reich: The Bad Nauheim Internment* (Menlo Park, CA, 1987). For Ashford General Hospital see Joseph G. O'Reilly, "The 'Shangri-La' of the Wounded Soldier," *The West Virginia Review*, vol. XXII, no. 6 (March, 1945); "Army Hospital," *Chesapeake and Ohio Lines Magazine*, vol. XXVII, no. 11 (November, 1943). For a description of both of these episodes and the years shortly after the war see Robert S. Conte, "Diplomats and Doctors, Draper and the Duke: The Greenbrier in the 1940s," *The Journal of the Greenbrier Historical Society*, vol. V, no. 1 (1987). On the 1948 re-opening party see "Life Goes to the Big Weekend at White Sulphur," *Life*, vol. 24, no. 19, May 10, 1948. The definitive biography of Dorothy Draper is Carleton Varney's *The Draper Touch: The High Life and the High Style of Dorothy Draper* (New York, 1988).

Many of the post World War II sources contain information on The Greenbrier's history; these include Cleveland Amory, *The Last Resorts* (New York, 1952); Sam Snead, *The Education of a Golfer* (New York, 1962); Fay Ingalls, *The Valley Road* (Cleveland, 1949); Andrew Hepburn, *The Great Resorts of North America* (New York, 1965); Ralph C. Martin, *The Woman He Loved: The Story of the Duke and Duchess of Windsor* (New York, 1973); Jeffrey Limerick, Nancy Furgeson, Richard Oliver, *America's Grand Resort Hotels* (New York, 1979): Carleton Varney, *There's No Place Like Home: Confessions of an Interior Decorator* (New York, 1980); Stephen Salsbury, *No Way to Run a Railroad* (New York, 1982); Andrea Chambers, *Dream Resorts* (New York, 1983); Robert A. Caro, *The Path to Power: The Years of Lyndon Johnson*, vol. I (New York, 1982); Sam Snead, *Slammin' Sam* (New York, 1986). The history of White Sulphur Springs is seen in the context of Greenbrier County in Ruth Woods Dayton, *Greenbrier Pioneers and Their Homes* (Charleston, WV, 1942; reprint ed., Charleston, WV, 1977) and Otis Rice, *A History of Greenbrier County* (Lewisburg, WV, 1986). For an intriguing view into an ante-bellum season at White Sulphur Springs—even though it is renamed "Egeria Springs"— see Mary Lee Settle's novel *Know Nothing* (New York, 1960).

Of the hundreds of postwar newspaper and magazine articles about The Greenbrier, the following are particularly informative: "The Magic That Gave Birth to The Greenbrier," *The Hotel Monthly* (March, 1949): "Politicians Without Politics," *Life*, vol. 29, no. 1, July 3, 1950; Al Hine, "The Greenbrier," *Holiday*, vol. 11, no. 5 (May, 1952): Irene Corbally Kuhn, "The Greenbrier: A Chateau in the New World," *Town and Country* (May, 1963); "That Incredible 59," *Sports Illustrated*, vol. 10, no. 22, June 1, 1959; "In the Grand Manner." *Golf*, October, 1964; "The Greenbrier: Legendary Resort in West Virginia," *Architectural Digest*, vol. 34, no. 1, January/February, 1977; Phillis Lee Levin, "Life's Comforts Carry the Day at Greenbrier," *The New York Times*, March 25, 1984.

Additional recent sources include reports from Liz Trotta, "Greenbrier: Recreation in History" *The World and I* (April, 1992) and from Jonathan Yardley, a chapter in *States of Mind: A Personal Journal Through the Mid-Atlantic* (New York, 1993). See also Brian McCallen, *Golf Resorts of the World: The Best Places to Stay and Play* (New York, 1993) and "The Greenbrier," *Golf Travel*, vol. 2, no. 11 (November, 1993). For information about The Greenbrier's interior decorator in the 1930s see Leslie A. Pina, *Louis Rorimer: A Man of Style* (Kent, Ohio, 1990). For more on World War II, see Louis E. Keefer, *Shangri-la for Wounded Soldiers: The Greenbrier as a World War II Army Hospital* (Reston, Va., 1995). Regarding the bomb shelter, see Ted Gup, "Last Resort: The Ultimate Congressional Hideaway," *The Washington Post Magazine*, May 31, 1992. And for more about Robert E. Lee's visits to White Sulphur Springs see Tim McKinney, *Robert E. Lee at Sewell Mountain: The West Virginia Campaign* (Charleston, WV, 1990) as well as Richard Adams' novel *Traveller* (New York, 1988).

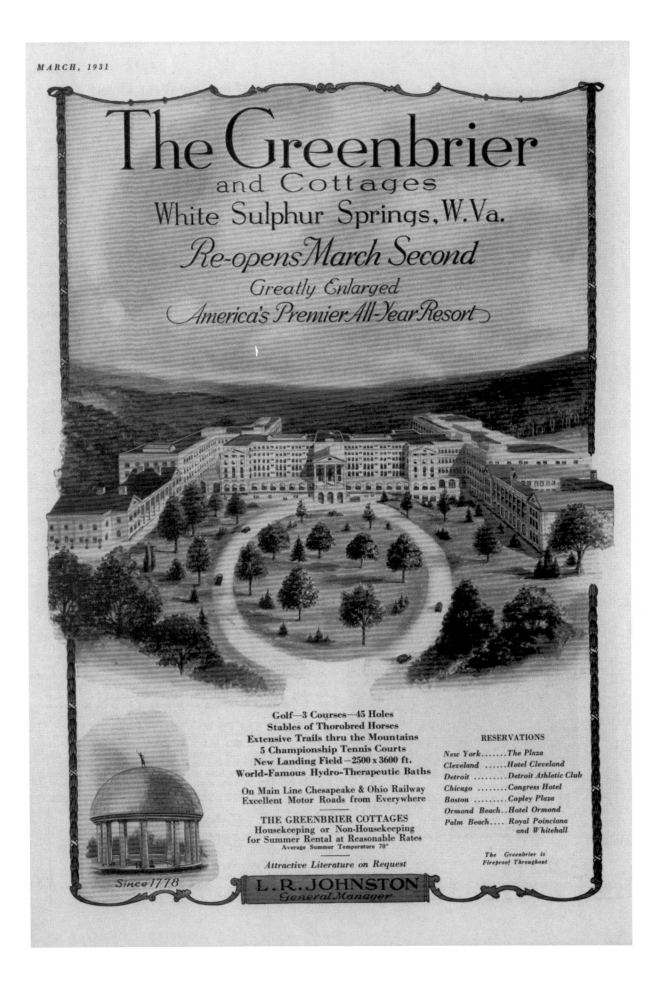

Index